She's Just Another Navy Pilot

She's Just Another Navy Pilot

§

An Aviator's Sea Journal

§

WITHDRAWN

Loree Draude Hirschman,

with Dave Hirschman

Naval Institute Press
Annapolis, Maryland

Naval Institute Press
291 Wood Road
Annapolis, MD 21402

Library of Congress Cataloging-in-Publication Data
Hirschman, Loree Draude, 1967–
    She's just another navy pilot : an aviator's sea journal / Loree Draude Hirschman, with
Dave Hirschman
        p. cm.
    ISBN 1-55750-335-4 (alk. paper)
        1. Hirschman, Loree Draude, 1967—Diaries. 2. United States. Navy—Officers—
Diaries. 3. Air pilots, Military—United States—Diaries. 4. United States. Navy—Aviation.
5. USS Abraham Lincoln (Aircraft carrier) I. Hirschman, Dave. II. Title.

UG626.H57 A3
359.9'4'092—dc21
[B]

99-58891

Printed in the United States of America on acid-free paper ∞
07 06 05 04 03 02 01 00   9 8 7 6 5 4 3 2
First printing

This book is dedicated to the members of
Carrier Air Wing 11 who lost their lives
in service to their country:

Lt. Kara "Hulk" Hultgreen

Lt. Glenn "K-9" Kersgieter

Lt. Cdr. Stacy "Sprout" Bates

Lt. Graham "Hobbs" Higgins

Lt. Cdr. Bill "B. B." Breaker

Lt. Cdr. James "Jimmy D" Dee

Lt. Tom Francis

Lt. Larry "Jedi" Anderson

Contents

Preface

This book began as a handwritten journal, a personal memoir of my first deployment aboard the USS *Abraham Lincoln*. Before and during those six months at sea, I kept notes of my experiences during what was a tumultuous period for the U.S. Navy, my shipmates, and me.

When I was commissioned as an ensign in the U.S. Navy, I had no idea that one day I might be a pilot in a combat aircraft squadron. Back in 1989 the best assignment I could hope for was to fly in a land-based support squadron. When the navy decided to allow women in combat squadrons in 1993, I was quick to volunteer. I wanted to serve my country and help make the navy's new policies work.

That first cruise on the *Lincoln* was the most unforgettable six months of my life—a true test of will under adversity. The very first day I flew on board the *Lincoln* was the day Lt. Kara Hultgreen died in her F-14 Tomcat while attempting to land. Her death and the subsequent debate that ignited concerning double standards set the tone for our six-month deployment. Many male aviators questioned our qualifications, and many female aviators felt that the women were set up to fail. It was often difficult to find the truth.

As an unseasoned pilot, or "nugget," on my first cruise, I was frequently bewildered by the complicated, fast-moving events that were unfolding around me. Looking back, much of my frustration, anger, sadness, and joy seems naive or misguided. Those emotions were real, however, and I have included them here because they mattered so much at the time. Similarly, small things such as e-mail, Cheerios, pizza, and chocolate sauce took on an almost comical significance.

Looking back on my journal with four years of additional experience, including a second deployment, I'm keenly aware of its shortcomings. My narrative doesn't tell the whole story of Air Wing 11, and it sheds little light on the varied experiences of my fellow aviators. More than five thousand people went to sea on the *Lincoln* in 1994 and 1995, and each of us remembers our time together differently. My purpose wasn't to speak for everyone, or for the navy. I have added an "Other Voices" appendix to include the perspectives of other members of the air wing.

Some of my journal entries are critical of other women who served aboard the *Lincoln,* and I may rightly be criticized for being overly harsh and judgmental. I realize that I was fortunate to have had a supportive squadron. Other female aviators did not. After the deployment I learned from a fellow junior officer that although many of my squadron mates had not endorsed the integration of women, as a group they decided that it would be better to accept the change as professionals rather than to fight it. I had no idea during my deployment that some of my squadron mates were not supportive of the policy of women in combat, because they were always supportive of me. Other women in the air wing were not as lucky. Their squadrons were not as accepting, and they made life painful for the female members. It was often difficult for me to empathize with them because my experience in VS-29 was so positive. I regret that I was not more sympathetic to their situations. We were all under a great deal of pressure, and so we tended to operate in survival mode, looking out for ourselves.

My experience on this nugget cruise was very different from my second deployment on the USS *Kitty Hawk* (CV-63) in 1996. This book focuses on the *Lincoln* cruise not only because of its historical significance but also because there were important lessons learned. First, strong leadership is the absolute key to the success of any major change such as integration. I firmly believe that the reason Air Wing 11 experienced difficulties was that there was weak leadership on many levels. In the past few years since integration occurred on aircraft carriers, our air wing has been the only one that experienced problems sufficient to warrant an investigation. The second lesson is, Don't assume anything. Too many of the men assumed that women were not qualified just because they were women, and plenty of women assumed that if they received a bad grade it was because of their gender, not their performance.

On both cruises I experienced teamwork between men and women, and I believe that the integration was successful. However, two problems arose that diminished our success: pregnancy and fraternization. Pregnancy is obviously an issue because of its effect on readiness, but as a single factor it is not significant enough to ban women from combat. My squadron did not lose any women to pregnancy on the *Lincoln* cruise, but a pregnancy test order early in the deployment caused bad feelings that persisted for the entire cruise.

Fraternization is technically a relationship between officers and enlisted, senior officers and junior officers, or instructors and students. But even relationships between junior officers in the air wing caused distraction—something not needed on a warship. I found out the hard way that even ordinary friendships had to be tempered because of the rumors that could result. On my second cruise my closest friend was a guy in my squadron, and even though we were only friends, both happily married to other people, some people started rumors that we were having an affair. Maybe if we had been at war people would have had something better to talk about. But in times of peace, anything unusual is a topic for discussion, and when women are the minority, they are usually the topic. It wasn't fair, but that's what we had to deal with.

I don't expect this book to change anyone's mind about the issue of women in combat. It is an emotional issue, and I realize that many people have views that nothing will alter. My goal with this book is to educate. I want to let people know that the integration of women on board aircraft carriers has gone well, and would have gone even better on the *Lincoln* if we had been assigned stronger leaders.

Flying on and off an aircraft carrier is stressful enough without the added pressure of media attention and critics who are waiting for you to make a mistake. The women on the *Lincoln* performed their difficult duties extremely well, they sought no special treatment, and they were a credit to the navy and their country. It's a tribute to the talent, honor, and dedication of the men and women in the navy that, a few short years after women went to sea for the first time, no one within the military talks of barring women from combat ships or airplanes. I am proud to be known as just another navy pilot.

Acknowledgments

I would like to thank the following people for helping me survive my deployments:

The sailors and officers of VS-29 for welcoming me and the other female members of our squadron. Your emphasis on teamwork and professionalism made our cruises successful and rewarding. I salute you all.

Capt. Chuck "Grunt" Smith, my first CO at VS-29, for making all those trips up to see the Air Boss in my defense. I will always be grateful for your patience and fairness.

Lt. Joe "Flojo" Keith and Lt. Larry "Jedi" Anderson. You helped me keep my sanity on cruise, and you looked out for me and believed in me. Larry, you are sorely missed.

Lt. Jana "Lola" Raymond. We had our difficulties, but it was only because of the stress we had to endure together. You are a true friend whom I have always been able to count on. Thank you for putting up with me for so long.

The Romanas family, the Massey family, Kathleen Spane, and Aunt Sharon for the care packages and constant support.

The VS-29 AV/ARM Division and ATCS Hippen. I hope I was able to make your lives easier while we were deployed. I enjoyed working with all of you, and it was a privilege to be your division officer.

The VS-29 Maintenance Department for providing me with up jets to fly. I wish the public really knew how much you sacrifice and how well you perform your jobs. You are the unsung heroes of the fleet.

All of the LSOs from CVW-11 for being so demanding. I am a better pilot because of your unyielding standards. Keep 'em off the ramp, Paddles.

The following individuals read my manuscript and assisted me greatly with their constructive criticism and suggestions: Craig Foster, Ron and Kathy Clark, Tricia Wood, Dennie Stokes, Christina Taylor, Jamie Johnson, Brenda Scheufele, and Sue McNally.

My deep appreciation goes to agent Alice Martell for her patience and persistence. I also want to thank Paula Crawford and the Women in Military Service Memorial Association, specifically Gen. Wilma Vaught and Linda Witt. Thanks to Mark Gatlin, Tom Cutler, Rebecca Edwards Hinds, Kimberley A. VanDerveer, and Susan Artigiani at the Naval Institute Press for greatly assisting in the completion of this book. Also, Mary Yates, my copyeditor, did a fantastic job of reading my mind and making my manuscript complete.

I want to thank my brother-in-law and coauthor Dave Hirschman for his insight and invaluable assistance. He kept me motivated throughout the process and helped me translate my journal and experience into this book.

The entire Hirschman-Melville clan has always been incredibly supportive: John Sr., Wilma, Martha, Jason, Gayle, John Jr., Fran, Don, Lesa, Micah, Vicky, Jerry, and Kelly.

I offer my eternal gratitude to my family for always supporting me across the miles and keeping me in their thoughts and prayers. Mom and Dad, you get all the credit for raising me so well. Mom, your prayers kept me safe and the archangels busy! Dad, you are my inspiration on how to be a good leader; thank you for your wisdom and guidance. I love you both very much! Pat and Ryan, thank you for your support and the funny notes that kept me smiling. Grandma, I greatly appreciated your kind and loving letters and your prayers.

Finally, my husband Harry. You gave me the strength to endure the many difficult times, and your love never once faltered. To you I owe the most. I love you!

She's Just Another Navy Pilot

Prologue

Her Next of Kin

25 October 1994 started as the kind of day that made me feel lucky to be a navy pilot.

I climbed into the cockpit of an S-3 Viking at the naval air station at North Island in San Diego, started the plane's two jet engines, and prepared to fly the airplane and three other crew members to the USS *Abraham Lincoln*. The nuclear-powered aircraft carrier that soon would become our home was waiting about fifty miles offshore. This was a warmup for the ship's air wing, a chance for aviators to practice landing and taking off from the moving deck of the aircraft carrier in the open sea. In six months our squadron was scheduled to fly aboard the *Lincoln* and steam across the Pacific Ocean, through the South China Sea and Indian Ocean and into the Persian Gulf. There we would enforce the "no-fly zone" over Iraq and monitor the volatile military situation in the Middle East.

Our cruise would make history, too. The *Lincoln* was about to become the first West Coast aircraft carrier to go to sea with female crew members.

I was among seventeen female aviators, and the only woman piloting S-3 Vikings—twin-engine jets that hunt submarines, drop bombs, and refuel other planes in flight.

The morning was cool and clear with steady trade winds and streaks of high stratus clouds that looked like huge white brush strokes on a deep blue canvas. I took off from the west-facing runway at North Island, turned south over San Diego harbor to avoid overflying the residential areas of Point Loma, then joined up with another S-3 headed toward the *Lincoln*. We climbed together to fifteen thousand feet and circled in loose formation about thirty miles south of the aircraft carrier.

Given its role as the first Pacific Fleet aircraft carrier to carry female pilots, people throughout the navy jokingly referred to the *Lincoln* as the *Babe-raham Lincoln*. The genesis of the nickname was the movie *Wayne's World* ("She's such a babe that if she was president, she'd be Babe-raham Lincoln"). I got a chuckle out of the moniker and even used it in letters to my parents.

The air was smooth at our altitude, and that made it easy to keep abreast of the other S-3 as we made lazy circles in the sky. Our Vikings, pejoratively known as "Hoovers" for the vacuumlike sucking sound their twin turbo-fan engines make, are hardly the glamour planes of the fleet. Compared with the supersonic single-seat F/A-18 Hornets I had flown in a previous assignment, or the sleek afterburning F-14 Tomcats made famous by the movie *Top Gun,* Vikings are slow and ponderous. But in the air, with the landing gear tucked neatly into the wheel wells and the flaps retracted, even plodding Vikings look graceful.

Through my plane's large canopy I had an excellent view of the lead aircraft. Like most carrier-based jets, it was painted a dull gray. The drab color did a good job of obscuring the many fuel leaks that always seemed to streak along the undersides of the wings and line the fuselages of our aging planes. The navy had been flying Vikings since the mid-1970s, and some of the planes at North Island had been in service since I was in elementary school.

I kept my head turned to the left and studied the lead S-3. Like all the planes in our squadron, VS-29, it had the silhouette of an ancient Viking

ship painted in black on the tail. Most of the tall-masted ship with the bil-
lowing sail covered the vertical stabilizer, and the rear of the boat stretched
onto the rudder. But to me the emblem resembled a cartoon rubber ducky,
and the side-to-side movements of the plane's rudder sometimes made it
look as though the little duck was waddling through the sky. Even though
I was becoming more tense as we approached the ship, the comical rubber ducky made me smile.

I had finished my final carrier landing qualifications in an S-3 a month
before, and this was going to be my first time aboard the *Lincoln* as a full-
fledged member of the Pacific Fleet. After four college years in the
Reserve Officer Training Corps, three years of navy flight training, and
two years in a land-based composite squadron, I was finally about to start
doing the job my country had prepared me to do: I was going to sea with
a fleet squadron. We were part of a five-thousand-member team aboard
a technologically advanced aircraft carrier. And that ship was at the heart
of a floating arsenal, one of the most powerful naval battle groups ever
assembled. Our ship alone had more firepower than the entire U.S. Navy
had delivered in all of World War II.

As an added bonus, I was going to be part of navy history: the first
group of female aviators on the West Coast to deploy at sea as fully qualified combat pilots. Women in the military—and especially in military
aviation—had overcome tremendous obstacles to get to this point. My
bookshelves at home were stocked with accounts of their heroism. Many
military women had given up hope that this day would ever come. But
thanks to their sacrifices and dedication during more than fifty years of
military flying, nineteen of us were about to fulfill their dream. We were
going to be allowed to go as far as our ability and imagination would take
us. The artificial gender barrier was gone, and we would be allowed to
succeed or fail on our own merits.

As usual, when our S-3s arrived at the holding pattern about twenty
miles from the ship, air-traffic controllers instructed us to stay at a high
altitude. Vikings are relatively fuel-efficient, and we could wait in a holding pattern while the gas-guzzling F-14 Tomcat fighters, which had to get
on the deck quickly, were guided in. Next came the F/A-18 Hornet

fighter/bombers, then the two-seat A-6 Intruder bombers and four-seat EA-6B radar-jamming planes.

Finally it was our turn to begin our approach, and my adrenaline surged as the *Lincoln*'s air-traffic controllers told us to drop down to a lower altitude. Even though I had already performed dozens of carrier landings, each one was an exciting challenge. The goal was to fly a perfect approach at exactly the right airspeed, then hit a spot on the deck while holding the plane at precisely the right attitude. There are hundreds of variables, so no two landings are exactly alike. Each approach and landing is graded, and the results are posted in every squadron's "ready room" for all to see.

Carrier landings differentiate navy and marine aviators from their counterparts in the other services, and we measure ourselves by how well we perform this critical task. No matter how good we are at bombing, dogfighting, hunting submarines, or refueling other aircraft, all of that is meaningless unless we can be counted on to bring our airplanes back to the ship at any time of day and in any kind of weather.

During my previous trips to "the boat," there had been several delays that kept planes in the holding pattern longer than expected. The deck crews were new to their jobs, and so were many of the pilots. It wasn't uncommon for operations to lag a few minutes behind schedule. But on this day, as we kept circling in seemingly endless lefthand patterns, the situation was becoming absurd. Our planes had plenty of fuel, so we were capable of staying aloft for hours; time wasn't a problem. But why had the ship's air-traffic controllers brought us down to a lower altitude if the deck wasn't clear to come aboard? It didn't make any sense. We orbited so long that my neck was getting sore from constantly looking left toward the lead airplane.

Then, at last, we were told to approach the ship for landing. There was a thin layer of clouds over the ship, and I followed the lead airplane through the wispy white cloud. We came out of the clouds about two thousand feet above the blue ocean surface.

My mouth went dry, and my heart was beating so hard that I could hear it thumping through the earphones inside my helmet. I tried to calm myself down by concentrating on the procedures as I entered the pattern for my first fleet carrier landing, or "trap." My limbs felt as though they had electricity running through them, and my stomach tightened. It was like a bad case of stage fright. This was going to be my first time aboard the *Lincoln,* and I wanted to make a good impression.

I brought my S-3 into tight formation with the lead aircraft, and together we streaked toward the ship at about 400 miles an hour, just eight hundred feet above the ocean. Whitecaps from the wind-blown ocean passed by us in a blur, and the choppy air near the water's surface made it feel as though we were racing cars down a rutted country road. As soon as the *Lincoln* disappeared beneath us, the lead plane banked hard left and began slowing down in preparation for landing.

I continued straight ahead about one mile, then swung my aircraft onto its side in a tight left turn, yanked the two throttle levers back to idle, and extended the speed brakes. The g-forces of the hard turn pressed us all down into our ejection seats at three times our normal weight, and I glanced at the airspeed indicator as it unwound. At 186 knots, my left hand found the round landing gear lever on the instrument panel and pulled it sharply downward. A series of mechanical groans and clanks followed as the hydraulic system pushed the wheels into the slipstream and locked them into place.

My goal was to touch down exactly forty-five seconds after the plane in front of me. That's the minimum amount of time the deck crew needed to move one plane out of the landing area and prepare for the next arrival. By evenly spacing our arrivals at the shortest possible intervals, aviators can reduce the amount of time the ship is required to steam into the wind —a predictable situation that makes the ship and its crew especially vulnerable to enemy attack.

The *Lincoln* was about a mile off my left wing and the lead plane was making its final approach to the steel deck when I grabbed the square flap handle with my left hand and pulled it all the way back to the landing position. My plane was traveling at 156 knots when I tugged on the lever, and it decelerated as though I had tossed out an anchor. In four seconds the flaps reached their full travel of 65 degrees.

I pushed the nose of the airplane down to maintain airspeed, and I tried to anticipate the altitudes at certain key points in the arrival pattern. As soon as we were abeam the ship's arresting wires, I banked the plane 25 degrees to the left and began a descending turn. I focused intently on the instrument panel. With 90 degrees of turn to go, my S-3 was 450 feet above the water. As I rolled into the "groove" on final approach, the ship's frothy white wake was 325 feet below. So far so good.

The naval flight officer, or "NFO," in the right seat made the "ball call" as the "meatball," an automated lighting device that showed the plane's position relative to the deck, came clearly into view.

"Seven-oh-five, Viking, ball," he said in a calm, clear voice. "Four point-oh," he added, letting air-traffic controllers know that we had a little under two tons of fuel remaining.

Everything looked right. The lights on the meatball were centered, just as they should have been, and I was properly aligned with the white painted center stripe on the black deck. My eyes quickly shifted between the gauges on the instrument panel and the rapidly changing view outside. Airspeed was 110 knots, fine. The rate of descent was roughly 600 feet a minute, good. I glanced at the numbers and, by force of habit, reviewed my procedures out loud: "Meatball, lineup, angle of attack."

Under my breath, I admonished myself not to screw up.

From this point on there was no reason to look at the instrument panel. The final portion of any carrier landing is purely visual, and I kept my eyes on the panoramic picture in front of me. The ball started to sink, indicating that I was getting too low, so I added a touch of power. But that changed the aircraft's pitch, so I pushed the nose down to compensate. Then the airspeed increased along with the rate of descent. I was flying like a rookie—reacting to the ball instead of using the airplane to actively place it where I wanted it to be.

Suddenly we slammed against the steel deck with a loud screech, and the forged metal hook dangling beneath our plane's tail caught the third of four arresting cables. Maybe it was beginner's luck, but I had caught the target wire. We came to an abrupt stop with the nose wheel only a few yards from the edge of the deck. I could feel the rolling motion of waves crashing against the ship's hull directly beneath us.

There was no time to savor the successful trap, however. We knew that the next plane was rolling into the groove just forty-five seconds behind us, and we had to raise the tailhook and clear the landing area quickly. The flight officer in the right seat pulled the lever that unlocked and folded the wings, and in my side mirror I could see them folding into a giant X above us. I added power and steered through a narrow gap between several parked airplanes as we rolled to catapult number one at the bow of the ship. Everything was hurried, but nothing could be overlooked. We unfolded the wings, then extended the launch bar on the front landing gear after I taxied the airplane to the catapult.

As soon as I got the hand signal from the launch director, I brought both engines up to full power. The jet engines whined, and the airplane rocked and shook against its restraints, then squatted down as the catapult went into tension. A pair of deck hands scurried in front of the plane, then ducked down to check the nose wheel and make sure the aircraft was properly attached to the catapult. Moments later, they scrambled away to safety.

I clicked the launch bar switch to "retract" so that it would raise up automatically and not interfere with the landing gear at the end of the catapult stroke. Next I moved the joystick all the way left and right, forward and aft, then around in a circle to make sure that the movement was free and unobstructed. I pushed the rudder pedals firmly back and forth with my feet. Everything felt normal. Then I scanned the gauges a final time to make sure that the jet engines were up to speed and none of the warning or caution lights was on. A few seconds later, the checklist was complete.

I saluted the yellow-shirted catapult officer and watched him slowly turn his head to look up and down the four-hundred-foot length of the catapult, making sure that nothing was in our way. Then I took a deep breath and prepared for the sudden acceleration of a catapult shot. As soon as the catapult officer was satisfied that all was clear, he bent down and gently touched the deck with his left hand, his long-sleeved jersey rippling in the stiff wind. At that moment, the "shooter" behind him hit the button that sent us on our way like a rock from a slingshot. In three breathtaking seconds, we lunged forward from zero to 130 miles an hour. The bow of the ship passed underneath us in a blur.

As our Viking began climbing into the salty air, the furious noises and strange sensations of the catapult faded away. We were flying again. The smooth, comforting sounds of the two jet engines and the wind passing over the wings filled the cockpit. The plane was under my control, and the horizon before us was wide and expansive.

I couldn't wait to do it again.

I made four traps and four "cat shots," as the catapult launches are known, before being told to fly home to nearby North Island. The short trip back to the coast gave me a chance to calm down, and landing on the eight-thousand-foot runway that runs parallel to the beach on Coronado Island seemed like child's play compared with setting the plane down on the ship. By the time our S-3 rolled to a stop in front of the hangar at our base and we shut the engines down, I was relaxed and happy with my day's work. My passes hadn't been perfect, but each of them had brought us aboard the ship safely. The day's events had increased my confidence that I could perform the demanding tasks required of navy pilots, and that with experience I would become a valued team member.

I bounded upstairs to our squadron ready room with the rest of the crew. The four of us were still talking and laughing when someone asked if we had heard about an F-14 crash. Crash rumors circulate through navy squadrons with amazing speed, and they are seldom unfounded.

A chill ran through me. There were three female officers in VF-213, the F-14 squadron assigned to the *Lincoln*. Two—Lt. Kara Hultgreen and Lt. Carey Lohrenz—were pilots, and a third, Lt. Christina Taylor, was a radar intercept officer, or "RIO." I had worked with Christina in a previous assignment at another squadron, and I prayed that she wasn't involved. But no one had much solid information. All anyone knew for sure was that an F-14 Tomcat had gone down a few minutes before we had arrived at the ship. That explained our long delay in the arrival pattern before landing.

The next morning the *San Diego Union-Tribune* printed a little blurb about the accident on the front page. The article said that an F-14 Tomcat had crashed while attempting to land on the *Lincoln*. The RIO in the back seat of the two-person fighter had been plucked from the 63-degree water and treated for mild hypothermia. But the pilot was gone—lost at sea. The paper said the pilot's name was being withheld pending notification of "his" next of kin. I was slightly relieved by the pronoun, because the only people I knew in that squadron were women; if it had been one of them, I assumed, the paper would have written "her" next of kin. I went to the VS-29 ready room and prepared to fly back out to the *Lincoln* for several more days at sea.

Naval aviation is a hazardous enterprise, and accidents happen. Several people I had met since starting navy flight training had been killed in aerial mishaps. All the losses were tragic, but there was little time to mourn; the missions had to go on. The navy had trained me to compartmentalize, and I hardly thought about the crash at all as I prepared for my next flight to the *Lincoln*.

It was another gorgeous fall day, and I landed on the ship that morning without any problem. After stepping out of the jet, I met Lt. Jana Raymond, a female NFO in my squadron, and we lugged my bags to the stateroom we had been assigned to share during the upcoming deployment. Jana had already been on the ship for a couple of days, and she knew her way around the catacombs better than I. We dropped my bags in our stateroom, and I followed her down a ladder to the second deck.

Jana and I had known each other for several years and had roomed together at the naval air station in Lemoore, California, during a previous assignment. She has brown hair and eyes and a smooth tan complexion. In appearance she reminds me of the actress Holly Hunter; they both have the same slight Southern twang, Jana having been raised in Kentucky. As we got down to the second deck, though, Jana turned and with her usual bluntness asked a question that cut right through me.

"So, did you hear about Kara?" she asked, a concerned look on her face.

Jana's words staggered me. From the tone and the terse wording of the question, I instantly knew that Kara Hultgreen was the F-14 pilot who had been killed in the previous day's accident. The pilot in the newspaper was really a she, not a he. My knees almost buckled, and I had to sit on the ladder and catch my breath.

"No," I answered. "Please tell me you're not talking about the crash."

Jana informed me that the navy had just called off the search for Kara's body. The rescue helicopters were back on deck, and spotter planes had returned to their land bases. I hoped desperately that Kara might be out there bobbing around on a raft, working on her tan and wondering why it was taking those helicopter drivers so long to find her. But in my heart I knew right then that she was gone.

Kara had been assigned to share a two-person stateroom during the upcoming cruise with Christina Taylor. Now Christina had been told to move in with Carey Lohrenz, the other female F-14 pilot in her squadron. Jana and I were moved into Christina's old room—the one she and Kara had been going to share. Some of Kara's belongings were still in the cramped quarters when we got there; it was hard to believe she was really dead. We put Kara's T-shirts and personal things into a bag and gave it to Christina to send back to Kara's family in Texas.

I hadn't known Kara well, but I had been impressed by her confidence and sense of humor from the moment we met. At twenty-nine, Kara was a few years older than most of the other female aviators. She had a tall, athletic frame, and she was outgoing and vivacious. She had been a vocal proponent of allowing women to fly combat planes, and she had testified before Congress several years earlier seeking to change the old laws. She seemed absolutely positive of who she was and what she wanted to accomplish. I'm sure that many of her fellow F-14 pilots saw in Kara a female version of themselves. She had the same fighter-pilot swagger and self-assurance. Her radio call sign was "Revlon," a nickname she picked up for wearing makeup in a TV interview. Others called her "The Incredible Hulk" or "Hulkster" in reference to her imposing size.

Some female aviators who, like Kara, began their navy careers when women were excluded from combat assignments had mixed feelings about serving on the front lines. They never considered the possibility that they might be shot down, become prisoners of war, or have to endure the strain and loneliness of being at sea for months at a time. Kara had thought about all of those things, though, and had been a forceful advocate for female aviators. To me she had always been a symbol of our competence and eagerness to serve our country.

I spent the rest of that afternoon in a daze. I couldn't eat or concentrate on my trivial tasks of unpacking. That night in my stateroom, when I finally went to sleep, I had the odd sensation of floating somewhere. There was nothing to look at, only blackness, and I was deeply afraid; I didn't know what was going on. Then there was a faint glimmer of light and shadows. I knew immediately that it was Kara, and she was telling me without words that everything was going to be all right. I felt her presence and her peace, and wherever she was I had a sense that she was OK. I don't know why I should have had a dream like that, especially about a person I didn't know very well. The memory of that dream is still vivid, and it calms me whenever I think about Kara and her sudden and violent death.

That Friday the air wing held a memorial service for Kara aboard the *Lincoln,* and the turnout was impressive. Officers from Kara's squadron, VF-213, stood shoulder to shoulder in their khaki uniforms in the forecastle, or fo'c'sle, at the extreme forward end of the ship. Many of them had been opposed to the idea of women flying with them, but their proud, pained faces showed that they regretted Kara's loss profoundly. The rest of us sat in folding chairs among the ship's heavy anchor chains. The ceremony was short, simple, and emotionally overpowering. I had difficulty getting through it, especially when the lone bugler sounded taps. We were acknowledging the loss of a fellow aviator, someone who had known the dangers of her profession but had pursued flying with passion and determination anyway.

The ceremony hadn't even ended when, back in San Diego and around the country, anonymous faxes began arriving at news organizations claiming that Kara had been "pushed" through flight training because she was a woman. These nameless messages insinuated that she hadn't really been qualified to fly F-14s. The malice and cowardice of these writers made me furious. How could people make such serious charges anonymously? How could they gang up on Kara when she wasn't around to defend herself? How could they pour salt in her family's wounds during their time of sorrow?

More than 60 percent of military plane crashes are caused by pilot error, but I had never heard of anyone questioning the qualifications of other pilots who died in mishaps. The furor over Kara's qualifications seemed incredibly unfair. Fortunately Kara's mother made her daughter's flight training grades public. That should have put a quick stop to any questions about Kara's qualifications. She had had some difficulty mastering the art of landing an F-14 on an aircraft carrier, but that's nothing new; it's a huge airplane, and bringing a Tomcat aboard a ship is one of the most demanding feats in aviation. Her grades throughout training had been above average, and she had finished third in her training class of seven. Kara had a degree in aerospace engineering from the University of Texas and had hoped to become an astronaut. She was a gifted flier who had proven herself in the navy and truly earned her place in a fighter cockpit. She didn't deserve to die so soon—or to become the target of such vicious slander.

For several weeks after Kara's accident, every time I flew toward the ship in preparation for another trap I would think of her. No one was better qualified to lead the female aviators on our ship than she. She was fearless and funny, charismatic and confidence-inspiring. She had appreciated the historical significance of our mission, and she had been dedicated to completing it. Now, suddenly, she was gone—and our chances for success seemed diminished.

Prove Them Wrong—Or Right

After Kara's accident, I felt more pressure than ever to fly well. Yet the harder I tried, the worse I actually did.

A week after Kara's memorial service, I was scheduled to fly a night refueling mission from the *Lincoln* off the California coast. I started the engines and began taxiing our S-3 toward a catapult on the bow when one of our plane's two generators quit. I was momentarily tempted to ground the plane for a mechanical inspection and skip the entire flight. But my crew and I were able to restart the faulty generator without too much difficulty, so we decided to proceed.

The night sky was murky and ominous as we approached the catapult, and I had a deep sense of foreboding. The ocean surface was rough and windswept, and low clouds blocked out the moon and stars. As we taxied forward to the catapult, I silently pondered a few of the unanswerable questions that had surely passed through the minds of all the naval aviators who went before me: What invisible forces conspired to bring me to this frightful place? What fate awaits me in that darkness ahead? What the hell am I doing here?

I concentrated on my tasks inside the cockpit and tried to vanquish these troubling doubts.

With my gloved left hand I pushed the S-3's two throttle levers forward as far as they would go. I listened to the engines whine and felt the airframe buffet and shake as I double-checked the gauges and tested the controls. The cockpit was bathed in a faint red light designed to enhance night vision. Finally I flicked on the external lights and held my breath as the catapult hurled us forward into the night. The launch felt normal, and the airspeed indicator on the instrument panel showed that we were accelerating at the proper rate. I wanted the plane to leap off the deck and vault upward, away from the blackness and the cold, churning water beneath us. But as soon as I pulled back on the joystick to initiate our ascent, all the lights in the cockpit went out, our plane had lost electrical power, and suddenly it was as dark inside the cockpit as out. I could hear the engines humming, so I knew that we wouldn't have to eject as long as I could keep the airplane under control.

My eyes found the dim standby gyroscopic gauge near the bottom of the instrument panel, and I used it to hold the wings level and begin climbing. I remembered from training that the gauge would run for nine minutes on battery power alone, so I had time to try to get to a higher, safer altitude as the others tried to sort out the problem. I called to the NFO in the right seat and told him that I had control of the aircraft. He knew he didn't have to pull the ejection lever that would blast all of us from the plane, and he began restarting the generator.

A long minute later, the electrical power returned. The red lights inside the cockpit came on again, and we all tried to calm down. We continued flying away from the ship and performed our tanking mission without any more complications. By the end of the ninety-minute flight I thought that I had put the fright of losing power behind me, and I prepared to bring our airplane back to the ship. The weather had deteriorated during the time we were away, however, and what had begun as a scattered overcast was now virtually solid. As we skimmed through the clouds, the blinking external lights exacerbated the dizzying vertigo I already felt. I had to concentrate on the flight instruments to keep the airplane right side up, but the sudden loss of electrical power had rattled my faith in the equipment. Beneath us, the ocean swirled like an infinite well of black ink.

Our S-3 was scheduled to be the last plane to land on the *Lincoln* that night, so in the back of my mind I knew that all the aviators would be watching our arrival on the ship's internal television system. Every squadron's ready room was equipped with a TV monitor that showed the ship's landing area and broadcast radio transmissions between pilots and the landing signal officers (LSOs) guiding them to the arresting wires. On nights like this, aviators throughout the ship would sit around the ready rooms eating popcorn and watching "terror-vision."

I tried to forget about the electrical failure and concentrate on making a smooth approach and accurate landing. I scanned the instruments as we descended through the clouds, then spotted the ship about two miles straight ahead. The deck was rising and falling as the ship plowed through heavy seas, and the rough air near the surface was equally turbulent. Our plane had plenty of fuel, and we were near enough to the coast that we could have diverted to land bases at Miramar or North Island if necessary. But I was determined to show that a female pilot—even a new arrival to the fleet like me—could handle these tough conditions.

On my first approach, the deck seemed to rush up toward our plane as the ship rose on a large swell. I instinctively added power, but it was too much, and our S-3 sailed a few feet over the top of the arresting cables on deck. This was a missed approach, or "bolter." I slammed the throttles full forward and took off again, promising not to let myself make the same mistake a second time.

Then, to my horror, on my second approach I missed the wires again.

"The third time's the charm," one of my crew members offered, trying to boost my confidence. But the third landing attempt wasn't lucky for me, either. Another bolter. Finally, on my fourth approach, I trapped successfully.

I parked the airplane, and the deck crew immediately chained the aircraft to the pitching deck to keep it from rolling. I climbed out, exhausted, wet with sweat, legs rubbery and weak. I was totally humiliated by my three failed landing attempts. It had been a terrible night, made worse by the knowledge that everyone in the air wing had had a front-row seat to my gaffes. After Kara's death, I wanted to build my shipmates' faith in female pilots. Now, because I had allowed myself to become too preoccupied, my poor performance was accomplishing just the opposite.

"Thanks for the extra flight time," one of my crew members joked, trying to lift my spirits.

"At least you were too high," someone else said. "You should've seen the F-14 that almost hit the ramp tonight." That was no consolation, either.

Back in our squadron ready room, Joe "Flojo" Keith, a senior S-3 pilot and LSO, punched me in the shoulder sympathetically and told me he thought he knew what I had been doing wrong. Instead of telling me about it right then, however, he wisely suggested that I get some sleep; we could discuss it in the morning.

I trudged downstairs, took a shower, and went to my stateroom. On my desk there was a package from my parents. Evidently Jana had found the box in the ready room and had thoughtfully brought it back for me to open. I tore at the brown packaging material and hoped to find something inside that would take my mind off my current difficulties. There was a can full of treats as well as letters from Mom and Dad.

My dad had served as a marine officer, and both my parents knew how important mail and care packages from home could be to morale. Even though the room was dim, I began reading the letters right away:

Dear Loree,

I've wanted to write to you for a few days now. That package Mom is sending you seems an appropriate vehicle—food for thought along with real food. Mom and I attended the memorial yesterday for Kara (I've enclosed the clipping from today's paper). It was moving in every respect. We introduced ourselves to Kara's mother, and Mom had already written to her. I hope we'll spend some time together later.

When I administered your oath of commissioning, I spoke of my pride in seeing you and your classmates join the officer ranks and of my delight as an active-duty officer that talent like yours would be with us. But as a father I knew—more than most other fathers present—that this is a dangerous profession. We are managers of violence, and sometimes accidents happen. I wish I had not been so prophetic, but I had to be honest.

As far as I know, Kara is the first of your comrades to be lost. If there are others, this is probably the closest to you. If it would help, let me share a few thoughts with you about losing comrades.

At your age, and in your calling, death seems distant and not relevant. You and your team have so much to do and to live for. Few think of or dwell on the possibility of death while you do so well that which you've been trained so well to do.

Then, like the thief in the night, death strikes and you must react. Then you come to grips with your own mortality. Often the first reaction to the death of a comrade is relief that it wasn't you. That is followed by guilt for feeling that way. Both are very normal reactions to the shock of losing someone close.

There follow feelings of anger—at the lost friend for being gone, at the system that allowed the loss, at others who don't seem to feel the loss the way you do. (I must add, regretfully, that the chorus has already begun about qualifications of women pilots. You and the other women will have tough, bitter days ahead of you. I wish I could help you, but you will do just fine. Maintain your poise and dignity—you'll find both in short supply in others.)

Once you've gone through the various emotions and trials of being one of the first, you'll have to come to grips with how you go on from here. Tough as it is, you must continue to do your job. Without notice or publicity you must just fly your missions and take care of your troops. Grieve in private. Be the officer and pilot you are capable of being. The greatest tribute you can give Kara is by being the best you can be. Many will expect less of you and are ready to excuse you and the other women from really performing now. Only you can prove them wrong—or right.

When you became one of the first, you took on a lot more than you probably expected. You are up to it. These difficult times will make you better. Get through them like a professional. When I was your age, I had lost many marines—some because of my decisions, my mistakes. It doesn't get any easier with time. It just makes you more determined to avoid the same errors and to continue to set the example.

I think of you constantly and pray for you each night. God bless all of you. I am so proud!

Love,
Dad

Dear Loree,

Happy Halloween! Enclosed in the box is my treat (peanut butter cookies and a tin of special nuts—bet you can't eat just one of these nuts). Couldn't think of a trick, although Dad suggested an exploding can of phony snakes—I put the zap on that fast.

I had such a strange birthday this year. (Your card was absolutely wonderful—I read each word of it, and it made me feel so loved by you—many thanks, my darling!) Kara's memorial service was at 5 p.m. on my birthday. It was held outside of the San Antonio Country Club on its terrace, shaded by large oak trees with lovely golf-green lawns sloping away to the golf course. The navy had an Honor Guard, and the Marine Corps provided the firing squad.

Prior to the service, the Navy Band played several patriotic selections ending with "I'm Proud to Be an American" and "Eternal Father." Short but very emotional eulogies were then given by Admiral Yakely (who said he knew you), Kara's best friend Mo, her two sisters, her dad, and finally her mother. The ceremony (attended by about two hundred people) concluded with the firing squad's three volleys, taps, and an F-14 flyover in the missing-man formation. [At aviators' funerals it is traditional for the flyer's squadron to fly a missing-man formation. A four-plane division approaches the site of the memorial service, then one of the aircraft, symbolizing the missing aviator, breaks off by pulling up toward "the heavens." The rest of the formation continues flying without him/her, with a space left in the formation.]

*This death really hit me hard even though I had never known Kara. Her
great sense of humor, the French braiding of her hair when on flight status,
her witty intelligence, and the love she had for flying couldn't help but
remind me of you. You are so very dear to me, my only daughter, my direct
line to the future and the source of my sweetest memories of the past. My
pride in what you do is never exceeded by my fear of its risks, but I do pray
daily for your safety.*

*I guess I found the total lack of any mention of God or an afterlife at
Kara's memorial very sad. Such a beautiful soul should have been alluded
to. Kara's spirit, so vital and strong, surely whispers in God's ear each day
now to protect and help her aviator buddies as they continue doing the
work she so enjoyed. Many of the women I talked to were particularly upset
at the manner of Kara's death. I prefer to believe she was too busy trying to
solve her problem to fully realize the grave danger in her last seconds of life.*

*I see in my mind's eye, directly beneath the water's surface, an enormous
archangel, one of the many who guard all our pilots, and his face shines
with such love for her as she lays her head upon his chest. With mammoth
wings furled protectively around her, Kara met God and now knows how to
really fly. We poor souls still plodding along from day to day on this earth
are left with the anger, the sadness, and the lost potential of Kara's passing.
My comfort is that I think of death as being very much like childbirth—
great pain and tears producing great joy in a new life. Kara has been
reborn into Heaven.*

*Dearest daughter, I treasure every bit of you. Stay safe, and if you ever
chance to hear a rustle of wings as you near your S-3, those are just Mom's
guys arriving on duty.*

Love always,
Mom

My parents' pride and faith in my abilities were sincere, and I'm sure
they meant for their thoughtful words to elevate my spirits. Yet on this
night their positive, hopeful expressions only deepened my despair. Dad
said the way to honor Kara's memory was to excel. By flying so poorly—
and so conspicuously poorly—I had dishonored my fallen shipmate.

Even though I seldom cry, alone in my room that night I put my face
in my hands and wept until exhaustion overcame me.

o n e

§

Getting Here

A Sixth Sense

Being a pilot was never one of my childhood aspirations; I dreamed of being an actress.

As the children of a career Marine Corps infantry officer and a teacher, my two younger brothers and I grew up on military bases around the world. We never lived in one place more than three years before it was time to pack up and go to the next assignment. Theater was one of the few constants in my youth, and it was an activity I participated in everywhere we went, from Hawaii and California to Virginia.

My dad, Tom Draude, has always been a quiet tower of strength in our family—a leader by example. We share the same affinity for tasteless jokes, and we inherited the same old-fashioned ideas about loyalty and devotion to duty and country. Dad comes from Kankakee, Illinois. He is the son of an immigrant plumber from Germany and a first-generation Irish-American nurse. He is the youngest of three children and the only boy in a strict Catholic family.

When my dad was a junior in high school, he saw a movie called *The Drill Instructor,* and he describes the film as an awakening for him. From that moment on he knew with absolute certainty that he was destined to be a marine. Their ideal of selfless duty was to him like a religious calling. When Dad graduated from high school, he won an appointment to the United States Naval Academy. As a "plebe," or freshman, there he was harangued by upperclassmen who demanded to know why he wanted to become a marine "bullet stopper" when he qualified for a promising and more gentlemanly career as a navy officer. My dad answered, with his usual midwestern earnestness, that he would rather scrub toilets as a lowly private first class in the Marine Corps than be the high and mighty chief of naval operations. I'm sure he paid for his temerity with hundreds—maybe thousands—of pushups. But his certainty about his future never wavered.

He graduated from the academy with distinction and soon went to Vietnam for the first of several extended periods. He was an infantry officer in Vietnam in 1964, 1965–66, and 1969–70. He was involved in some of the most intense fighting of that brutal conflict. He is such a thoughtful, gentle, and loving person that it's difficult for me to picture him in that role. He seldom talks about his experiences in Vietnam, but when he does, he is candid and composed, factual and analytical.

He won two Silver Stars for bravery in combat. The first was in 1966 when, as a company commander, he gave the order to "fix bayonets" and storm an enemy position. The attack succeeded—but at a price. One of his squad leaders was killed during the assault, and my dad ran out and retrieved his friend's body while the battle raged. Three months later his small company repelled a much larger North Vietnamese battalion in a horrific close-quarters fight.

Decades later, near the end of Dad's military career, he helped lead the First Marine Division during the Persian Gulf War. He crossed Iraqi fortifications and minefields with his troops and was one of the first flag officers to arrive in liberated Kuwait City. His nickname is "Sage," and I like to think it's because others recognize the value of his learned advice.

When my dad retired from the marines in 1994 as a brigadier general, many of the men who had served with him in Vietnam came to the ceremony. Few of them had chosen to pursue military careers, and most had long since left the service. They lived all over the country and worked in a variety of fields. But I remember the ease and familiarity they shared— even though they had known each other so briefly, during such a tumultuous time, so long ago. They had followed divergent paths and had become very different people, but they were still a band of brothers. I hoped that someday the people I served with in the navy would share the same sense of camaraderie and unity of purpose.

My parents met sometime after Dad's first tour in Vietnam, and they were married in 1966. My mom, Marysandra or "Sandi," also came from a military family; her father was a career army officer. Mom was a schoolteacher, and her job was the perfect complement for my dad's career.

Her personality too is a complement to Dad's; they're entirely different, but an unstoppable team. Where Dad is even-keeled and reflective, Mom is more emotional and demonstrative. Dad is German and Irish; Mom is pure Italian. I'm more like him in disposition and temperament. But every now and then, especially when I'm perfecting the minute details of some plan or obsessing about getting the house spotlessly clean, I'll suddenly realize that I've fulfilled that old truism: I've become my mother.

Mom taught at junior and senior high schools wherever Dad's career took our family. She demanded the best from her students, and they responded. She was able to find something good in each individual, even if it meant having to search really hard. Whenever we moved, Mom coordinated everything. She made exhaustive lists and took care of all details. She managed the kids, the movers, and the travel plans. Everything fell to her because Dad was usually consumed by his new responsibilities at work.

I was very young when my dad went to Vietnam the second and third times, and frankly I don't remember his absences. When he returned from his last extended trip there, however, my brother Patrick was only one year old and didn't know who Dad was; Pat was terrified and screamed whenever Dad tried to pick him up or hold him. I know that had to be very painful for Dad because family is more important to him than anything.

When I was in the sixth grade, Dad went on a one-year assignment in Okinawa. The rest of the family stayed at Camp Pendleton in Southern

California where we had friends and a well-established support network. That was a tough year for our family, though. Dad was able to return home only once, and then only very briefly. Years later he went to Saudi Arabia and Kuwait for seven months before and during the Persian Gulf War. But by that time my brothers and I were adults; although we still missed him and worried about him, we knew why he was gone and what he was doing—abstract ideas that would have been incomprehensible to us as young children.

The main things Dad taught us were to stand up for what we believed and never, ever quit. Once, when I was twelve years old, I joined a Little League team. I liked baseball, but I didn't play well enough to make the "major league" team, as I had hoped. Instead I was assigned to another team with a bunch of boys up to four years younger than I. I towered over them like a mother hen, and for a self-conscious preteen like me, it was a mortifying experience. I didn't want to finish the season, but Dad put his foot down: I was a member of a team. Joining had been my choice. Even if I wasn't the best player, I had made a commitment to my teammates. I had given my word, and there was no way I was going to get out of my obligation to them.

The only other time Dad really laid down the law with me was after high school. I wanted to pursue an acting career, but my parents were dead set against it. I had received a Naval Reserve Officer Training Corps position and an academic scholarship to the University of San Diego that would essentially cover all of my college costs. My parents felt that I would be throwing away a rare educational opportunity if I didn't go. A few times I was tempted to leave school and pursue acting despite their opposition. But I had promised them that I would graduate from college first, and I couldn't stand the thought of backing out of that commitment and disappointing them. I also had more pragmatic considerations, like how to feed and clothe myself without any means of financial support.

I majored in mathematics at the University of San Diego, a private Catholic college, and excelled at ROTC. The military regimen in ROTC was familiar and comfortable to me. It was all I had known growing up on marine bases. Few career choices in the navy appealed to me, however, until our ROTC group took a field trip to the naval air station at Miramar in San Diego County.

The place was amazing. Miramar called itself "Fightertown USA," and it was the home of the F-14 Tomcats—the supersonic fighters immortalized in the movie *Top Gun*. The two-seat fighters carry state-of-the-art missiles that can knock other planes out of the sky from more than fifty miles away. Their computer-controlled wings automatically sweep back to drag-resistant, aerodynamically efficient settings at high speeds and extend when the Tomcats slow down. Their powerful engines shake the ground and shoot flames twenty feet behind them when they go to full power.

But what really stuck in my mind about Miramar was how excited the people there were about their jobs. They believed that becoming a naval aviator was the greatest accomplishment in the world, and they wore gold wings on their uniforms proudly. The things they described flying off aircraft carriers, being in the front line of U.S. military strategy, and taking on Soviet-built fighters around the globe—sounded immensely challenging. I joined the aviation club in my ROTC unit the very next day. A few months later *Top Gun* came out, and it seemed that everyone wanted to be like Tom Cruise and fly an F-14.

Very few women had become navy pilots at that time, but there was talk of expanding female roles to include flying the newest, most advanced aircraft in the inventory. Some even predicted that eventually the navy would allow women to hold front-line combat assignments. The possibility that I could be a pioneer of sorts intrigued me, but it was not a major factor in my decision to pursue aviation; I just wanted to work with motivated people on meaningful assignments.

I graduated from college in the summer of 1989 and immediately was commissioned a navy ensign. After passing academic and physical tests, I entered flight school at Pensacola, Florida, the cradle of naval aviation. Whatever type of aircraft they end up flying, all aviators begin their careers at Pensacola. The place buzzes with youthful energy. Ensigns all seem eager to embrace the pilot stereotype by studying hard and partying hard.

I went through eight weeks of academics, physical fitness, and water survival training there. The academics were demanding. Our classes consisted of engines, aeronautics, and navigation. You didn't need a technical background to do well; in fact, some aeronautical engineers struggled in the classroom because they tried to read too much into the questions.

Water survival, an aspect of the training made to seem intimidating by the movie *An Officer and a Gentleman,* was actually fun for me. I'm a good swimmer, so swimming a mile, covering seventy-five yards in flight gear, even the Dilbert Dunker—which puts students in a simulated cockpit, then dumps them into a pool upside down—didn't faze me. My biggest personal hurdle was the land obstacle course. I'm not a fast runner, and sprinting through all that deep sand was tough. But I was determined to become a pilot, and if that meant that I had to practice the obstacle course every day, that's what I would do. A friend even volunteered to run with me, screaming all the way to provide extra incentive.

My first actual flight in a navy plane came right before Christmas of 1989. The aircraft was a T-34 Mentor, a two-seat single-engine propeller plane used by all primary navy flight students. At first the cockpit with its multitude of dials, switches, and levers seemed too complicated to master. But by studying methodically and focusing on one instrument at a time, I began to understand the machinery and how all of it worked together.

My roommate, Ens. Julie Cane, and I built a fake "cockpit" in our living room with a cardboard instrument panel, a fork for a throttle, and a wooden spoon for a joystick. One of us would play the role of the pilot while the other acted as an air-traffic controller. We practiced procedures and radio calls until they became automatic. We lived in Milton, a small town about thirty-five minutes away from Pensacola by car, so that we wouldn't be tempted to go out on work nights. We didn't even have a TV, because we didn't want the distraction.

A month after that first introductory ride, I made my first solo flight. It was very quiet in the plane with no instructor talking at me, and looking down on the trees, the green earth, and the aqua blue ocean was like opening a door to an entirely new world. Everything below me was small, distant, and slightly unreal, like the backdrop of a movie set. This was a separate existence, in which I controlled where I went and what I saw. If

I wanted to fly upside down, I just rolled the plane over, and suddenly the ground was above the Plexiglas canopy. Geographical features and landmarks that were invisible to people stuck on the ground now were laid out on the horizon for fliers like me to appreciate.

That first solo flight lasted only an hour, but it altered my perspective forever. I sang rock-and-roll songs as loud as I could almost the entire time I was aloft. I even brought a camera and snapped a picture of myself at the controls. Being alone in the sky was magical.

After a student solos for the first time, the instructors hold an informal "tie-cutting" ceremony to celebrate the cutting of the ties that bind us to earth. Students bring the ugliest tie in their wardrobe, knowing that it's going to be destroyed. I selected a hideous red tie from a local thrift store for the occasion. My instructor, Lt. Jim Prince, was a quiet, laid-back guy with a dry sense of humor who was about to leave the navy for an airline career. Before a crowd of about twenty fellow students and instructors, he cut my tie and made a few subtle jokes about my flying skills.

Then, for a moment, I got to turn the tables on my instructor with a speech of my own. He was such a mellow personality that it was difficult to make fun of him, so I did what any normal aviator would do: I made jokes about his height (about five feet five inches). First, I related a story about how we once flew along the Pensacola shore so that he could check out the waves, and I acted like I was trying to see over the edge of the canopy as he had. Then I announced that the folks at United Airlines were so pleased that Lieutenant Prince was going to be joining them that they had sent a special gift for me to present to him. I went to the front of our squadron's ready room and retrieved the child's plastic booster seat that I had hidden. The others roared with laughter, and true to his good nature, my instructor laughed right along with them.

As the weeks went by, students progressed to formation flying, aerobatic maneuvering, and pure instrument flight. I enjoyed all of it immensely. Each day brought new topics, new possibilities. The environment was invigorating, and as students we could feel ourselves learning, maturing, and gaining experience at every step along the way.

Once, on an instrument training flight, I was sitting in the back seat of the plane with a dark canvas hood draped over me to shut out any view of the outside world. I had been under the hood for about an hour focusing entirely on making precise climbs, descents, and turns. Then the instructor told me to take a break and look outside. I pulled back the hood and was amazed at the view. We were on top of a snow-white layer of clouds, the sun had dropped below the horizon, and the sky was glimmering pink for miles in all directions. It was a beautiful sunset, and the airplane and I were part of it. Learning to fly was like being given a sixth sense, a new way to interpret the world. I felt like a child who had just learned to walk and would never again be satisfied crawling.

But primary training also introduced me to an aspect of aviation that I hadn't considered: friends and acquaintances dying in aerial accidents. The first day I was to perform stalls and spins in a T-34, another student was killed in a midair collision at a nearby airfield. We heard about the accident before we took off, but flying activities continued as scheduled. As my instructor and I climbed to altitude for our first spin, we passed over the runway where the fatal accident had so recently occurred. I looked down and saw the morbid scene. Salvage trucks surrounded the wreckage like buzzards.

Dying is more than a remote possibility in military flying. Like everyone else, I knew I had to come to terms with that fact in order to continue. It gave me some comfort to know that when my dad was my age, he had led troops in combat and many of his friends had been killed. Yet Dad had survived with his dignity, humanity, and sense of humor intact.

I knew that my challenge was to do the same.

§

My dad's final assignment in the Marine Corps was at the Pentagon.

There, President George Bush appointed him to a commission that had been formed to study the role of women in the armed forces and decide whether women should be allowed to serve in combat roles. After months of contentious debate, Dad voted that women should be allowed to fly combat aircraft and serve on combat ships. Even though he is a traditionalist in many ways, he said his positive experiences dealing with military women during the Persian Gulf War convinced him that qualified women should be allowed to do more.

The following text is taken from his report to the commission:

I wish to quote, "It is essential that there be maintained in the Armed Services of the United States, the highest standards of democracy, with equality of treatment and opportunity for all those who serve in our country's defense." These are not my words and they are not about women in combat. This Presidential quote opens the 1948 Executive Order regarding racial integration in the military. However, there are interesting parallels which I invite to your attention: The President was talking about racially integrating the Armed Forces, which had been closed to black Americans, not for what they had done but because of who and what they were. Similarly, women are currently being denied the opportunity to fully serve their country solely because of their gender.

The President used the words "equality of treatment and opportunity" not "military necessity" because the impetus of military necessity would not come until two years later with the Korean War. Military effectiveness was significantly improved by racial integration when the talents, courage and dedication of black Americans were finally used without restrictions. I have every confidence that the same enhanced effectiveness would result from gender integration of combat aviation and all combatant vessels.

To best ensure our national security, we must give women the same chance to prove to our great Nation their talents, their courage and their dedication. . . . I believe we must fill our ranks with our best, regardless of gender, and God forbid, send our best to fight and win our wars. In doing so I will proudly risk far more than other Commissioners—I risk my son [Patrick had become a Naval Intelligence officer] and my daughter.

Each week when Dad called me on the phone in Florida, and every other time we spoke, he made a point of telling me that he was proud of me. Those sentiments warmed my heart and humbled me. But at the same time, I hoped he realized that the more I learned about the unique demands of my profession, the more I appreciated his achievements.

I was proud of him, too.

Hairball

It was hardly love at first sight when Harry Hirschman and I met in 1991.

Both of us were assigned to the naval air station at Kingsville, Texas, waiting to start jet flight training. I was in charge of scheduling the morning that he breezed into the office and asked me to leave him off the next month's duty schedule; the reason he gave escapes me now. We chatted for a few minutes, then he went on about his business. I don't even remember whether I granted his scheduling request or gave him double duty for having the audacity to ask for preferential treatment.

Harry and I come from completely different backgrounds. He was an aviation prodigy who learned to fly as a kid, pumped gas and washed airplane windshields in exchange for flying time, and worked as a civilian flight instructor during college at the University of California at Los Angeles. His parents divorced when he and his three brothers were quite young, and he was raised by his mother and stepfather in the shadow of Los Angeles International Airport.

Harry grew up riding skateboards and surfboards. He was the Bruin bear mascot in college, and it sounds as though he majored in sports events and parties. He was a member of ZBT, the Jewish fraternity, and from all accounts was a smart guy but an average student. After college he worked briefly as a stockbroker. But he wanted to go Mach 2, so against his family's wishes he took the navy flight aptitude test and in 1991 went through sixteen weeks of aviation officer candidate school.

I had heard about Harry several months before we actually met. During primary flight training at Pensacola, other students and instructors used to talk about this one particular ensign who was far ahead of everyone else in virtually all areas. He was a whiz at formation and aerobatic flying, and a natural at cerebral instrument flight. Like most of the other students, I found that it was all I could do to keep up with the demanding curriculum. We all resented this one guy whose scores were blowing the rest of us out of the water.

Later I came to find out that Harry was the guy setting all those records.

But looking at him, you would never guess he was such a hot shot. He is about five feet nine inches tall and has sandy blonde hair, a crooked nose, and soft brown eyes—not exactly the steely-eyed, chisel-chinned type of pilot/hero you would expect from the movies. Harry is approachable and funny. He loves kids and dogs, and he has an innate ability to charm them both. He has an offbeat sense of humor and the endearing quality of being able to take his work seriously but not himself. Even his radio call sign, "Hairball," told me this guy was different. Most pilots want macho nicknames that broadcast to the world how tough they are; then there's Harry, proud to be known as an indigestible wad that would gag a cat.

When we began jet training in T-2 Buckeyes, Harry was in the class behind me. We saw each other in social settings and tended to gravitate toward the same group of friends.

The culmination of jet training comes when students make their first real aircraft carrier landings in T-2s. It is the most intense part of flight training. All students make their first landings alone in their two-seat planes. There is tremendous pressure, and the margin for error is very slim. A year before our first carrier landings, a student pilot and several people on deck were killed when the student lost control of his T-2 and smashed into the USS Lexington.

May thunderstorms in South Texas postponed my class's first carrier qualification, or CQ, attempt, so Harry's class caught up with us. We spent a month flying our planes together as groups of students took turns landing on a runway at Kingsville that was painted to look like the deck of a ship. Time after time we would approach the simulated deck, set our airspeed, pitch angle, and rate of descent, then slam the landing gear against the concrete. As soon as the tires hit, we would add full power and take off again. We made dozens of approaches, one plane behind the next, day after day.

The practice runway even had a "meatball" sighting device, just like the deck of a real aircraft carrier. The ball, or Fresnel lens optical landing system, showed a round amber light in the center of a row of smaller green lights. If the plane was too high on approach, the ball appeared above the horizontal row of green lights. If the plane fell too low, the ball dropped below them. Navy pilots watch the ball every time they approach the ship, and they must react instantly to the most minute changes. We went through the procedures time after time knowing that our true test —the first real aircraft carrier landing—was coming soon.

It was at this point that I really started to pay attention to Harry. He was confident without being a braggart. He was supportive of the other students without being condescending. He listened to the instructors without being a brown nose.

Up until then I had resisted dating anyone at Kingsville. I was the only female student there, and I knew that whatever I did, good or bad, would affect the perception of other navy women who followed me. Whether or not it was fair for me to carry that burden, I felt it keenly. The gal who had been in training at Kingsville before me had been kicked out for poor flying, and I wanted to avoid that fate. During my first year and a half in Texas, none of the other students had piqued my interest enough to make me set aside my concerns. But gradually, as Harry and I spent more time together, my reluctance faded.

Our combined classes flew T-2s to the naval air station at Oceana, Virginia, and we planned to make our initial CQs on the USS *John F. Kennedy*. But poor weather in the mid-Atlantic frustrated our efforts again. We had been at Oceana for a week waiting for the low clouds and rain to clear, and I was beginning to have some very strong feelings for Harry. I thought he was kind of flirting with me, but I really didn't know how he felt about getting involved in a long-term relationship.

Finally, on our last night at Oceana, I decided that I had to at least bring the matter to his attention. A group of flight students had walked to a nearby Dairy Queen that steamy July evening, and Harry and I were the first ones through the line. We were slurping Blizzards when I told him that I was sorry that the CQ phase of our training hadn't ended yet, because as soon as it was over I planned to ask him out on a date. Since the weather in Virginia hadn't cooperated, I pointed out, now I would have to wait for another chance to see him socially.

Harry looked into my eyes as I spoke. He seemed to be hanging on my every word, studying me. When I finished, he was silent for a moment as he weighed the deeply personal things I had just told him. Then he burst out laughing. It wasn't just a chuckle, either; he threw his head back and let out a big belly laugh. He made some smart-ass comment too, but I couldn't understand what he was saying because he was so convulsed in laughter. It wasn't exactly the response I had hoped for, but at least he knew my intentions. I had taken the first step by planting the idea in his head.

After several weeks of additional practice in Kingsville, we flew to San Diego for another CQ attempt, this time aboard the USS *Ranger*. The weather wasn't cooperating in San Diego either, and it looked as though we might have to go back to Texas again without having landed on a real ship. Then, late in the afternoon of the last day we were scheduled to be on the West Coast, four of us were told to hop into our T-2s and fly out to the *Ranger* in formation. I ran from the ready room to the flight line along with Harry and two other student pilots.

Our four jets took off together, and we headed straight west, across the beach and out over the ocean. The orange summer sun was beginning to set in the Pacific when we spotted the ship. It was steaming west into the gentle evening trade winds. Air-traffic controllers aboard the *Ranger* immediately cleared us to make our first carrier landing attempts.

The first time I approached the ship, my heart was beating so hard that it seemed to shake my whole body. I knew that I had prepared myself as well as possible for this moment. I had practiced these types of approaches for months and had memorized all the procedures. But the ship looked so small in the vast ocean. Somehow I had expected a bigger target.

My initial approach went well, and soon my plane was nearing the arresting cables. My T-2 hit the deck so hard, and the wires brought it to a stop so quickly, that I was literally thrown forward against the seatbelt harness. It was a violent collision that sounded and felt like a high-speed automobile accident. But all that was normal, I learned; that was the way navy landings were supposed to be.

Once my plane came to a stop, there was a confusing scene as the deck crew sent me and the other brand-new pilots taxiing around with a flurry of rapid hand signals. One of their favorite pranks with neophyte aviators is to taxi them to the very edge of the ship. In the T-2, the nose wheel is under the pilot, and sadistic deck hands will sometimes command pilots to taxi forward until they are perched precariously over the ocean about sixty feet below.

My first catapult launch was the best part of that unforgettable day. It was like the fastest roller-coaster ride I could ever imagine times ten. I screamed with glee during that first cat shot. Each of the T-2s orbited the ship, and all of us were able to make at least two traps and cats before sunset. After the final catapult shot, the four of us brought our T-2s into a tight formation again and headed back toward shore with the throttles pushed all the way forward. At our altitude of five thousand feet, the evening sun glimmered off our orange and white airplanes while darkness began to engulf the ocean beneath us.

It had been an incredibly exciting and rewarding day. And sharing it with Harry seemed to deepen my feelings for him. When we returned to Kingsville, however, Harry still hadn't taken any type of decisive action about me, or us. I knew that he was the "big tuna," and it was time to reel him in. But I had already made my feelings clear to him, and now I had to give him time to make up his mind.

We saw each other nearly every day in Kingsville. He was sharing a house near the navy base with several mutual friends, and I went there frequently to study, eat pizza, watch TV, and just hang out. All of us recounted the tiniest details of our recent, fleeting brush with carrier aviation. Prior to landing on the *Ranger* we had all believed that we were capable of flying jets off ships at sea; now, in our own minds at least, we had demonstrated it.

In the future we would learn to operate a variety of different kinds of airplanes from the decks of aircraft carriers. While each new type of aircraft would pose unique challenges, those steps would be smaller than the giant leap we had just taken. The next plane we would fly, the delta-winged TA-4 Skyhawk, was faster and less forgiving of pilot mistakes than the T-2. Some of the Skyhawk instructors derisively referred to the T-2 as the "Gerber Safety Jet" because of its relative stability and docile handling characteristics. But we weren't concerned or intimidated by the prospect of flying the twitchy Skyhawks. Our confidence was at an all-time high.

Harry and I are both night owls, and at his house we would stay up talking long after the others had gone to bed. I felt so comfortable with him; he was so smart, compassionate, and focused. His mother, Wilma Melville, was a private pilot, and I think that gave Harry a little perspective on what the prevailing attitudes toward women in aviation were. He was a great coach, and he gave me good-natured little pep talks whenever he felt I needed them. Once he scribbled an encouraging note on the back of a barf bag and left it under the windshield wiper of my car for me to find after a particularly grueling flight.

On about the third night that Harry and I stayed up late talking, he started caving in. We were sitting on a ratty white couch in the living room of his rented house. The floor was covered with flight manuals and discarded pizza boxes. We had been playing "Flinch" —a stupid game that our little group had started playing during our trip to San Diego. I'm a little fuzzy on the origins, but one person would make an OK sign with his thumb and index finger and hold it somewhere below his waist. If another person looked at it, the person making the sign would get to punch the onlooker in the shoulder; if the person making the sign couldn't get the other to look, the one making the sign got punched.

Anyway, I had been winning at Flinch that night, but instead of cashing in my punches all at once, I told Harry I would keep them for a rainy day. He went to the kitchen for a glass of water, and I followed him there; I was thirsty, too. He was standing at the sink when he turned around with this mischievous smirk on his face and said, "How about trading in those punches you owe me for a kiss?"

I could hardly believe what he was saying. So I asked him if he was sure that's what he wanted. He smiled and nodded that, yeah, he was positive.

He was still leaning up against the kitchen sink, and I walked over to him, wrapped my arms around his neck, and planted a long, soft kiss on his lips. He hugged me and kissed me back, and it was fantastic. We held each other and kissed some more. It confirmed my intuitive sense that he was the guy with whom I wanted to spend the rest of my life.

We have been a couple ever since that night.

At first I was adamant that we keep our relationship a secret. We avoided all public displays of affection, and except for Harry's roommates, I don't think anyone really knew of our intimacy. Whenever we were at work, we made it our policy never to sit together at meetings and always to act professionally toward each other. I was afraid to the point of paranoia of being regarded as "Harry's girlfriend" instead of a fellow aviator.

As the months passed and we knew that our time together in Kingsville was drawing to a close, Harry and I became less secretive about the true nature of our relationship. The two of us went places together off the military base without other people around. We didn't advertise the fact that we were a couple, and most people probably didn't think much about it, since Harry and I had always been part of the same group of friends. But we didn't take any unusual measures to conceal our relationship, either.

We had no idea what the future would hold for us. But I had been raised in a household in which it wasn't unusual for a spouse to be called away for many months at a time. Those were hardships that I considered normal. I was willing and even eager to deal with them, just as my parents had always done. I knew that two strong people could love each other, remain committed to each other, and strengthen their relationship despite prolonged separations.

Yet it was a foreign concept to Harry, and I figured it would take him a while to get used to the idea.

Tailhook '91

The annual navy convention in Las Vegas has become infamous for the inexcusable excesses that took place there in 1991. Lt. Paula Coughlin, a helicopter pilot and admiral's aide, was groped and fondled while being pushed down a gauntlet of drunken aviators.

But my memories of that convention are far different.

Harry and I went there to attend aviation symposiums and forums as well as to meet old friends and senior officers who could influence our careers. I saw a lot of friends from ROTC, and the weekend was like a big reunion. I collected all kinds of airplane videos, coffee mugs, and T-shirts and lazed around by the outdoor pool. We didn't stay at the Hilton, where most of the abuses took place. Being extremely junior officers, we chose cheaper accommodations.

Before and during the convention, I was warned by people who had been to previous Tailhooks to stay away from the third floor of the Hilton. The gauntlet was a recurring annual event, and aviators lined the hallways outside the elevator and tried to put their squadron stickers and emblems on the breasts and panties of any female who happened by. It sounded like an out-of-control fraternity party, and I had no desire to go there.

The only ugliness I experienced took place in another hallway: I was getting out of a crowded elevator, and someone grabbed my butt. I was surrounded by people, and I couldn't tell right away who had done it or whether that person was even in the navy. I figured it was an isolated event, so I didn't make a big deal out of it.

That day there was an "admirals' symposium," at which the highest-ranking officers in the navy showed up to candidly answer questions from anyone present. It was a great opportunity to ask them anything without fear of reprisal. None of them was wearing a military uniform, so it was open season; no subject was off limits.

A female aviator in the crowd asked if women in the navy would ever be allowed to fly combat planes in front-line squadrons. The crowd whistled and jeered and tried to shout her down. The top admiral said that if "forced" to open combat assignments to women, the navy would comply. But he didn't think it was a good idea, and he wasn't about to initiate such a change. I figured the best I could hope for during my career was to become a flight instructor or to fly in a noncombat support squadron.

On the night that Paula Coughlin was being molested at the Hilton, Harry and I went out to dinner with a former astronaut and a test pilot. They told us about the experimental programs they had participated in, and we told them about current navy flight training practices. It was a wonderful evening. We had no idea that history was being made on the third floor of the Hilton, or that the ensuing scandal and its bizarre repercussions would soon create the political climate for opening combat aviation to female pilots.

A month later, as allegations about Tailhook were making newspaper headlines and nightly newscasts, the Naval Investigation Service began interviewing everyone who had attended the convention. I had almost forgotten the butt-grabbing incident, and when I mentioned it to investigators, they wanted to classify me as a "victim" of Tailhook. They even went so far as to have Harry and me demonstrate for them the exact manner in which my butt had been grabbed. We went into a room with two investigators, and I goosed Harry firmly from behind. I told them I was willing to repeat the exercise, but they said they got the picture. I told the investigators that I was not a victim, and that strange as it might sound, I had had a really great time in Las Vegas that weekend.

SERE School

Survival. Evasion. Resistance. Escape. All pilots and navy air crew who operate combat planes learn these skills and practice them under simulated conditions.

After getting my wings in Texas, I was sent to SERE school outside New Brunswick, Maine, in June 1992. The setting was absolutely gorgeous, with deep green forests, stunning mountains, and clear, cool streams. SERE school was no vacation, however.

I was one of eighty-three officers and enlisted air crew going through the rigorous school; there were only three women in the class. We spent a lot of time in classrooms, where we talked about survival techniques and strategies for evading capture. Then we hiked deep into the woods for more practical instruction on resisting enemy pressures if we ever became prisoners of war.

The next few days were a blur of stress, hunger, fatigue, and confusion. At the conclusion, however, one of my fellow prisoners, a marine corporal, said he was impressed that I had made it through the ordeal; he had assumed that any woman would buckle under the relentless psychological pressure and physical discomfort. Afterward, I knew that if I ever ended up in a hostile situation, I could endure more punishment than I might have otherwise thought.

SERE school made all of us confront the prospect of becoming a prisoner of war. Most of our country's potential adversaries are not signatories to the Geneva Convention, and they have no rules for or history of humane treatment for war prisoners. In the United States, many opponents of women in combat voice concerns that female pilots and soldiers would be raped and tortured in captivity, and men would give up military secrets in order to protect the women.

Personally I find those arguments to be quite shallow. During the Persian Gulf War, two American women were imprisoned by the Iraqis, and the reaction of the American public was not much different from their reaction to the news of the male POWs.

But I have to wonder, is being raped worse for a female prisoner than a male prisoner? Is sexual assault more traumatic or debilitating than other forms of physical or psychological torture? I don't know. Being a prisoner means being subjected to the worst manipulation your enemies can imagine. If rape is on their list, I think it pales in comparison to the horrors that American heroes like Adm. James Stockdale have already endured. Stockdale, a former navy fighter pilot, survived eight years of imprisonment and torture in North Vietnam. For four of those years he was in solitary confinement. Yet his captors never broke his spirit, and Stockdale risked his life to help other American prisoners avoid despair.

His wife, Sybil, remained devoted to him and raised their four children throughout their long ordeal. I'm in awe of their strength and tenacity.

Someday an American woman pilot will become a prisoner of war somewhere. It could happen any day in Bosnia, Haiti, the Persian Gulf, North Korea, or Somalia. When it does happen, I hope Americans are psychologically prepared for it, and that people at home will honor the pilot's willingness to defend her country and make personal sacrifices. But I don't think her suffering will be any greater than that of male prisoners. All of them will deserve their nation's compassion and respect.

Biased and Misguided

Harry and I could hardly believe our good fortune at the end of flight training at Kingsville: both of us were sent to Lemoore, California, where we would learn to fly front-line F/A-18 Hornets—the newest, most technologically advanced airplanes in the navy inventory. These versatile single-seat planes can carry bombs and missiles and fly at supersonic speeds.

Harry and I looked forward to learning to master Hornets together, even though our careers were starting to go in different directions. Harry knew that he would be assigned to a combat squadron when he finished training, and he would learn to operate from an aircraft carrier and use all the plane's air-to-air and air-to-ground weapon systems. I, on the other hand, would only learn to fly Hornets from land bases. At the conclusion of my shorter training period, I would be assigned to a "composite squadron" that used Hornets to simulate enemy strikes against ships and other targets. It was the best assignment a female jet pilot could hope for, and the worst for a male jet pilot. There was no reason for me to learn Hornet air combat tactics, bombing, or carrier landings because at that time women were barred from front-line positions, and our squadron's mission didn't necessitate combat training.

The only navy F/A-18 base in the western United States was at the naval air station at Lemoore near Fresno, a flat agricultural area in California's

Central Valley. Remote as it was, the place seemed like a giant improvement over the hot, dusty desolation of South Texas. On clear days we could see the twelve-thousand-foot peaks of the Sierra-Nevada mountain range to the east. But the real attraction was the airplanes. The Hornets were awesome.

On my first flight in a two-seat Hornet used for teaching, the instructor pilot, or IP, took us rocketing over the Sierras to a military practice range in Nevada. The acceleration was incredible as we climbed at more than 30,000 feet a minute. The bubble canopy allowed for tremendous visibility in all directions, and the plane responded crisply to every control input. Instead of the myriad dials and analog gauges I had become accustomed to in Vietnam-era TA-4 Skyhawks and T-2 Buckeyes, the Hornet cockpit was full of computers and digital displays. They called it the "electric jet," and with good reason.

We swooped low over the windswept eastern slope of the mountains and buzzed a natural hot springs. The IP hauled back on the control stick, and the plane shot straight up into the sky. We climbed more than twenty thousand feet in a few seconds, and the corkscrew path of our rolling airplane must have resembled the painted lines on the world's tallest barber pole. The thrill of that first flight in that nimble Hornet was unforgettable, but the exhilaration didn't last long.

I was the first female pilot to go directly from flight training into VFA-125, the squadron for new Hornet pilots at Lemoore, and the senior officers there quickly made it plain that they resented my presence and would do whatever they could to get rid of me. I certainly hadn't expected open arms and a key to the city when I arrived at Lemoore, but I wasn't prepared for the hostility, deceit, and antagonism I faced there. When I would greet any of the instructors in the hallways, they would walk by without answering or look away. Several were being investigated by the navy for their actions at the Tailhook convention, and the instructors at Lemoore treated me like a disease.

The trouble began when someone placed an eight-page article from the *Marine Corps Gazette* on the bulletin board in the squadron ready room. The opinion piece was a diatribe about why women should not be allowed to fly tactical military aircraft or serve in combat roles. It was spread across the bulletin board, each page front and back, with certain sections highlighted as though they were being endorsed. I found the article itself kind of funny; the author's strident tone was so biased, and his conclusions seemed so illogical. But I wanted to know why it was being displayed so prominently, and whether I would be allowed to respond by placing pro-female articles on the same bulletin board. I had thought that the bulletin board was limited to informational items like rooms for rent, cars for sale, that sort of thing.

I wasn't alarmed by the article. In fact, something similar had happened during advanced jet training when we were practicing bombing in TA-4s. Someone tacked a poster of some partially naked women on the bulletin board. I didn't get mad when I saw that, either. Instead, I bought a copy of *Playgirl* magazine and put the centerfold on the bulletin board with a bull's-eye over the male model's crotch. It gave the guys a taste of how they might feel if they were in my position, and most of them seemed to take it pretty well. They laughed about it, and so did I.

Also in intermediate training, another student once suggested the call sign "Drano" for me on a call-sign sign-up sheet. I wasn't sure what it meant. Did he mean to imply that I was caustic and abrasive like the harsh drain cleaner? I had always tried to be friendly and sociable, so I didn't think so. When I asked another pilot about it, he acted kind of squeamish. Finally he told me that the name stood for "pipe cleaner," a euphemism for a blow job. That hurt my feelings, but I didn't whine about it or try to get the guy into trouble. I figured I could give as good as I got, and any problems or gender issues that came up could be handled at our level, just between us aviators. I had developed a pretty thick skin and wasn't about to run away screaming "sexual harassment" or call in the Thought Police. (Eventually my squadron mates settled on the call sign "Rowdy," which rhymes with Draude, my maiden name.)

But it wasn't another student pilot who posted the polemic article at Lemoore; it turned out to be the executive officer. When I asked him about it, he said the purpose was to stimulate discussion of current events—not to slam me in particular or women in general. I thought that sounded rather odd. Posting the article certainly hadn't changed the fact that no one was talking to me; if anything, it had widened the chasm between me and the instructors. I took him at his word, though, and told him that I would appreciate the chance to respond in kind. He said that would be fine, and so the next day I posted a recently published short letter to the editor from a newspaper that took the opposite view.

But the executive officer wrote a disclaimer on my little note, saying, "This is the opinion of Lt. (j.g.) Loree Draude." The eight-page article was gone, and the instructor pilots wrongly assumed that I had insisted that they take it down. I hadn't, but the damage was done; I was branded a troublemaker and accused of bossing around the top officers in the squadron. The whispering campaign against me went into high gear.

From that day on, none of the IPs would speak to me except to communicate information required for our flights. When I walked into the ready room, the place would instantly become silent and icy. Instructors would get up and leave. They treated me like a leper, an enemy. Behind my back, they said the only reason I had been assigned to Hornets was that my dad was a marine general. Once again, the accusation was totally untrue.

In the airplanes, the IPs were even more antagonistic. They weren't trying to teach me; they were looking for excuses to ground me. They didn't offer advice or helpful hints as my previous jet instructors had done. They just critiqued me and kept a running tally of my mistakes. Each flight was like a final exam. Everything I did or didn't do was endlessly analyzed, scrutinized, and dissected. It seemed it was up to me to teach myself how to fly the Hornet.

The IPs seemed to intentionally put me in ambiguous situations so that whatever choice I made, I could be criticized for reaching the wrong conclusion. One morning I was scheduled to undergo a routine physical examination at the same time a ground school class was being offered. I asked the scheduling officer which event had priority, the flight physical or the lecture. He gave no definitive answer, so I kept my appointment with the flight surgeon and took the physical so that my medical clearance to fly wouldn't expire. Later I was lambasted for having skipped the lecture, even though other students routinely missed ground school without being penalized.

As the weeks went by, the IPs seemed more determined than ever to make me fail. As a middle-class white girl, I had never felt discrimination before. I knew in an abstract sense that it existed, and I had come across plenty of individuals with bad attitudes. But I had never been confronted by officially sanctioned malevolence, hypocrisy, and double standards until I got to Lemoore. I tried to convince myself that I could persevere, that I could win the IPs over by working hard and proving my competency. But the more I tried, the clearer it became that the cards were stacked against me.

The tension was awful, and it was beginning to affect Harry, too. The IPs knew we were a couple, and, not coincidentally, his grades began to suffer. Harry had been the top flight student in the entire navy in 1992, the year we went through training. He was a star in T-34s, T-2s, and TA-4s. But in the F/A-18 training squadron, his scores were consistently average or below average. Both of us studied as hard as we could and spent extra time reviewing procedures in ground-based simulators. But it was an uphill struggle.

If anything, the adversity strengthened our relationship, though. Harry put up with a lot of crap, but he did his best to defend me and stand up for the underdog.

My chief tormentor at Lemoore was Lt. Cdr. Matthew "Pug" Boyne, then the operations officer for VFA-125. He is about my height, with close-cropped dark hair and large brown eyes. He has a friendly face and a ready smile, but his outward warmth seemed insincere. Whenever I approached him he would grin and act as if everything was wonderful and he was my good buddy. Then he tried to get me kicked out of training and end my navy flying career. He assumed that because I was female, I was unqualified to fly fighters. Then he set out to prove it.

There was only one squadron for a female Hornet pilot like me to go after training: VAQ-34, a composite squadron based at Lemoore. As I neared the end of training I made a point of walking to that squadron's ready room and introducing myself to the officers there. They were short of pilots at the time and seemed eager for me to arrive.

Then, with only two flights remaining before the end of the Hornet instructional course, Pug pounced. A "Human Factors Board" was convened to decide whether outside influences were interfering with my ability to learn. The four-member board was told to decide whether I should be allowed to keep flying, as I argued, or whether a Field Evaluation of Naval Aviator Board, or FENAB, should be convened with the possibility of drumming me out of the navy. Pug wrote that I should be FENABed and not allowed to undergo combat training in the F/A-18. I couldn't understand why he was mentioning combat training when that was not part of my syllabus. I guess that by that point he could see the writing on the wall and wanted to ensure that I would not come back if the combat exclusion law was repealed.

I wrote a five-page memo describing the unfair criticism that had been leveled at me. Part of it read as follows:

Yes, I have made mistakes on my flights, but mistakes that are classified as "good learning points" for others are seen as [reasons for grounding] me. I resent the higher level of scrutiny of my performance because I am a woman. I earned my place in F/A-18s. I'm not here on a quota and I'm not here because there's nowhere else to put me. I'm here because I'm a good pilot, and my training command record proves it.

Although these few months at VFA-125 have been rough, I still do not doubt my abilities as a pilot. I only doubt the professionalism of some Instructor Pilots who do not want me here. For those Instructor Pilots, nothing I do will be good enough, nothing I say will be acceptable, and every mistake I make will be one more reason for them to believe women should not be allowed in tactical aviation. I accept that I cannot change their minds, but I will not accept their efforts to slowly, methodically drive me out. I did not come to this squadron with my fists up looking for a fight, or to be an advocate for women's rights.

There is only one solution to our current situation that will be good for Naval Aviation: allow me to complete the two remaining flights in the syllabus. I am wanted and needed at VAQ-34.

The evaluation board was equally divided, two to two. The skipper of the squadron broke the tie and allowed me to keep flying and finish training.

I insisted that the skipper of the Hornet squadron evaluate my final flight. I wanted to show him that I could fly an F/A-18 as well as any new pilot. I had found it odd that although he knew how much difficulty I was having with his instructors, he had never flown with me himself to form his own opinion. He consented to fly my last flight with me, and we went out on a night hop together, in separate, single-seat jets. We flew in formation, made aerial rendezvous and instrument approaches—everything the syllabus required and more. When we landed, I felt that I had proved my point. The skipper apparently agreed.

I went on to VAQ-34 and flew Hornets in simulated electronic warfare missions. The more I flew, the more at home I felt in the airplanes. Then, less than a year after I joined VAQ-34, the squadron was dissolved because of budget cuts. At the same time, however, Defense Secretary Les Aspin lifted the combat exclusion law for women. I hoped to go back to VFA-125 and learn to use the Hornet as a weapon. Harry had finished his training successfully, and he was part of an active squadron at Lemoore.

But the instructor pilots got the last laugh; they made sure that when the navy's female pilots received their "combat transition" assignments, I was sent elsewhere to fly some other type of aircraft. Friends of mine who worked in the navy's personnel department told me that instructors from Lemoore called the assignment makers and told them I was a troublemaker and a poor pilot. Although I have no evidence that Pug was involved, I can't help but feel that he was part of the reason that I was sent to San Diego to fly S-3 Vikings instead of being allowed to stay in Hornets.

I was crushed when the VAQ-34 commanding officer informed me of my new assignment. I was on a trip to Miramar at the time the combat transition assignments were due. I called him from a pay phone to find out where my new orders would take me. I knew something was wrong right away because he wouldn't take my call. When I finally got him on the phone, he reluctantly passed along the bad news. It felt like being back in junior high, being told I had to play on the minor league team all over again.

I was faced with a decision: I could fight the orders and call for an investigation into the harassment I endured at VFA-125, but that would guarantee that I would not fly for a long time while the administrative details were settled, and I would not be doing my country any service by sitting around waiting for all the paperwork to be processed. Also, by the time I had received my orders, two other women who were senior to me had started Hornet training at VFA-125, and I was afraid an investigation would agitate the instructors and harm those women's chances for success. I chose to accept the orders to S-3s.

Every time I made the tedious five-hour drive from San Diego to Lemoore to visit Harry, I found myself stewing about how Pug and his cronies had outmaneuvered me. Returning to Lemoore at all used to make me uncomfortable. I hated seeing the smug faces of the instructors who had humiliated me and made my time there so miserable.

But I also realized that the better I performed in my next assignment, the more success I achieved in Vikings, the more distant those bitter memories of Lemoore would become.

Fairy-Tale Times

Harry and I had been dating for more than a year when I suggested that at our two-year point we ought to sit down and evaluate our relationship and where we were headed.

At that point we were both still in F/A-18 squadrons at Lemoore. And knowing Harry, I figured he would wait until the absolute last possible moment before addressing any serious subject. I didn't mean to set a deadline or use the two-year point as an ultimatum; I just thought it would be a good idea for us to set some time aside to give our relationship some consideration. I was happy with the way things were going, and I was confident that he was, too.

Little did I know that Harry was already thinking far ahead of me. He had told my dad months before that he intended to propose to me, and he asked for and received Dad's permission. Harry told his parents too, and John and Wilma quietly gave him the diamond from his great-grandmother's wedding ring. Then, on 16 April 1993, about four months before my self-imposed evaluation date, Harry and I drove from Lemoore to Santa Barbara for what he promised would be a memorable weekend.

We met his parents there and saw a play, *The Road to Mecca,* and then went out to dinner. Afterward Harry's folks got into their car and started driving home to Ojai, about twenty miles away. We were following in Harry's car, and he told me he needed to stop and use a bathroom. He steered off the highway and pulled into the driveway of a fancy seaside hotel. We both got out and walked toward the lobby, and on the door there was an envelope with the name Hirschman on it.

Harry smiled and confessed that he had made hotel reservations for the night—but the surprises were just beginning. The next morning, when I walked outside, our car was gone. Harry told me that he had had trouble sleeping the previous night and had driven around. That sounded weird; I had never known him to have trouble sleeping, and besides, I would almost certainly have woken up if he had left or reentered the room. But I didn't question him, and we went to a nearby restaurant for breakfast. Afterward a limousine was waiting for us in the parking lot.

"Here's our ride!" Harry beamed as he hopped into the back of the white Lincoln Continental.

Harry was not rich. At the time he still had student loans to pay off from college. But when he decided to splurge, he could spend like there was no tomorrow. (So could I, and my credit card rating proved it.) We spent the morning riding around downtown Santa Barbara like a couple of rock stars. I hopped out for brief shopping forays at the pier and the Biltmore Hotel. I was getting into the impromptu spirit of the weekend and just having a lighthearted good time.

But when we got back into the limo, the driver took us south toward Ojai—not back to Santa Barbara as I had expected. And Harry's mood began to change, too. He sat back against the leather seat, held my hand, and told me that our time together "so far" had been wonderful, and he was looking ahead, "trying to think of ways to make it even better."

Slowly it began to penetrate my thick skull that he was about to ask me to marry him. The hotel, the limo, the ride to Ojai—it was all part of an elaborate setup. The joviality and giddiness of the morning evaporated as I realized that a major life change was upon us.

The limo drove up the winding ten-mile road from the coast to the Ojai valley. We went through the familiar orange and avocado groves toward his parents' house. But when we got there, the driver ignored the gravel turnoff to their driveway and kept going up a steep road toward the Thacher School. There's a chapel there, and that's where Harry's older brother Dave married Martha and his uncle Don married Lesa. During our previous visits Harry had never taken me to see the chapel that is so dear to his family; he said that he would do it when the time was right. I suddenly realized that this was my time.

The limousine finally stopped under a line of oak trees near a horse stable. I couldn't see the chapel itself, but there was a red rose attached to each of the two stone pillars at the entrance to a narrow pathway, and the entire route was lined with flower petals. We walked together up the steep hill that led to the chapel. As we held hands and moved up the trail, my emotions began to overcome me. I was overjoyed and deeply honored that Harry wanted to spend the rest of his life with me. But I was also apprehensive about the future, and a little sad that my familiar, relatively carefree youth was about to end.

When we reached the top of the hill, the view to the west was magnificent. Jagged mountains framing the Ojai valley spread out on either side of us, and the citrus groves were like square green carpets below. It was a cool, cloudless day, and we could see for miles.

At the chapel, the flower petals stopped at a wicker basket. The basket held a bottle of sparkling apple cider and two tall glasses, a batch of warm chocolate chip cookies, and a tiny black velvet bag. Harry insisted that we sit down on the wooden benches, drink some of the cider, and have a snack. I tried to do what he wanted; he had gone to such incredible lengths to make sure that everything was just so. My stomach was in a knot, though, so I couldn't eat any of the fresh-baked cookies—even though chocolate chip was my absolute favorite.

Finally Harry opened the velvet bag and gently removed an antique silver ring box. He got down on one knee, said he couldn't imagine living the rest of his life without me, and asked me to marry him.

I burst into tears and said yes.

We knew that our lives together wouldn't be easy. But the obstacles facing us would be far less imposing if we faced them together. We held each other in a long embrace, and I admired the diamond engagement ring that Harry slid onto the third finger of my left hand. It was a simple ring, but such a powerful symbol. We took in the view for a few minutes, and I did my best to regain my composure. Then we gathered up the basket and its contents and walked back down the rocky trail.

When we reached the oak trees where the limousine had parked, I was surprised to find that the car was gone. Harry seemed unconcerned, though; we were still living out his clever plan. Then I heard the clip-clopping of horse hooves on the narrow road. It was Harry's folks driving a carriage, and they gave us a ride to their house just two miles away. They explained to me that they had taken Harry's car from the hotel parking lot the previous evening, baked the cookies, and placed the rose petals, the wicker basket, the food, and the ring at the chapel. They even stood guard nearby until we were on our way up the trail. I was thrilled to share the happiness of that day with them.

Fifteen months later our family and friends gathered at that same outdoor chapel for our wedding. The ceremony took place on another gorgeous afternoon. The entire chapel seemed to be covered with flowers. The wedding was a mix of the traditional and the unconventional. I wore a formal white gown with my gold pilot's wings pinned over the left breast, and Harry was in his dress uniform. We walked under an arch of navy swords. My dog, Stoney, was the ring bearer, and at the reception I surprised Harry by wearing my flying boots under my dress instead of silk slippers.

Dad and I danced together, and he looked proud and handsome in his uniform covered with medals and campaign ribbons. Harry's friends lifted him above the dance floor and paraded him around in an exuberant Jewish hora.

I still laugh, and I still get misty-eyed, when I think about it.

Whenever I went to sea, I kept my engagement and wedding rings stored in my locker; I didn't wear them while flying because rings are a safety hazard. Every so often, though, I would take them out and admire them. If I was really lonely, I would wear them to bed. They reminded me of my husband and those fairy-tale times in Ojai.

You'll See

I had no idea what to expect on 1 November 1993 when I checked into VS-41 in San Diego to begin Viking flight training. My bitter experience at Lemoore had hardened me, but I tried not to prejudge the Viking community the way the Hornet community had prejudged me. To my delight, it quickly became evident that the Viking aviators embodied the qualities that had drawn me to aviation in the first place. They were a funny, competitive, smart bunch of team players. They expected me to work hard, fly well, and contribute to their team.

Another pleasant surprise to me was the S-3 Viking itself. The stubby plane with its bulbous nose and oversized tail looked to me like an aerial version of a minivan. The first time I flew the plane, however, Capt. Jansen Buckner, the skipper of the S-3 training squadron, showed me how versatile it was and how much it could do. His enthusiasm was infectious, and I smiled as he deftly took the airplane through a series of aerobatic maneuvers. The plane felt similar to the T-2 Buckeye, one of my favorite planes from flight training. It seemed stable and docile, but with a little coaxing a pilot could draw out its rowdy side.

At Lemoore each day had been a fatiguing battle; going to work at VS-41 was just the opposite. I couldn't wait for each day to begin, and the time went by quickly.

Soon after I arrived, I wanted to talk with Captain Buckner and try to dispel some of the rumors that had followed me from Lemoore. Before I could get the first sentence out of my mouth, however, he stopped me. "You're talking about the past, and that's a subject I'm not particularly interested in," he said. "You're in my squadron now, and I promise you that for better or worse, you'll be evaluated on your performance. Nothing else matters."

He backed up that assurance every day. I still had to study diligently during S-3 training, but I felt sure that the instructors were there to teach me and not to look for excuses to ground me. I had flown Hornets for 140 hours before going to Vikings, and that experience helped, too.

The final hurdle in training was night carrier landings. The deck of the ship at night is a confusing, bewildering, dangerous place, and even the most senior navy aviators admit that they never become totally comfortable with night operations.

I practiced simulated night carrier landings on runways in San Diego and on San Clemente Island and counted down the days until my first real attempt. Luckily the night turned out to be perfect for a new arrival like me. The sea surface was as calm as a lake, winds were light, and there wasn't a cloud in the sky. Moonlight made the ship and its distinctive outline almost as clear as day.

After my first trap, I looked to the NFO in the right seat and said, "This ain't so bad. What's the big deal about night landings?"

He rolled his eyes and chuckled knowingly. "You'll see," he said. "Maybe not tonight, but you'll see."

§

Lt. Jana Raymond and I finished S-3 training at about the same time, and we checked into VS-29 on 1 October 1994. The squadron was based at Naval Air Station North Island, the same place where we had done our training.

All the members of the VS-29 Dragonfires were away on a practice exercise that day, and Jana and I walked through the deserted hallways of the normally bustling facility. The walls were covered with pictures of Vikings at sea, awards and emblems, and pictures of the squadron members with their names underneath. I tried to memorize the names and faces of the people with whom I would soon be going to sea.

I had finally made it to a fleet squadron as a fully qualified combat pilot, and I was eager to get to work. I was curious about how I would fit into the squadron, and I was concerned that I would get the same chilly reception I got during Hornet training at Lemoore. I had no idea what the aviators in VS-29 had heard about me, and I was worried that they would resent me for the heavy-handed "sexual harassment" and "equal opportunity" training the navy had recently forced them to undergo.

On 11 October, VS-29 held an "all officers meeting," the first since Jana and I had joined the group. About thirty-five aviators gathered in the ready room. We were shaking hands and introducing ourselves to individual squadron members when someone called out, "Attention on deck!"

Cdr. Chuck "Grunt" Smith entered the room, and I jumped to attention along with everyone else and stared straight ahead. About six feet tall, wiry, with a thick brown mustache and a quiet, intense bearing, Smith seemed all business. He had the reputation of being a workaholic who regarded the squadron as his second family. "Seats," he grumbled, and everyone relaxed and found a chair.

Other officers took turns speaking from the podium about a long list of administrative items. Then Smith got up and went to the front of the room. "We have two new aviators with us in the wardroom today," he said, looking at Jana and me. "Why don't you stand up and introduce yourselves."

We stood up and prepared to address the group, but before I could get the first word out of my mouth, everyone in the room shouted "sit down" in unison. They laughed, and I did what I was told and took my seat again. My apprehensions disappeared all at once as it became clear that I would be treated the same as the long line of aviators who had preceded me. It was good to know that VS-29's collective sense of humor hadn't been smothered by political correctness. These guys were willing to insult Jana and me in person rather than behind our backs, and that was a welcome change.

After the squadron had undergone the navy's sexual harassment lecture in preparation for integrating women, one of the junior officers had printed up and laminated some "red and yellow" cards as a joke and a sarcastic response to the training. According to navy policy, a "red light" comment or action was something clearly over the line that was offensive and would make someone feel uncomfortable. A "yellow light" was a cautionary statement: you're not over the line, but whatever you had done or said came close. The policy was not really applied or enforced among us aviators, for we thought the system was a joke. If someone offended you, the way to handle it was to take the person aside and talk about it— not wave red and yellow cards around. Most of the time the offense was not intentional.

We used the red and yellow cards in a joking manner, not to be in adherence with the policy. Jana and I received our individual red and yellow cards, or "Dragoncards," when we checked in to the squadron. We called them Dragoncards because the idea for making the cards was unique to our squadron, the Dragonfires. We decided that we had to carry them with us at all times, and if any member of the squadron was caught without a card, he or she had to buy the next round of drinks in port. We would whip out our Dragoncards if a particularly bad joke or comment was made, but it was to signify being impressed rather than being offended.

After a week or two in the squadron I sensed that some of my squadron mates were still being overly cautious around me, and I started looking for a way to make them relax. One day I was told to present a lecture to the other officers on some obscure technical topic, and I decided to take a chance. One of the more flamboyant NFOs in the squadron was nicknamed "Dobber," and I made him my target. Dobber was from Louisiana and thought of himself as quite the lady killer. His typical civilian attire consisted of a polyester aloha shirt, khaki shorts, knee-high socks, and sneakers.

I started my lecture by telling everyone that I had recently discovered that Dobber had been engaged a few months ago. The people in the audience looked startled, especially Dobber, but I continued as if I hadn't noticed. Yes, Dobber had been engaged but broke it off when he found out that his fiancée was a virgin. His mother, upon hearing about this from Dobber, told him, "Good boy! If she's not good enough for her family, she ain't good enough for ours."

Dobber turned beet red and lowered his head, laughing. The rest of the ready room joined in, and to my delight I saw a few yellow cards thrust into the air. Even the skipper smiled and chuckled. After that day I noticed that my squadron mates wouldn't glance my way anymore if they swore or told an off-color joke. I think they realized that they didn't have to worry about accidentally offending me.

Stonewall

It's kind of embarrassing to admit, but the first few times I went to sea, I missed my dog as much as I missed any person. Maybe it was because I had spent more time at home with Stoney than just about anyone else in recent years. Maybe it was because we had been through so much together. But I preferred to think that it was mainly because he was such a fun, good-hearted guy.

Stoney is mostly Labrador retriever with some other kind of medium-sized dog mixed in. I got him from Harry's older brother Dave in 1991. Stoney was a puppy then, maybe twelve weeks old, a stray that Dave had picked up a few blocks from his home in Memphis, Tennessee. Stoney almost got run over by a car one Saturday morning on Stonewall Avenue —hence the name Stonewall, or Stoney for short. Dave took the little guy home, cleaned him up, and fed him. And a few weeks later, when no one answered his classified ads for a found black puppy, he gave me a sales pitch. Dave said that he and his wife, Martha, would have happily kept Stoney as their own if they hadn't had two big dogs already.

I was in Kingsville doing advanced jet training at the time. I was living in a house outside the navy base with a fenced backyard, so I agreed to take Stoney. The very next day he arrived at the airport in Corpus Christi in a huge plastic "live animal" container. There was a rawhide bone inside, a water dish, a food bowl, a cute red collar, and a note from Dave and Martha predicting that someday Stoney would grow up to fill the entire crate.

I couldn't wait to come home each day to find Stoney wagging his tail. He didn't care if I had flown less than flawlessly; he just licked my face and showed his constant willingness to retrieve Frisbees, tennis balls, or anything else I would consent to throw. I taught him to sit, stay, speak, roll over, crawl on his belly, and shake hands. I bought a foam pad for him to sleep on and put it on the floor next to my bed. He would crack me up each morning by nuzzling up to me in bed, putting a tennis ball by me, and lifting one eyebrow in a silent plea for action.

When Stoney was about one year old, I got quite a scare when he started developing a constant soreness in his hips. He would limp, and sometimes at night he would whimper as he lay on his pad. I gave him aspirin and other medications, but nothing seemed to work. He was developing hip dysplasia, and I feared that I would have to euthanize him.

Then Harry's mom, Wilma, recommended that we start a canine exercise program. Swimming helped build the muscles in his back end. And the more he worked out, the healthier he became. In San Diego we went running on the wide white sand beach every morning and evening, and I threw his ball into the surf and watched him bound into the waves after it. The long stretch of sand that parallels the runway at NAS North Island was another favorite. He would play with other dogs and chase flocks of seabirds while I watched the arriving and departing jets.

When I left him in Ojai just before going to sea on the USS *Abraham Lincoln,* I asked Harry's folks not to tell me if anything bad happened to Stoney while I was gone. If my dog got sick or died while I was away, knowing about it would be too upsetting. Besides, there was nothing I could possibly do about it out there in the middle of the ocean. It seemed better just to think about Stoney having a great time playing with the other dogs in Ojai and splashing in the pool. If for some reason I never saw him again, I would face that loss when I returned.

I gave Harry detailed instructions about what to do if Stoney passed away. I told him to have him cremated, then bury his ashes under an oak tree on one of the hills overlooking the outdoor chapel in Ojai where we got engaged, then married. I also made Harry promise to put a brand-new yellow tennis ball with Stoney's remains. Harry listened thoughtfully for a while, but when I got to the part about the tennis ball, he just smiled and put an arm around my shoulder.

"I'll do whatever you want," he finally promised. "But I'm sure they have plenty of tennis balls in Doggy Heaven."

§

A few months before the USS *Abraham Lincoln* was scheduled to go to sea, I learned that Pug had become the executive officer for VFA-94, one of the Hornet squadrons assigned to the ship. I would be dealing with him on the ship, seeing him at air wing functions and in the ship's passageways. I could hardly stand the thought.

Harry left for his first cruise aboard the USS *Constellation* in the fall of 1994. I was out at sea on a two-week training exercise aboard the *Lincoln* when his ship departed. The *Constellation* was scheduled to return to San Diego a few weeks after the *Lincoln* began steaming west toward the Persian Gulf. We figured that our ships would pass somewhere in the western Pacific.

Our schedules would allow us to be together for only a few weeks in all of 1995.

Dress Rehearsal

19 February 1995: An Active Imagination

The radar operator in our plane's four-person crew was the first to detect the unusual activity on the ocean surface. We were patrolling an area northwest of the USS *Abraham Lincoln*'s path today, and the powerful downward-looking radar in the nose of our airplane started picking up multiple unidentified targets moving swiftly across the ocean surface.

We were practicing antisubmarine tactics on a beautifully clear morning a few hundred miles off the California coast. The ocean surface was as glassy as a mirror. I brought our Viking down to about two hundred feet above the water as we swept along at our normal cruise speed of 250 miles an hour. We extended the MAD boom—the "magnetic anomaly detector" that slides out of the tail of our aircraft like an enormous stinger. With it the sensor operator can scan the sea beneath for large metal objects like submarines. But the MAD boom didn't pick up any sign of a submarine in our area.

Long, evenly spaced ocean swells passed rapidly beneath the nose of our plane, and the straight lines blurred by like fence posts seen from the side window of a car. The lower we flew, the more pronounced the sensation of speed became. We were moving faster than a racecar at the Indianapolis 500, but the ride was smooth and quiet.

The radar operator vectored me toward the strongest blips by calling out the compass bearings and the distances while I aimed the aircraft straight toward them.

"Two six zero degrees, six miles," he called into the intercom. "Come right five degrees, four miles."

About two miles away I caught my first glimpse of our target: a pod of California gray whales on their annual winter migration from Alaska to Baja California. We passed directly over the top of the majestic animals —each of the adults weighing fifty tons or more. Tall plumes of water vapor shot skyward each time one of them spouted. It was an unbelievable sight. Each whale had a tiny dorsal fin on its dark rounded back, and their tails, or flukes, seemed as broad as the wingspan of our airplane.

As we came upon the first group of whales, I slowed down and banked the plane steeply to the left so that the sensor operator behind me could peer out his small window and down into the deep blue ocean beneath us. Through the still surface, each whale was clearly distinguishable through twenty feet of water or more. I kept the plane in a series of tight spirals, first to the left, then to the right, so that everyone could get a good look at the amazing creatures below.

Later we came upon a large group of dolphins playfully cavorting around a huge school of fish. Some of the dolphins were leaping entirely clear of the ocean surface before gracefully splashing down. The trained dolphins at Sea World in San Diego couldn't have put on a better show. Our S-3s were fantastic planes for sightseeing. I banked the plane in a hard left turn, and the canopy allowed me to look straight down onto the water. I could hardly believe my good fortune—being paid to go whale watching.

We also spotted a flock of seagulls making lunch out of something on the ocean surface. Those gulls reminded me of airborne rats. I was always concerned about the possibility of sucking one (or more) of them into the jet intakes and damaging an engine. A few months earlier, while practicing landings at El Centro, I caught a glimpse of a dark shape closing on us at our altitude just an instant before a bird splattered against the windscreen directly in front of my face. I instinctively ducked, even though it would have been impossible for me to get out of the way in time. The poor bird never knew what hit it, and lucky for me, the strike didn't damage the canopy.

On this day our submarine patrol flight lasted more than four hours, so I was quite ready to land when we were finally allowed back to the ship. I got waved off during the first two approaches because there was traffic in the landing area. The third time was clear, though, and I got an OK (3) grade. That's an OK pass and a 3-wire—what every pilot, especially a new arrival to the fleet like me, strives for.

The navy system for grading landings is strict and uncompromising, and all pilots are judged on every landing throughout their careers. The grading system is based on a numerical scale, just like academics at school. The absolute best grade any pilot can get is an underlined OK. An underlined OK is worth five points, but such high marks are extremely rare. They are usually given only when a pilot makes a good landing with a major malfunction like a dead engine, partial hydraulics, or other extenuating circumstances that compound the difficulty.

Under normal conditions the best a pilot can hope for is an OK, or "okay" pass, worth four points, for a well-flown approach and landing in which the plane stays on glidepath, on speed, and on centerline with minor deviations. It's the equivalent of an A in school. A grade of (OK), a "fair" pass, worth three points, is for an average approach and landing in which the pilot makes substantial deviations from the ideal profile but corrects them quickly.

The next step down is a "bolter," worth 2.5 points, in which the pilot fails to make an arrested landing because the tailhook doesn't catch one of the arresting wires. Bolters are usually caused by pilots missing the landing area because they fly too high or let the nose of the airplane fall and the tail rise just before touchdown. Sometimes an approach will be fine but the tailhook skips on the metal deck and bounces over the wires. That's known as a "hook skip" bolter, and it doesn't count against the pilot.

A pilot gets a "no grade" or "gash," worth two points, for a below-average but safe approach and landing. A "waveoff" occurs when a pilot must abort a landing attempt for being too far from normal approach parameters.

The worst possible grade is a "cut pass," or zero, in which the pilot makes unsafe deviations close to the ship or past the waveoff window. The waveoff window ends at the "point of no return," where the pilot is too close to abort an approach safely. When a pilot makes gross deviations near the ship, touches down short of the wires, or fails to add power on landing, the result is a cut pass. Such events are rare, but they do happen. A cut pass often results in a review board being formed to evaluate the pilot before he or she is allowed to fly again.

Each squadron color-codes its grades and displays them next to the pilot's name on its "greenie board" (so called because in every squadron, OKs are coded green). Greenie boards are posted in every fixed-wing squadron ready room, and they are a constant source of pride and humiliation to aviators. In our squadron an underlined OK pass earned the pilot a blue mark, an OK was green, a grade of (OK) was yellow, a bolter was orange, a waveoff was red, a no grade (commonly known as a "shit stain") was brown, and a cut pass showed up as white. During the most recent grading period, I received five OKs, four (OK)'s, one bolter, and one no grade.

On the *Lincoln,* each squadron's combined landing grade point average was calculated and posted daily. All pilots in our air wing were required to maintain at minimum a 3.0 landing grade point average. If anyone fell below that level, a review board was automatically convened. Most air wings didn't have a "minimum" GPA as ours did. If someone was having a rough time, a review board would be held to evaluate the struggling pilot's performance, but there were no hard and fast rules about when the boards convened.

In some air wings the bottom ten pilots were automatically dropped at the end of a cruise. A 3.0 GPA sounded easy enough to maintain. But as I came to learn, the averages could play tricks on you. A consistent pilot who flies a series of average passes could suddenly get into trouble with one or two bolters or waveoffs. Then the cutoff line was suddenly a very real threat.

The rookie pilot, or "nugget," who gets the highest landing grades during the six months at sea is named the Top Nugget. Like everyone else, I wanted to win that prize. But the main goal was making consistent, safe passes. I had made fifty-three traps at that point in my navy career, and I was still very much a beginner.

My adrenaline would surge during each approach. I was usually concentrating too hard to be scared. I've always had an active imagination, and on the ground I enjoyed letting my mind wander. But in the cockpit, and especially during approaches to the ship, I became totally focused and didn't allow myself to think about anything else. The three crew members on my plane were counting on me to get them aboard safe. They entrusted me with their lives each time they got into my airplane, and I would never have forgiven myself if I had let them down. In the back of my mind I also knew that my peers were watching each landing—and so was the skipper.

After Kara's death, Commander Smith took me aside to talk about stress. He knew I was under a lot of pressure. All of the female aviators were under the microscope; this was our first cruise. And to compound the stress for me, Harry had just left on a deployment to the Persian Gulf. His ship had pulled out of port while my air wing was at sea practicing, and I felt terrible that I hadn't been able to say good-bye in person. Commander Smith recognized my difficulties, and he told me he would do everything possible to help me succeed. At the same time, he made it clear that I would have to break through on my own. No one else could do the hard work for me.

He concluded his low-key pep talk with an admonition to keep doing my best and keep improving. If I slacked off, everyone would be able to tell: "You'll be walking a little funny," he kidded, "because you're going to have my boot up your ass."

§

After my most recent flight, I ate a ham sandwich and slept for three hours. I can usually sleep soundly day or night. But for some reason I had a really bizarre nightmare. I dreamed that I was in one of the back seats of an S-3, and our plane began tumbling out of control. I yelled to eject, but no one did anything. I watched the altimeter unwind to less than four thousand feet. (That in itself was weird, because there is no altimeter in the back of an S-3, and I never flew in that seat.) The next thing I knew, I was watching my folks pull into the driveway of our old house in Montclair, Virginia, in a limo.

I could tell it was a dream. But as peculiar as the events seemed, they became even stranger. All of a sudden I was back on the ship and my landings were being evaluated. But instead of flying an airplane, I was riding a broomstick like the Wicked Witch of the West. Everyone was out there on the flight deck watching me and criticizing the way I was flying this broomstick. Then some admiral came up and told me that I wasn't cutting it and my days as a navy pilot were over. I begged him to let me keep flying, but he just laughed. Then I started yelling back at him, calling him a son of a bitch, among other things. That's when I woke up. I don't usually spend much time interpreting dreams, and dreams like this one make that seem like a good practice.

I went to the wardroom at 7:30 P.M. and learned that I had missed dinner. Then I went to Administration and did some research on which of my sailors had won awards or upgraded their qualifications during their time in our squadron, VS-29. I believed that the main reason sailors left the navy was that they didn't get the recognition they felt they deserved. I was glad to make an extra effort to make sure that my sailors got noticed for the things they did well.

20 February: Soggy Underwear

Jana and I were in Chris "Jolly" Taylor and Lt. Debbie Monroe's room having a junior officer gripe session when the question of how to pee in the cockpit came up. Debbie brought it up because her CO had returned from a flight and left his used piddle pack in the cockpit for the plane captain (the sailor who prepared the jet for the next flight) to remove. I told her the story I had heard about one of the senior officers in her squadron who was infamous for relieving himself on the cockpit floor during long flights. I can't imagine what his plane captain had to say about that.

I was curious to hear what Jolly did, because she is six feet two inches tall and flies in the cramped back seat of an F-14 Tomcat. They often refuel two or three times on long flights, and I wondered how she managed. Her method, she said, was simply to use the head (the bathroom) before takeoff, avoid drinking anything in flight, and grit her teeth.

I had seldom thought about such matters in training because our flights usually took ninety minutes or less from beginning to end. But S-3 missions can last five hours or more, so the question was now a lot less abstract. The navy formed a study group to consider "urine collection device" options for female aviators while I was training in S-3s. Women had been flying navy planes for twenty years, but suddenly, with the advent of female combat pilots, our leaders decided it was time to analyze how we pee.

Each of the gals in the group was given a grocery bag filled with different sorts of strange-looking contraptions. They included pads of varying thickness, incontinence diapers, and a curious plastic gadget designed to collect urine through a tube, then drain into a bag filled with a polymer dust that gels upon contact with liquids.

The device was a female-adapted version of the "piddle packs" guys had been carrying in cockpits for years. Piddle packs began as nothing more than zip-lock bags with sponges inside; later they replaced the sponges with a high-tech polymer powder. Women used to be issued regular piddle packs with the idea that if nature ever demanded it, we could somehow manage to fly the airplane while holding a baggy between our legs and not lose a drop. Fortunately, by going to the bathroom before each flight and avoiding liquids in the cockpit, I was able to avoid that particular situation. I figured frequent exercise would keep my bladder as strong as cast iron.

Nevertheless, I was glad the navy was taking our situation seriously, and so I tried to help. I took my goody bag and each of the devices for a "test drive" of sorts. Rather than subject the other three members of my S-3 crew to my initial experiments, I decided to try them in the privacy of my apartment.

First came the pad, a huge hulk of absorbent material that made it almost impossible to walk straight. I waited until I really had to use the bathroom, then sat on the toilet with the lid down. Even though my bladder told me I had to go, my body refused to cooperate while I was fully clothed. All that great potty-training my parents had drilled into me as a kid had obviously done its job. It took a few minutes, but I finally overcame my resistance—and the pad held the liquid remarkably well. Like a paper towel that had just mopped up a large spill, however, it was quite damp and uncomfortable to sit on.

The next item I tried was the plastic funnel device. Once again, when I really had to go I donned my flight suit and then sat down on the toilet. Just as in the first experiment, getting started wasn't easy. But the funnel itself worked great, and all the urine went straight into the bowl. I figured it would work just as well in the plane when connected to the piddle pack, so it graduated to the next level of testing.

Our squadron flew to El Centro the next day to practice simulated aircraft carrier landings on a remote runway painted like the deck of a ship. Between flights I stood with the landing signal officers watching other pilots practice approaches. The LSOs were busy, and there were no port-a-potties around, so I went behind a small wooden shed and whipped out the funnel. I was wearing a flight suit and full survival gear and decided to leave all of it on to simulate the situation during a real mission. I unzipped the flight suit from the bottom about five inches up. That was as far as the zipper would go before encountering the survival vest I wore on top of it. I squeezed the funnel into position and tried to position myself as though I was sitting on an ejection seat.

I began to urinate. Then I began to worry. Several seconds went by, and I still hadn't seen a drop of urine in the plastic bag! I stood all the way up—something I would be unable to do in the jet—and finally the pee began draining properly. When I was done, I reached around the back of my flight suit and felt some dampness on my rear end. That's just great, I remember thinking. I had managed to urinate all over myself, and now I had to fly home in soggy underwear.

Luckily I still had some time, and it was a bright sunny day in El Centro. I took off my survival gear and stood outside in the breeze trying to dry off my flight suit. The half-hour flight home to North Island wasn't too uncomfortable. Once we got there, I barely had enough time to race back to my apartment and change my underwear and flight suit before my next flight. After that little fiasco, I have refrained from using the urine collection device in the actual airplane.

Going to the bathroom became a standard part of my preflight ritual. I've flown individual missions of more than six hours' duration without having to resort to that plastic funnel thing. I even timed how long it took to get from the ready room to the toilet wearing my flight suit, torso harness, and survival gear, undress, use the bathroom, and then suit up again. It took me three minutes and ten seconds—but in a pinch I could cut that to about two minutes and thirty seconds. Not too shabby.

Once while I was in the bathroom just before a flight (the guys joked about my "dumping down" to takeoff weight), I heard the door fly open in the stall next to me. There was an urgent rustling as I watched the black boots next door. I heard some jostling noises and an unzipping and saw a survival vest hit the ground. Then some unbuckling and more unzipping and the torso harness fell on top of the vest. Another quick unzipping sound came next, followed by a long sigh as the aviator was finally able to relieve herself.

I could certainly appreciate the gravity of her situation.

§

We had a surprise inspection of sorts after Commander Smith was informed that a small-caliber bullet had been found in our squadron's male berthing area. He ordered the inspection, known as a "Health and Comfort" inspection, to find out if anyone was hiding a pistol. I waited for two hours in the avionics technicians' workspace with my division while their rooms were searched. Nothing turned up.

This was the first time I had ever seen Commander Smith angry. He didn't yell or lose his temper, but he swore a couple of times, and I had never heard him do that before.

22 February: A Trapeze without a Net

It's amazing how a person's brain learns to tune out certain sounds aboard ship.

I was the duty officer in the ready room from 7:30 P.M. until 7:30 A.M.—then slept like a rock until 2 P.M. I slept right through several launches and recoveries. That in itself was pretty incredible considering the screeching noise and shuddering vibrations that went through the ship every time an airplane took off or landed. During catapult shots each plane's engines were screaming at full power, and the steam catapult sent shock waves that rattled the walls and floors violently. The first time I walked down a passageway close to the catapult at the same time that a jet was launched, I nearly jumped out of my boots. With thirty-ton jets taking off with afterburners firing only a few yards away, my policy of wearing earplugs to bed was understandable.

There was also a metal hatch in the wardroom right above our stateroom, and sometimes I would have sworn the sailors were picking it up and slamming it just to get our attention. I never heard anyone open the hatch gently and close it normally; each time, it got yanked open and banged shut. Maybe they figured that if they had to be up and about, the rest of us should at least be awake. If I was really tired, the sounds didn't bug me. But if I was having a hard time falling asleep, or if the noises awakened me, I wanted to go out and kill someone. My desire for retribution never provided quite enough motivation to get me out of bed, though. I would just find myself grumbling and cursing and wishing I was somewhere else.

At all times on the ship, generators, vents, and pipes created a constant, very loud humming sort of white noise. At any given time there would be banging, drilling, clanging, bellowing, and screeching as systems were being worked on. This went on day and night.

The loudest place of all was the arresting gear room. Each time a plane landed, there would be a piercing screech as the arresting cables paid out and brought arriving airplanes from 140 miles an hour to a halt in two seconds. It sounded like a hundred thousand metallic fingernails being scraped along an amplified chalkboard. People would hear the gear spooling up and would cover their ears when they walked by.

Despite the constant barrage of otherworldly sounds, some noises cut right through the din. A ringing telephone or chirping alarm clock could awaken me instantly even though I could sometimes sleep through much louder catapult shots or arresting gear sounds.

§

At breakfast I traded barbs with a few of the other aviators in our squadron.

"Bert"—so named because his bushy black eyebrows resembled the *Sesame Street* character's—made some wisecrack about me while I happened to be munching on a piece of fruit.

"Watch out," another pilot warned. "She's got a pear!"

"She's got a pair?" Bert replied with feigned innocence. "A pair of . . . what?"

One of the things I liked best about navy aviation was the camaraderie. Aviators were always teasing each other and making jokes. Usually it was all in fun, and the practical jokes never seemed to end.

One time Jana got mad because someone had been stealing her Diet Cokes, and she left a big sign on the refrigerator in the ready room telling the "lowlife" who had taken the drinks to bring them back. The guys started calling her "Lola Cola" and would sing to the tune of the Kinks song "Lola," "Lola, someone stole my cola. . . ." The next time she was on duty, someone put a sign on the outside of the ready room door that said, "Free Diet Cokes Inside! See squadron duty officer for details!"

I almost always found something to laugh about in the ready room. Even when things were totally bleak, someone would find a way to point out something humorous about our shared predicament. One time when one of our pilots committed a particularly boneheaded blunder, someone drew a little question mark on a Post-It note and stuck it on his squadron picture on the ready room wall.

My flying was going well at this point, and my landings were improving. I had flown a three-hour-plus aerial refueling mission the previous day and made a night landing. The flight itself was pretty dull—mostly orbiting the ship. I figured it took us about five minutes to make one complete circuit around the ship. We were up there for about two hundred minutes, or forty trips around the *Lincoln*. When I'm bored, I do mathematics in my head. It's an old habit, and I feel that it helps keep me mentally alert in the cockpit.

I also brought some Gummi Bears along and shared them with my crew. Flying the S-3, I sometimes felt like Mom taking the kids out for a Sunday drive in the family station wagon. Some of the crew members were so young—especially the enlisted guys, who were just twenty or twenty-one years old. They were very professional, and they performed their difficult, technical jobs admirably. But hearing their aimless banter as they gobbled candy in the back seats reminded me just how young some of them really were.

At one point the sensor operator, or SENSO, in the seat behind me started complaining that his helmet didn't fit and it was giving him a headache. "My head hurts like hell!" he sulked.

I nodded sympathetically and added, "Well, it's your face that's killing me." We all got a chuckle out of that old line.

When I first transferred to S-3s from the single-seat Hornets, I was disappointed at being switched to the relatively slow, lumbering planes. It felt like a real step down from the state-of-the-art strike fighter. I always figured that if you were going to be stuck out in the middle of the ocean, it would sure be nice to be able to rip around going supersonic. And if you were going to be stuck flying antisubmarine planes, you might as well have the luxury of being stationed on land like the crews of P-3 Orions —the hulking four-engine turboprops that perform many of the same tasks we did. But the more accustomed I became to Vikings and the people who operated them, the more I enjoyed the interaction of our multiperson crews and the challenges of being at sea.

"Hawking" other planes that were low on fuel was one of the most rewarding missions we performed. When an attack jet returned from a long mission, the pilot usually had only enough fuel to make one or two landing attempts before running dangerously low. We followed the attack planes down and put our S-3s above (like a hawk) and to the right. If the attack jet boltered, the pilot knew that we would be at his one o'clock position, on altitude and on time. That way we could quickly top off his fuel tanks and allow him to make as many landing attempts as he needed.

It was tricky for the hawks to maintain the proper position relative to the other plane, because the approach speeds varied so widely. It was a dynamic situation that had to be constantly managed. The last thing a fatigued pilot in an airplane low on fuel wanted was to have to hunt around the night sky for a tanker. A couple of times, after successful hawking missions, other aviators would come up to me and thank me for saving their lives with timely tanks of fuel. They didn't need to say thanks; aerial refueling is part of any S-3 driver's job. But it was nice to receive the acknowledgment.

§

In S-3s, each crew member's job is clearly defined.

The "assistant" tactical coordinator, or COTAC, a naval flight officer, sits in the front right seat next to the pilot and operates the radios, navigation equipment, and radar.

The tactical coordinator, or TACCO, in the back right seat handles the weapons and tactical communications. The TACCO is often the most senior crew member and the mission commander. The SENSO in the back left seat is an enlisted person who listens to sonar buoys and identifies undersea targets and surface ships.

As the aircraft commander, I was responsible for getting our plane into position to accomplish our mission, then bringing us back safe onto the ship. I also kept a "big picture" view of the tactical situation to assist the TACCO.

When I first came to VS-29, I flew with Larry "Jedi" Anderson, one of the more experienced officers in our squadron, on a night training flight. The conversation in the back of the plane got a little colorful that night, and Jedi was afraid the four-letter words were offending me or making me uncomfortable. So he wrote a note reminding himself to talk to the rest of the crew after the flight and tell them to avoid swearing. Then, on my first approach to the ship, I added too much power, missed the arresting wires, and boltered. "Fuck!" I shouted, realizing that I had bungled the landing and would have to make another attempt. "Goddammit!"

Jedi reached over and quietly erased the note he had written to himself.

Word spread quickly that not only did I not mind swearwords, I was quite adept at using them. My crews continued to express themselves freely.

§

My most recent night landing presented a few unusual challenges. The sky was getting particularly dark, and a wall of storm clouds approached from the south. There was lightning on the horizon, and the flashes kept making me jump because the far-off lightning bolts looked exactly like the white strobe lights on the wing tips of other airplanes. The electrical storm gave the illusion that another plane was nearby at our assigned altitude creating the danger of a midair collision.

I stayed focused, though, and made it aboard on my first try.

The carrier's four arresting wires were about 40 feet apart, so there was only a stretch of 160 feet in which an arriving plane could touch down with any chance of coming to a safe stop. At this point we were too far out to sea to fly to shore if for some reason we weren't able to land on the ship. These were what was known as "blue water operations," and all land bases were out of range. Being so far out at sea was like performing on a trapeze without a net: you might have done the routine a thousand times, but without the safety net, it was like a whole new game.

23 February: Letter from Harry

(This letter was written from on board the USS *Constellation* in the Persian Gulf.)

Dear Loree,

Happy Valentine's Day!

Here's a letter to keep you from forgetting how much you are loved and missed by the fella who is lucky enough to wear your ring, but unfortunate

*enough to be on the other side of the planet on the day made for people
in love.*

*I just got the care package with an amazing letter from you (the one
with the poem). Wow. That one will keep me going for a while! I'll have to
keep it handy for when I need a little boost. You really knocked my socks off
with that one. Your perfumed letter arrived two days ago. You should have
seen me sitting in a corner of the ready room sniffing the envelope. I did it
for more than ten minutes, just imagining you. I almost hyperventilated! I
know you know how much I enjoy getting your letters, but it's worth saying
again. . . .*

*I was the squadron duty officer today. Long day. Tomorrow I go to
Dhahran, Saudi Arabia, for a two-day air force exchange. It should provide
a nice little respite from the grind out here on the ship. They say Dhahran
is a dusty little flyspeck of a place—but I'm sure it will feel like paradise
compared to the Connie.*

*I'll try and call you as soon as I get to shore. . . . I can't wait to see you
again.*

Love you,
Harry

23 February: Emergency Procedures

In airplanes, things never seem to go wrong one at a time.

My flights were either absolutely trouble-free, or they were nonstop
emergency-procedure fests. On my most recent flight we had a whole
series of equipment problems that seemed to pile up on top of one
another.

A few minutes after I started the engines, it became apparent that our
inertial navigation system, or INS, was faulty. The INS is our main navigation instrument. It's a handy tool that constantly displays the plane's
speed, heading, and distance from the ship. We had an avionics technician
come onto the plane, and he fiddled with the INS for a few minutes.
Whatever he did seemed to work. The INS computer indicated that it
was up and running, and the greenish lights on the instrument panel displayed the data we needed.

We moved into position and had a normal catapult shot. But the rapid acceleration of the cat must have caused something to jiggle loose in the INS, and it went on the blink again.

We climbed to altitude but stayed close to the ship. An A-6 Intruder pilot was having trouble getting aboard, and if he didn't land soon, he would be short of fuel. We kept close by in case the Intruder pilot needed to take some fuel from us. But he finally managed to land, so we didn't need to stick around. We got our INS realigned, then headed out to refuel some F/A-18 Hornets.

The Hornets were on "combat air patrol," or CAP, orbiting high above the fleet to defend against attackers. Since they weren't likely to encounter any bad guys in our position a few hundred miles off the coast of San Francisco, they decided to attack each other. As we approached the area, I could see them "yanking and banking"—trying to twist their supersonic jets into position for simulated gun or missile shots. It looked like they were having a great time leaving miles of curved white contrails in their crossing paths.

The Hornets must have been burning lots of fuel doing their antics, because they knocked off their simulated fight as soon as the CAP controller said that their "Texaco" had arrived on station. Texaco was our S-3, of course. The Hornets fell neatly into line behind us. We extended the midair-refueling basket—a long hose at the end of a reel. One by one the Hornets took turns moving into position behind us and pressing their refueling probes against the basket.

Midair refueling looks difficult, but for anyone accustomed to formation flying, it's not complicated. But as with just about everything in navy flying, there can be hidden dangers.

The month before, a Hornet in VFA-22 received some apparently minor damage during midair refueling when the basket knocked against its pitot static tube. The metal sensor sticks out about four inches from the nose of a Hornet. The damage didn't seem significant at the time. The plane landed on the *Lincoln,* and Lt. Glenn "K-9" Kersgieter got in and prepared for a night catapult launch.

Unknown to anyone at the time, however, the damaged probe was feeding erroneous information into the plane's flight control computer. And when K-9 shot off the catapult, the computer wrongly determined that the plane was too slow and automatically pitched the nose down. K-9 never had a chance. A half-second after his plane left the *Lincoln,* it disappeared into the blackness of the sea directly in front of the ship. He had a split second in which he could have ejected before hitting the water. But no one thinks or reacts that fast.

One moment, everything was fine. The next, K-9 was dead.

At K-9's funeral there was a lot of grumbling among the aviators about the fact that few admirals or top navy officials had seen fit to attend. Many of them, it seemed, had made it to the memorial services for Lt. Kara Hultgreen in Texas and her burial in Arlington Cemetery near Washington. By contrast, the services for K-9 were low-profile and subdued. I don't think anyone meant to slight K-9 or minimize his family's tragedy. He was a popular, gifted aviator and a good friend to those who knew him well. He came from a large religious family, and I hoped that their faith gave them comfort. But K-9 had never had to lobby in front of Congress for the opportunity to fly jets off a carrier, as Kara did. The large navy attendance at her funeral was a show of respect for a pioneer. If she got extra attention during her funeral, it was not just because she was a woman. Why begrudge her? The two deaths were equally tragic.

The sun dipped below the horizon, and our refueling mission was complete. All the thirsty Hornets were topped off, and they charged back up to the thin air and fading light above thirty thousand feet and resumed their dogfights. I pointed our S-3 back toward the ship. Our INS was still on the blink, but we had an AHRS (attitude and heading reference system) to help guide us home, and it kept us pointed toward the ship.

"Don't worry," said the COTAC, who was sitting in the front right seat next to me. "I've got one thousand hours in S-3s, and I've never had an AHRS fail."

Of course as soon as he said that, the AHRS dumped, too.

I had to rely on the standby gyroscopic instruments to keep our wings level on the way back. But the cockpit lights were on, so it wasn't too bad. We were only about thirty minutes away from the ship, the sky was still pink from the last rays of the setting sun, and the clear horizon made it easy to avoid vertigo.

My skipper was already airborne when we approached the ship, and he said he would meet our plane and lead us to the *Lincoln*. Then suddenly both the INS and the AHRS started working properly again. We rendezvoused with the skipper's S-3 close to the ship, and we took turns doing quick "package checks" of each other's refueling stores. He was going out on an aerial tanking mission, so we soon went our separate ways.

I started my approach to the ship, and everything was going well at first despite the fact that the sunlight was totally gone. I could see the *Lincoln* about five miles ahead of us—a speck of white light in a sea of blackness. There was a scattered cloud layer at about eight hundred feet above the water, and it created the illusion that the horizon was much higher than it actually was. From the cockpit my approach to the ship looked to be too high. I instinctively reduced power to quicken my descent, but when I glanced at the instruments, they told me I was getting too low.

The situation was pretty confusing, and for an instant it really freaked me out. But I added power and stabilized the approach as the instruments dictated. The closer we got to the ship, the darker the ocean around it became. Sweat was beading on my forehead, and I felt dizzy from vertigo. When we finally arrived on deck, the sea and sky seemed to merge in absolute, impenetrable darkness. I got an OK (3) on the landing. The landing signal officers must have cut me some slack because the conditions were so tough and I responded correctly when I started getting low.

I was ravenous after the long flight and wolfed down a bowl of ravioli, with Cap'n Crunch cereal for dessert.

24 February: My Own TV

The Golden Gate Bridge looked spectacular as we sailed into San Francisco Bay on our way to the naval air station at Alameda. This was our last at-sea period—our final dress rehearsal—before leaving for the Persian Gulf in six weeks.

I bundled up and stood on the windy deck, snapping pictures like a tourist the whole time. I don't think there's a more beautiful city in America than San Francisco on a clear day. I wanted to remember the sight because it would give me a preview of the end of our cruise the next fall. We were planning to return to Alameda when our six-month deployment was over.

Later in the day I was scheduled to get off the boat and hop on a C-9, a navy transport plane, and ride down to San Diego. I kept thinking how great it was going to be to see my dog, Stoney, again, to sleep in my own bed, and to use my own shower. Everyday things like talking on the telephone, shopping at malls, and going to movie theaters seem so important when those activities are unavailable. I decided I would even splurge on a massage when I got home; nothing soothes my tension better than that. The only sadness was realizing that Harry wouldn't be around.

§

On my most recent flight our S-3 located and tracked a nuclear submarine. I was following it visually, making wide oval patterns above it while its periscope cut through the waves on the ocean surface. We were in an almost constant left turn, and I kept the wing tip pointed at the periscope and watched its tiny wake for about twenty minutes. We made radio calls back to the ship and asked for permission to drop a simulated torpedo on the submarine, but the admiral leading our side of the war game told us to keep tracking the sub visually.

The sub was headed straight south and hadn't changed its course for several minutes. Then all of a sudden it went "sinker" and tried to dive away from us. I lost sight of its periscope when it quickly retracted under the water. I was looking straight down, trying to find some hint of where the sub might be, when I suddenly noticed its black cylindrical outline below the ocean surface. It was about twenty feet down, but the blue water was so clear that I could easily make out the sleek nuclear sub's distinctive shape with the single huge propeller churning behind it. It was an amazing sight, and it was kind of hard to believe that there were real people in that hunk of metal. It was fascinating to watch, but the temptation to stare was overridden by the need to watch my altitude, since we were very close to the water.

We laid down a series of sonar buoys around the fleeing submarine and tracked its descent. A few minutes later another Viking was called in to drop a simulated torpedo on the sub we had found. Our plane didn't get the kill, but we got credit for the assist.

I've often heard people wonder aloud whether women—being the kind, gentle, nurturing creatures we are—could ever pull the trigger in a combat situation. Personally I have no doubts at all. I'm not a mean or malicious person, but I wanted to kill that sub so bad I could hardly stand it. If it had been an enemy posing a real danger to our battle group or our country, I wouldn't have hesitated to send it and its crew to the bottom of the ocean forever. The submarine and I had been pitted against each other in a high-stakes contest, and only one of us could win. The way aviators look at it, either the sub dies or our staterooms and stereos get wet.

After the war games ended, all the flying was over. Our whole squadron had a chance to vegetate in the ready room that night and catch up on TV shows and movies. I watched at least eight *Seinfeld* episodes; one of the guys in the squadron had taped them and edited out the commercials.

I finished the at-sea period with six OK landings, five (OK)'s, one bolter, and one no grade. That put my landing grades at 3.35. I wanted to bring that up to a 3.5 by the time the grading period ended—probably about the time we got to Hong Kong on our way to the Persian Gulf. That was going to require some steady improvement and consistency on my part.

I realized that I had had a rough start, and that the stress of Kara's crash and Harry's departure for the Persian Gulf had probably distracted me. But I was encouraged by the fact that I had worked hard, and that my landing grades seemed to be improving. Then again, sometimes it was hard even to care about grades. When flying at night while the dim starlight was blocked out by a cloud layer and the deck was moving around as the ship plowed through huge ocean swells, I was just happy to get back safe on deck.

three

Over the Horizon

14 April 1995: A Few More Tizzies

I knew it would be my last real shower until Hong Kong, so I just stood there in the bathroom of my apartment and luxuriated in the steamy warmth as the water ran at full blast over my head and soapy skin. I turned up the temperature as high as I could stand it and let it pour over me until the water heater was empty and my skin looked like that of a prune. That afternoon I flew out to the USS *Abraham Lincoln* as the ship began steaming west on the beginning of our long voyage over the horizon.

For me there were no prolonged, emotional good-byes. Harry had been at sea for months on the USS *Constellation*. And I had already written a will, called family and friends on the telephone, and received their good wishes before starting out on this historic mission. I had stored up their love and vowed to carry it with me during the loneliness that I knew would come.

My flight out to the ship turned out to be a minor comedy of errors. The first S-3 I boarded at the naval air station at North Island had a faulty auxiliary power unit generator, so my crew and I hopped into another airplane. Then the second jet developed a major hydraulic leak in the starboard wheel well, so we bagged that one, too. Finally the third plane was mechanically sound, and it got us airborne.

When we arrived at the ship, I made two "touch and goes"—practice approaches and landings in which the pilot allows the plane to actually touch down on deck with the tailhook retracted, then adds full power and takes off again without coming to a stop. It's just like a regular approach except that the tailhook stays up. After that I made several more traps and cats.

When I got to our four-person stateroom, I was surprised and pleased to find that the guys in my squadron had already hauled all my boxes down to my living quarters. They later took care to inform me, many times, that I owed all of them beer at our first port call—and I gladly promised to pay in full. Helping me move was a thoughtful and unexpected gesture.

Like all living quarters aboard navy ships, our four-person room was cramped. It was about nine feet square with several metal lockers lined up against the bulkheads. The lockers were painted a pale shade of yellow that matched the bulkheads and the tile floor; my roommates brought some blue carpeting and used it to cover that yellow tile. Four of the seven lockers had fold-out desks. The sleeping compartment was separated from the rest of the room by a thin blue curtain, and there were two bunks on each side.

Jana and I had almost finished unpacking at about 10 P.M. when the two female pilots who would share the room with us came aboard. They flew E-2C Hawkeyes, large twin-engine propeller planes that carry huge round radar discs above their fuselages. Their crews act as airborne traffic controllers, directing planes to their targets and rendezvous points and warning pilots of potential threats.

Our first few minutes together were strained and awkward, and I hoped that this getting off on the wrong foot would not be a portent of things to come.

Jana and I introduced ourselves and started telling the new arrivals what space was available for them and their belongings. Since we were senior in rank to our roommates and had arrived first, Jana and I had staked out the two bottom bunks. But as soon as Lt. A. J. Brooks, the first of the Hawkeye pilots, got there, she started protesting. She said she had a bad knee and insisted on having one of the lower bunks.

Jana and I were a little taken aback because it sounded like A. J. was demanding a bottom bunk—not requesting one. But I decided to give her the benefit of the doubt. She was probably wiped out after a long day of flying, and she had had some mechanical problems on her plane that complicated her arrival; she could be forgiven for being a little prickly. I took a top bunk with the understanding that Jana would swap with me in exactly three months. It seemed like a reasonable compromise.

Unfortunately, Jana decided right from the start that she didn't like A. J., and she began giving her the silent treatment. That was an ominous sign considering that we were only on day one of our cruise, with 180 or more to go. I tried to cut A. J. some slack, and she started to come around. I think she realized that Jana and I had been less than enchanted with her at our initial encounter.

When Lt. Sue McNally arrived a few minutes later, she and A. J. started divvying up their space. One of them made the seemingly logical, innocuous suggestion that they store some of their things in the long locker between them, but they soon came to regret it. Jana had already put some of her stuff in that locker, and she pitched an absolute fit. She let everyone know immediately that she was tired of moving, and her stuff was going to damn well stay right where she had left it.

Jana and I had been moved to different quarters the last three times we had been aboard the ship. It was an aggravating pain in the butt to have to pack up and move all the time. I think Jana was taking it personally, and she was absolutely not going to move her belongings any more.

After her tantrum, things got real quiet.

Our roommate situation wasn't going to be easy. A. J. could be very pleasant when she wanted to be. She was about five feet six inches tall and had long brown hair that I envied (I had cut mine the year before), fair skin, and fine, delicate-looking features. But her face was usually twisted into a scowl, and she was awfully moody. I knew already that Jana had a quick, explosive temper but recovered quickly. Sue seemed friendly and reasonable, though.

We were feeling the pressure of being on a combat ship as it steamed toward the unknown, and each of us responded differently. I tended to withdraw, Jana vented and exercised, A. J. complained, and Sue tried to smooth things over. We knew we needed to be flexible and accommodating, especially with each other, but cooperation was scarce at first.

From the outset I worried about the friction between A. J. and Jana. I was concerned that it would create a split in our stateroom. And I knew that if Jana threw a few more tizzies like the one she had put on that first night in our stateroom, she was going to alienate herself. I was disappointed because I had looked forward to the four of us bonding and becoming good friends, but it didn't look as though our personalities would mesh well.

§

Aside from flying, my other responsibility on the ship was overseeing the sailors in the avionics and armament shops. There were thirty-five electricians, avionics technicians, and ordnance men, and my job was to take care of their well-being. The young ones were about nineteen years old, the same age as my younger brother Ryan, and I enjoyed the fact that they reminded me of him. They liked to put on a brave face and project a hardened, rebellious image—and with most of them, it was absolutely transparent.

I had worked with enlisted troops in previous jobs at other squadrons and had always found them refreshing. Over the years I had developed a talent for cutting through navy bureaucracy, and it felt good to put that knowledge to use as their advocate. Even though I had been the avionics/armament division officer for only a month, I felt that the troops knew I would stick up for them, and that my concern for them was genuine.

The young sailors impressed me with their technical skill and the huge responsibilities they shouldered. I sometimes felt guilty that they worked so hard and got paid so little. As a pilot, I got to fly and got a bigger paycheck, too. The few times the subject came up, however, the sailors told me that they wouldn't fly off a carrier at night for all the money in the world.

The older sailors had been on cruises and had far more training than the young airmen I had previously supervised. At first I was concerned that I had nothing to offer these gruff, tattooed, tough-talking sailors. They had more experience dealing with the navy than I did, and I knew they might resist taking directions from a female officer. But from the beginning my experience with them was cooperative and productive.

Sailors like the ones working in the *Lincoln*'s three avionics and ordnance shops are the heart and soul of the navy. They are responsible for the nuts-and-bolts job of making all the complex machinery work. They toil day and night in stifling, hot, noisy, windowless shops. Their jobs are physically demanding, and their sleeping quarters make a four-person stateroom like the one I had look spacious. At their best, the sailors are teamwork personified. They put their egos aside for common goals, and their interactions seem devoid of the petty political jealousies and personality conflicts that have always afflicted career-minded officers.

One of the electricians who worked in the avionics shop told me that his toddler son had been born with a kidney defect and would soon undergo surgery. As the date of the operation approached, the sailor became increasingly worried and distracted. Stress and concern were eating him up. I remembered hearing that the *Lincoln* had a video link to Balboa Hospital in San Diego so that doctors on the ship could consult with their more experienced peers on shore in case of medical emergencies. I knew that the sailor's boy was being operated on at Balboa, so I arranged for the sailor to talk "face-to-face" with his son before and after surgery.

The sailor was greatly relieved to see his son on the video monitor. He reassured the boy before the surgery, and the real-time images of his son afterward allowed the sailor to see with his own eyes that the operation had been a success. Within hours the sailor was back at work fixing airplanes. I was confident that his mind was clear, and that he could concentrate on his tasks. At the same time, it gave me a sense of accomplishment to know that I had helped make his burdens a little bit lighter.

18 April: Kind Words

The first major clash between the women on the *Lincoln* and its top officers came about as the result of an order that we submit to pregnancy tests. The order came as something of a shock, since all of us had taken similar tests when we checked into our squadrons. Now we had to repeat the tests again right away.

Some of the women on the *Lincoln* were furious and regarded the order as an unlawful intrusion into their private lives. They believed it to be a clear sign that the navy didn't trust us and was treating us differently. I found it odd that while our superiors were willing to put us at the controls of multi-million-dollar jets with the lives of other crew members at stake, they didn't trust us to manage our own bodies. I was pushed to the center of the controversy when Commander Smith summoned me to our ready room at 1 A.M. and told me to relay the order to the other women in our squadron.

Smith seemed upset by the suddenness of the order and the underlying message it seemed to convey. His hands were tied, however, and he and the other squadron leaders had to comply. He asked me to make sure that the tests were carried out promptly the next morning.

Personally I was ambivalent about being ordered to take the pregnancy test, but I was prepared to do it. The USS *Dwight D. Eisenhower* had been the first navy aircraft carrier to go to sea with female crew members, and about the time the ship left port, there were several pregnancies. Pregnant women were barred from combat assignments, and those on the *Eisenhower* were sent home immediately. New crew members had to be substituted at the last minute, and that must have been a hardship for the replacement sailors. All warships are composed of many teams, all of which must intricately coordinate their actions. Anyone who fails to perform for any team—no matter the reason—endangers everyone.

If any of the women aboard the *Lincoln* were pregnant, I figured they owed it to their shipmates to let the navy know right away so that they could be replaced near Hawaii instead of halfway around the world in the Persian Gulf. The whole battle group would be better off.

It became painfully clear, however, that some of the women on the *Lincoln* regarded the pregnancy tests as a personal affront. A few of the female pilots were extremely angry about the order, and a group of female chief petty officers was incensed, too. Unfortunately, a female chief petty officer from my squadron called the navy's Sexual Harassment Hotline—an 800 number—to complain before I had a chance to speak with her.

I had the unpleasant task of informing Smith of the anonymous call to the hotline. He was furious, and I was upset, too. The hotline was supposed to be used as a measure of last resort after all other means of solving problems within the chain of command had been exhausted. Instead of confronting the issue directly, this woman had gone straight to the phone.

Smith angrily printed his name, rank, and Social Security number on a piece of paper and handed it to me. He wanted me to give the paper to the person who had made the hotline call and tell her to get back on the phone and relay the additional information about who had ordered the tests. If anyone was going to take a hit over this controversy, he insisted it should be him.

I felt horrible. Smith was a tough disciplinarian, but he had been absolutely impartial, fair, and evenhanded to me and the other women under his command. He had a reputation for demanding a lot of his junior officers, but in return he backed us to the hilt. Aboard the *Lincoln,* whenever the Air Boss summoned one of the pilots in our squadron to his office to be verbally harangued for screwing up an approach or making some other kind of mistake, our skipper walked up nine flights of ladders and absorbed the Boss's wrath himself. Later he would talk to the offending pilot and offer constructive criticism, not bombast and invective. Very few squadron commanders were willing to become human heat shields for their junior officers. My mistakes had been keeping him in top physical shape before our cruise began, but Smith seldom mentioned the heat he was taking for me, because he wanted to reduce the stress he knew that I felt.

Smith was regarded by his peers as an excellent aviator, and the pilots in our squadron held him in high regard. His manner was somewhat stiff and formal but at the same time thoughtful and even approachable. He seemed to me the perfect person to lead our squadron through this difficult period, and if he were to become the scapegoat for this latest flap, I would have been crushed.

I understood and was sympathetic to the privacy issue. But there were real military readiness concerns, too. In situations in which the rights of individuals conflicted with the good of the group, I felt that individuals should be willing to do what's best for their team, their shipmates.

The pregnancy test order created a lot of hostility among the women in the air wing, and after obtaining legal advice, the commander of the air wing (CAG) soon backed down. The pregnancy tests became optional instead of mandatory, and that compromise diffused the situation—at least temporarily. It left us feeling uneasy about our CAG and his ability to lead an integrated air wing. I don't think his attitude toward women was malicious, just clueless. I had hoped the navy would assign better leaders for this cruise; instead, we got men like CAG and Pug.

§

The stress and difficulty of the first few days at sea drove one of the female sailors in my squadron to an emotional crisis. I heard she was having a tough time, and our most senior female chief asked me to meet with her in the VS-29 ready room.

The sailor told me that the cruise was shaping up to be more lonely and dismal than she could stand. She said she was contemplating an "unauthorized absence" when the ship pulled into port or doing "whatever was necessary" to get out of the navy. Did she mean she was going desert, or hurt herself, or even kill herself? It was impossible to be sure, but I suspected that she would either take drugs or try to get pregnant.

We sat down in two chairs at the back of the vacant ready room, and I listened as she talked at length about her deep disappointment. She didn't like the people she had been assigned to work with, she was dissatisfied with her job, and she hated being at sea. As she talked, she began crying, and her shoulders shook with each sob. She had signed on with the navy for three years, and so far she had served only six months. She was miserable, depressed, and desperate.

I could sympathize with her. Six years earlier I had made a similar confession to Lt. Kathryn Hobbs, my instructor at the Reserve Officer Training Corps at the University of San Diego. At that point I wanted to get out of the navy, too. But my instructor persuaded me to stick it out for six more months. During that time I went on the field trip to Miramar that directed my career toward aviation and changed my life.

I patted the young sailor on the back and gave her as much encouragement as I could. I tried to convince her that she didn't have to be miserable, and that she could do things to improve her situation. I reminded her that her parents were probably very proud that she was serving her country in the navy. Certainly they would be hurt and disappointed if she broke the law in order to get out of her navy contract. I recommended to the sailor that she take some of the college correspondence courses that the navy offers; it would be a great way to break up the monotony of living and working on a ship.

She nodded her head compliantly but still seemed melancholy at the end of our thirty-minute conversation. I think I may have gotten through to her a little bit, though. Mostly she needed someone to listen to her and assure her that she was not alone—that other people on the ship cared about her and were willing to help her.

I hoped she would make the right choices.

§

The flying had been going well for me to this point, even under some demanding conditions.

One night there was a solid overcast layer from eight hundred feet to about twenty-five hundred feet. I had a ninety-minute flight, then came back over the ship at about 9 P.M. There I met up with an A-6 Intruder that was acting as an aerial tanker, and I put a few thousand pounds of fuel into our S-3's tanks before my first landing attempt. I became especially glad that we had the extra fuel as I listened to the radio and heard another A-6 bolter several times.

The seas were high, visibility was getting low, and there was absolutely nowhere else to go. The ship was too far out to sea for any hope of flying to a land base if for some reason we were unable to get the plane safely onto the deck. Finally the A-6 trapped successfully—and that meant it was our turn.

Navy flight training had prepared me well for my assignments, and I had confidence in the people I worked with. But I have to admit that night carrier landings always made me tense. And the more of them I performed, the more certain I became that I would never be completely comfortable with them. No matter how well I memorized the procedures, I couldn't make myself enjoy night landings.

Even though we had enough fuel on board to make lots of landing attempts, I knew that the alternatives to a successful landing were extremely unpleasant. We could eject and hope that our parachutes would open and that the rescue helicopter crews could find all four of us in the middle of the dark ocean. Or we could have the ship's crew set up a barricade on deck and try to fly into it. A barricade is like a giant butterfly net made of thick straps and cables. It stretches across the width of the deck, and if the plane touches down in time, the net should be able to snare it and bring it to a halt. But it's used only as a last resort, and we were nowhere close to desperation time.

An air-traffic controller on the *Lincoln* used the ship's radar to guide us to a point about five miles behind the deck. There I began our approach, using sensitive cockpit instruments to judge our plane's alignment and distance from the carrier. I was on centerline and on glide slope at the beginning, but that was the easy part; the alignment and glide slope become narrower and the signals become increasingly twitchy as a plane nears a ship's deck. The stars and the moon were clearly visible at higher altitudes, but as we began our approach, our S-3 dropped down into the murky fog.

Finally, about a mile from the ship, the white lights on deck came into view. It was momentarily tempting to lift my head up and dive toward the arresting wires when I finally saw them. I caught myself doing just that and knew I had to resist the urge. I focused instead on the ball, the lighted guidance device that showed the proper glidepath, and I monitored the cockpit lights that showed the plane's correct attitude.

Fortunately I caught a 2-wire on the first attempt, and I have never been so glad to feel an arrestment. Being shoved against the seatbelt harness felt as comforting as a big bear hug from my dad. It was a wonderful improvement over the night off the California coast when I boltered three times in a row under similar conditions. I went back to the ready room and received kudos from the skipper, the executive officer, and other pilots. It turned out that they had all gathered for an upcoming briefing and had watched my landing on the closed-circuit TV. They seemed almost as pleased and relieved as I was.

The compliments from the other pilots were especially gratifying to a new arrival to the fleet like me. The best reward for any aviator is acknowledgment from his or her peers for a job well done, and I deeply appreciated their kind words. I was beginning to feel like a valued member of a team, and that fact alone made the hardships and inherent risks of this profession seem worth the sacrifices.

25 April: Waiting for the CODs

I got very little mail when our ship passed close to Hawaii, and the lack of contact with the outside world had an unusually powerful and demoralizing effect on me.

It's amazing how much care packages, letters, or even postcards from family and friends meant to me when I was at sea. Whenever I got letters, I read them over and over. I thought about the people who had written them and tried to imagine what they were thinking, what they were doing, what their days were like. I pictured them in their surroundings as they sat down to write. It was a great way to mentally step out of the predictable and seemingly endless repetitive cycles of life aboard ship.

The flip side of that, of course, was that not getting mail could be a shattering disappointment. Intellectually I knew that it wasn't really the case, but being passed over at mail call made me feel forgotten and unappreciated. And even though the ship was always packed with people, it could be a profoundly lonely place. My life revolved around a tense stateroom, a crowded ready room, a busy wardroom, and the nerve-racking flight deck.

Almost all our mail at sea was delivered by ungainly airplanes known as CODs, for "carrier on-board delivery." Hopes rose all over the ship when the boxy twin-engine turbo-prop airplanes showed up carrying bags of mail and tons of supplies. "Mail call" was the second most anticipated phrase on the ship, right behind "liberty call." The CODs could fly out to the ship only when we were within about a thousand miles of land, though, so we didn't get to see them as often as we would have liked.

On what had started out as 24 April, we crossed the International Date Line and skipped ahead to 25 April. I made a mental note reminding myself to call my dad on the twenty-sixth to wish him a happy birthday. There were several "Sprint" phones on the ship, and we could buy credit cards for them at one of the ship's stores. (There were three stores on the ship: a "luxury" store that sold stereos and other electronic items; a *Lincoln* store that sold T-shirts, hats, and other paraphernalia with the *Abe's* name emblazoned on them; and a sundries store that stocked laundry detergent and toiletries.) The phones were operational most of the time, but sometimes our geographical position would cause us to lose satellite coverage.

I had flown three times during the preceding week and had had one more dark night landing, but all the flights and landings had gone well. I was feeling in sync with the airplane and the crews. But I was allowing little things on the ship to get me down. I got all lathered up in the shower one morning, then the water supply cut out and I had to rinse myself off in the sink. It was a small inconvenience, but at the time it made me angrier than it should have. Then there was the horrible grinding noise that came through the wall of our stateroom at all hours. It turned out there was a service elevator there for bringing provisions to the wardroom. But the noisy elevator seemed most active early on the mornings after I had been flying all night. Or maybe there would be one of those general quarters drills that the ship kept holding early in the morning, which meant that the pilots had to scurry to their ready rooms, put on gas masks, and suck rubber for a couple of hours. It was all making me very cranky, and it was not helping the tension between me and my roommates.

Another reason for my crankiness was that I hadn't been working out as regularly as I did on land. I had access to an exercise bike and a stair-climbing machine in a remote corner of the ship, though, and I promised myself to make more frequent use of the equipment. Physical exertion always cleared my mind and lifted my spirits. Exercise got me tired enough to sleep well, and then I would wake up energetic and refreshed.

Gordo, one of the pilots in our squadron, got to fly to Hawaii briefly when we were near the islands. While he was refueling there he was able to fire off an e-mail message I had written to Harry. My message was short and chatty and concluded with "I love you madly." That's really all I had to say. Harry's ship, the USS *Constellation,* was scheduled to pull into Pearl Harbor a few days later. That meant that Harry was only a couple of weeks away from the end of his cruise. I missed him so much.

I wished I could have sent Harry e-mail from the *Lincoln.* The reason I couldn't was that our communications officer was totally unreasonable. Our ship had numerous satellite links and some of the most sophisticated telecommunications equipment in the world, and it didn't make sense not to use it. E-mail messages from home would have given everyone such a lift and helped avoid the disappointment of not getting anything from the CODs. On Harry's ship they sent and received as much personal e-mail as they wanted. That was the way it should have been for us, too. But our Comm-O had issued a dictate against personal e-mail, and that was that. There didn't have to be a reason.

27 April: Navy Showers

I got lost several times during my first few weeks on the *Lincoln*.

From the dock, the ship looks absolutely immense. But on board, it feels like a place built for midgets with long legs. The ceilings are so low that just about everyone has to duck going through the doorframes, and the steps are so high that they are hard to clear. Most of the passageways are too narrow for people to pass in opposite directions unless both move toward the walls.

It took me about two weeks to get familiar with the layout of the ship and proficient at locating particular places by their code numbers.

First, a little terminology: rooms on navy ships are called "compartments," floors are "decks," walls are "bulkheads," ceilings are "overheads," bathrooms are "heads," halls are "passageways," and stairs are "ladders." Those nautical terms have been used aboard ships for centuries, and they have endured from the days of wooden ships to nuclear aircraft carriers.

Each compartment has a number to identify its location. The frames, or wall divisions, on the carrier are numbered from 1 to 250, fore to aft. Then, from the keel at the center of the ship, the frames are counted outward from the middle. On the left or port side, the numbers are even. On the right or starboard side, they are odd. Each level or deck of the carrier is also numbered starting with the hangar deck in the center. Going up from the hangar deck, the levels are O1, O2, and O3, which is right below the flight deck, all the way up to O9, where the top of the control tower is located. Below the hangar deck the levels are known as the second deck, third deck, and so on down to the seventh deck. So there are a grand total of sixteen floors or decks on the *Lincoln* and more than thirty-two hundred spaces and compartments.

The stateroom where I lived was numbered O2-96-4-L. That meant it was a "living compartment" (hence the letter *L*) on the O2 level, ninety-six frames back from the bow, two frames to the left of the keel. It sounds bizarre, but after a while the system made sense to me, and it became quite easy to use.

Sometimes a compartment would be hidden behind an elevator or some pipes, and I would really have to search to find the entrance. The ship's crew gladly assisted us aviators who seemed incapable of finding our way around. There were even maps on the bulkheads with "You Are Here" signs on them. But the signs were so hard to read that they were virtually useless, and I wondered sometimes if they had been put in place just to mock us.

The *Lincoln* was built in Newport News, Virginia. Construction began in 1984, and the ship was launched for the first time in 1988. It took more than forty million man-hours of labor by thirty thousand shipyard workers to build this *Nimitz*-class aircraft carrier—the largest in the navy's inventory.

The *Lincoln* is 1,092 feet long, 206 feet high from the bottom of the keel to the top of the mast, and 257 feet wide in the middle. The flight deck covers 4.5 acres. Two nuclear reactors supply the power to four main engines, and they can move the ship across the ocean at a maximum speed of more than 30 miles an hour.

Whenever the *Lincoln* turned sharply, the differential speed of the two propellers sent a strange shudder throughout the ship. There was a deep reverberation and a low moaning sound, and the entire ship rocked and swayed as it crossed its own wake. In heavy seas the ship pitched and rolled with the powerful forces of wind and sea. The slow, uneven up-and-down and side-to-side motions created the sensation of constantly being slightly off balance. In an odd way the ship felt like a planet unto itself, with its own invisible, shifting gravitational pull.

The *Lincoln* had a distinctive smell that quickly permeated my clothes and virtually all my belongings from the first day I came aboard. The smell was a mixture of metal, jet fuel, grease, recirculated air, cleaning solvents, paint, and seawater. The odor wasn't particularly unpleasant— just singular and unmistakable.

All of the female officers on the *Lincoln* were assigned to two-, four-, and six-person staterooms on the O2 level. The rooms had previously been occupied by midlevel officers and senior lieutenants. But most of the female officers on the ship—like me—were lower in rank. And the fact that we were given these relatively quiet and spacious desirable quarters on the O2 level, or "Sleepy Hollow," created some justifiable resentment among the male junior officers—most of whom resided on the O3 level. The worst thing about the room assignments was that it gave people who didn't want women on the ship a clear example to point to of us getting preferential treatment. I'm sure the navy was trying to be considerate when these rooms were delegated to us. But in reality the rooms made matters worse. There was no reason that female officers couldn't have been given a block of rooms on the O3 level, right below the flight deck, like all the other mid- and low-level male lieutenants.

Our four-person stateroom had the kind of credit card–style key system that has become so common in hotels. Each bed, or "rack," had a thin twin-sized mattress, white cotton sheets, a pillow, and a scratchy gray wool blanket. My roommates and I all had enough foresight to bring our own linens and rack accessories. In addition to my own sheets and blanket, I brought some foam egg crate padding to make my bed more comfortable. A. J. had a fluffy feather bed that she put under her sheets.

I figured that the more time I spent sleeping, the faster the cruise would go by, so I tried to make my rack as homey as possible. There's an old saying for long deployments: "Eat 'til you're tired, sleep 'til you're hungry." Even that strange truism was starting to seem logical.

There was one bathroom, or "head," near our staterooms that all forty-five of the female junior officers on the *Lincoln* shared. All the ship's heads had a strong saltwater smell because that's what was used in the sewage system. The female head near our stateroom had a mildew problem that made it especially pungent. We ended up getting some toilet cleaner that sprayed a citrus scent into the commode every time we flushed.

In the head there were five toilets, five shower stalls, and one sink with a mirror. The showers had specially designed nozzles that allowed water to flow only when the button on the showerhead was held down. The mechanism kept us from wasting precious fresh water. But even so, the occupants of the *Lincoln* used about four hundred thousand gallons of fresh water each day. Everyone on the ship quickly learned to take "navy showers": pushing the button for a few seconds to get wet, lathering up, then rinsing. To wash your hair, you repeated the process with shampoo.

Navy showers weren't too bad except when they cut off the water supply before you were done with the rinse cycle. They pulled the plug on the water supply fairly frequently for a variety of maintenance reasons. Then you had to towel yourself dry and wait however long it took for the water to come on again. After getting stuck a couple of times, I made a habit of bringing a bucket with me into the shower stall. The first thing I did was fill the bucket with fresh water, so if they cut off the water supply, at least I wouldn't have to go back to my room soapy and sticky.

If my roommates were asleep in our stateroom, I dried my hair in the bathroom using the wall-mounted hand-drying machine. It usually took three full cycles to get the water out of my collar-length hair. Otherwise I used a small electric blow-dryer in the stateroom.

My main diversions on the ship were reading, studying Chinese, listening to music, writing in my journal, and working on my personal computer. I had brought several Anne Rice books, a couple of John Grisham novels, and *Forrest Gump* by Winston Groom.

I had also brought my entire collection of 175 CDs. I usually listened to Green Day or the Cranberries in the morning and Sarah McLachlan or Enya at night. It was great to hear their soothing voices after a tough flight. I generally listened in bed using a CD player with headphones so that the sound wouldn't disturb my roommates if they were sleeping. Lying there in the dark, I could mentally transport myself anywhere I wanted to go. Jana had brought her mini-stereo and CD player, too. Unfortunately, she and A. J. couldn't stand my New Age tunes, and I couldn't acquire their taste for country.

I had also brought a box of videos, since "roll 'ems" are an important social aspect of every long deployment. At night, after all of the aircraft were back on deck, the squadron duty officer was often in charge of selecting and showing a movie. Certain films became cruise classics, and they were replayed time after time until we could recite the dialogue along with the actors on the screen.

Some of the movie lines carried over into other aspects of life aboard ship. If someone told me the stairs I was taking reached only the tenth deck, and I replied in an English accent, "Well, these go to eleven," they would probably recognize the line as coming from *This Is Spinal Tap.* Movies that were replayed most included *The Princess Bride, Caddyshack, Scarface, Terminator, Apocalypse Now, The Meaning of Life, Raising Arizona,* and *Pulp Fiction.* My collection also included *Willy Wonka and the Chocolate Factory* and *The Lion King.* The other aviators complained whenever I put those tapes in the VCR, but squadron members with kids had a soft spot for *The Lion King,* and it attracted some of the largest ready-room crowds of any film on the ship.

For me, the most precious device on the ship was my personal computer. A month before shipping out I had bought an IBM notebook computer with a 486 DX50 microprocessor. I used the word-processing program to write squadron reports, and I installed a data base for tracking all kinds of information in the avionics shop. My computer had an accounting program that I used to keep track of my finances, and it had a built-in modem that I used in port to send and receive e-mail. I even had Harry buy me one of those fancy color printers so that I could churn out graphics with my reports and illustrate my letters to him.

If the *Lincoln* ever sank, I probably would have grabbed my little black computer and CD player before jumping into the lifeboat. The gadgets were indispensable.

2 May: Power Rangers

One of our ship's F-14 Tomcats crashed a couple of days ago when the pilot lost control during a simulated dogfight. Lt. Cdr. John "Sprout" Bates and his RIO ejected safely, and they were picked up by a helicopter within twenty minutes without serious injuries. A $30 million airplane was gone, but none of us seemed concerned about the money. After losing Kara and K-9, we were just relieved that no one was killed.

I reached my goal of a 3.5 landing grade average about halfway across the Pacific, and as we continued heading west and south across the seemingly endless expanse of blue ocean, I hoped to raise it higher still. Any chance for me to win a Top Nugget award was long gone. Several nuggets posted consistently better landing grades than I, and three pilots in our air wing had perfect 4.0 averages. From this point forward, earning better grades was a matter of personal pride, and the reward would come from the satisfaction of having raised my own standards.

Everyone on the ship settled into a comfortable routine, and the days passed quickly. I was busy overseeing the avionics shop, preparing for flights, and debriefing with other pilots, crew members, and landing signal officers.

I was also beginning to relax and enjoy my time aloft more. The sky in the South Pacific was filled with the kind of puffy white clouds I so enjoyed punching through and maneuvering around. We practiced dropping some live 500-pound bombs on a tiny island that served as a gunnery range. I hit the island smack in the middle with a pair of Mark 82 bombs, and we got some good video of the impacts. I planned to compile the best images and create a video for everyone in our squadron when we got home.

The S-3 carried bombs ranging from 500 to 2,000 pounds each, and they could be stored in a bomb bay or mounted on underwing pylons. Usually we kept a few 500-pounders in the right bomb bay and a torpedo in the left. The torpedoes could be used against submarines or any gunboats that tried to make a run toward one of our ships.

A typical bombing run starts with a tight turn as I visually acquire the target and the COTAC in the right front seat selects the station from which the bombs will be released. I double-check the COTAC's handiwork and maneuver the jet to a predetermined heading, altitude, and airspeed.

Once I see the target, I pull the nose up sharply, then roll the plane almost onto its back so that I can scan the entire area below. I click the "master arm" switch to the on position so that individual bombs can be released from the plane. Then I let the nose of the airplane fall into a 30-degree dive. In front of me the windscreen suddenly fills with earth or ocean. At this point I level the wings and jink (turn sharply) left or right, up or down, to get the plane on exactly the right course and altitude.

Inside the cockpit the noise level increases and the airplane begins shaking as aerodynamic buffeting lets me know that the plane is accelerating toward its maximum structural airspeed. The altimeters unwind like cartoon clocks, and the COTAC calls out the altitudes as we roar downhill. When the COTAC calls "Pickle," we have arrived at our bomb release altitude. I press the weapons release button on the joystick with my right thumb, pause for a second while the bombs fall clear of the airplane, then yank the stick back and begin a hard, climbing turn. We typically pull about 3.5 g's as we climb, so my 140-pound body gets squashed into the seat with more than 500 pounds of force.

At this point I always turn my head to the left so that I can watch the impact of the bombs on the target. Then I call "Off, safe" as I turn the master arm switch to the off position so that we don't accidentally drop anything else.

We also practiced antisubmarine or "undersea warfare" missions in preparation for our arrival in the Persian Gulf. Iran had obtained several Kilo-class submarines from Russia, and those subs could pose a threat to shipping in the region. The Kilo subs have diesel engines and are extremely quiet and difficult to track when submerged. But they are limited as to the amount of time they can stay submerged. If my crew was ordered to track and sink one, I felt confident that we could take the sub out quickly and effectively.

As the *Lincoln* moved deeper into the tropics, the days became steadily hotter. Jana and I got up early each morning and walked on the flight deck just after sunrise. It was a good way to enjoy the few hours of relatively cool weather, and the low rays of sunlight and the sea breezes put me in a good frame of mind. It was amazing how little any of us aboard the ship saw the sun during the course of a typical day. Most of our time was spent inside windowless rooms until it was time for us to fly.

One of the pilots in my squadron found a covert e-mail connection and downloaded a lot of messages. I got eight glorious pages from Harry, his parents, in-laws Dave and Martha, and even Bill Delaney—a friend of Harry's who had served with my dad as a marine tank commander in the Persian Gulf. It made me angry that I couldn't answer them; there was absolutely no reason for that prohibition of personal e-mail.

Harry was scheduled to arrive in Hawaii in less than a day, and I planned to call him on the telephone. I fantasized about how great it would be to hear his voice. He wrote his letters in the same informal, irreverent way that he spoke, so it was easy to hear his voice in his written messages. I tried not to dwell on how much I missed him.

Harry planned to spend a few days at his parents' place in Ojai when he got home to California. Having grown up on military bases around the country, I have never felt particularly attached to any geographical region. But Ojai would always be special to me—and to us.

In preparation for our next port call in Hong Kong, I concentrated on studying Chinese, and I was making steady progress in writing and comprehension. But my pronunciation was very weak. The classes were enjoyable, though, and I looked forward to putting my classroom lessons to the test when I got to meet and interact with real people in Singapore and Hong Kong.

I felt myself adjusting to the pace, rhythm, and feel of life aboard a warship. I got so comfortable going up and down ladders that I didn't even slow down approaching them. In each of the ship's narrow passageways, there were electrical boxes, with latches and knobs all over. Most of them seemed to be placed at head and knee level. During my first few days on the Lincoln I was constantly smacking my head and banging my shins. Later I began instinctively picking up my feet every five or six paces to avoid the twelve-inch-high "knee knockers" at the bottom of each doorway, and I developed an intuitive feel for the head-level circuit boxes. I maneuvered around people in crowded passageways without having to feel for those darn metal boxes. It may not sound like much, but my developing sense for avoiding painful collisions improved my life tremendously. I suspected that when I got to shore, however, I would step up each time I went through a doorway and duck each time I walked down a hall.

I rearranged some things in my stateroom and changed my bed sheets from Ralph Lauren teddy bears to Power Rangers. Since our racks were twins, I found the best selection of sheets in the children's section of department stores, and I thought it would be humorous to liven up my rack a bit. Chris Taylor, whose squadron was called the "Black Lions," brought *Lion King* sheets. I couldn't find anything with Vikings or Dragons, so I had to settle for Power Rangers. At least the TV characters were printed on soft cotton—far more comfortable than the scratchy navy-issued whites.

I had been flying twice a day for the previous couple of weeks. Usually I did one daytime flight and one at night.

4 May: Chocolate on the Line

The pranks in the ready room gradually escalated as our cruise progressed.

Whenever someone left a coffee mug or a water bottle on a table in the ready room, other people usually took it upon themselves to stash the article in the freezer. Over time the practice came to include hats, gloves, clipboards—anything and everything. And if the ready room residents were feeling particularly cruel, they would soak the forgotten articles in water and twist them into odd shapes before depositing them in the freezer.

It was silly but entertaining to watch people wander into the ready room and start looking bewildered, wondering where they had left something. The uniform hats or "covers" we wore were among the most highly sought after targets. The fabric covers could be molded into strange shapes, and they quickly froze solid.

One of the guys complained that others in the squadron were littering the computer table with the perforated edges of paper printouts from our flight summaries. Naturally I began saving the scraps of computer paper for several days, then stuffed this sizable collection of confetti into his mailbox.

The guys in my squadron teased me all the time about my fondness for sweets, especially chocolate chip cookies and chocolate ice cream. I was in the wardroom with a group of friends from the F-14 squadron when one of them got up and politely asked if anyone would like something from the food line. I asked for a cup of soft-serve ice cream with a little chocolate syrup on top.

Two minutes later this guy came back to the table with a heaping bowl of ice cream drenched with chocolate sauce. There was so much sauce, the bowl couldn't contain it, and some of it had dripped down the backs of his hands. He plunked the bowl down on the table in front of me, and everyone started chuckling. Then one of the RIOs made the mistake of challenging me to eat all of it.

"I bet you can't," he taunted. "If you can, I'll trade patches with you."

The F-14 guys were very proud of their Tomcat patches, so I went right to work. This guy obviously had no clue who he was dealing with. As I began consuming this mountain of chocolate, the RIO started looking nervous. When I got toward the end, I began taunting him by eating slowly as though I were getting full, then scraping the bottom of the bowl with my spoon. Finally I finished the last drop and flipped the bowl over while the others at the table cheered my victory.

I showed mercy on the guy by letting him keep his patch. But I think I proved my point. "Never go against Rowdy when chocolate's on the line," I told him. (Even that was a variation on a line from a movie, in this case *The Princess Bride:* "Never go against a Sicilian when death is on the line.")

10 May: Letter from Harry

Dear Wife:

As of yesterday we're only fifty-seven hundred nautical miles apart and getting closer every day. I wonder how close we'll get.

Enclosed is a copy of a picture that showed up in the Sydney newspaper. An old friend of mine from Los Angeles moved to Australia a few years ago and we lost touch. But he recognized me from the picture in the paper and called the quarterdeck. It was great to catch up with him and meet his bride. You'll meet them when the Lincoln comes to Australia, and I'm sure you'll like them.

I didn't do squat in Sydney. We only had two days there, and I was on duty the entire first day. I got off the ship briefly to visit my old pal on day two, but then it was right back to sea.

I'm looking forward to doing Australia right with you in September. Or doing it wrong with you. Or just doing it with you. I can't wait to see you again. We're going to have a great time Down Under. I'd like to take a tour of the Australian Outback. We'll go see some kangaroos and emus. Are you up for it?

Last night I was laying in my rack looking at the picture of you like I usually do before going to sleep. I started reminiscing about the night you first told me you loved me. You were so vulnerable back then. It was a hot, humid night in Kingsville, and we were at my house. You kind of tiptoed over to me and said it real softly. I kind of heard you and kind of didn't. I was surprised, so I asked you to say it again. And you stepped real close and put your arms around my neck and our bodies touched real lightly. You put your lips up to my right ear and whispered softly but clearly, "I love you."

I've fallen so deeply in love with you over these short three years—deeper than I ever thought I could. Our lives are completely folded together. That's why being apart is so tough. Yet it's such a comfort to know how strong you are. It keeps me from worrying. There is nothing that you can't do.

I've sent e-mail to you but haven't received anything since you've been afloat. Is your system working OK? I've been sending and receiving OK to everyone else. Please send the tentative dates for your port calls as soon as you get them. I can't wait to hold you in my arms.

I love you,
Harry

17 May: Letter from Harry

Dear Loree,

It looks like our point of closest approach was 2,062 nautical miles on the twenty-sixth of April. I checked today, and our ships are just over twenty-one hundred miles apart.

Damn we were close! I could feel ya. Warmed me up inside.

I loved the e-mail you sent via Gordo. I don't know why, but it gave me a *heartpunch like I haven't had in a while. Things are slow on my end. We're winding down although I flew twice today. I'm right in the middle of my squadron as far as landing grades for this cruise (eight of eighteen pilots). That's a nice, low-key place to be, although I should have done a bit better.*

To tell the truth, I hadn't even looked at the list until the commanding officer showed it to me. Even then I didn't notice what my GPA was, and I haven't looked at it since. I really haven't been too wrapped around the axle about the grades (although I appear to be a minority on that count). I really enjoy flying a solid pass, but I know when I do that even without the grade.

I did a bunch of flying over Iraq our last few weeks in the Persian Gulf. Fly in—tank—find target—fly out—trap. After a while it got pretty routine, and I guess that was the whole point. Two of the four pilots in our stateroom are on shore, so that leaves just me and Dozer. We've had a few chats lately. It's amazing how little any of us talk to each other when we're at sea. I think the cramped quarters keep us from wanting to communicate, or even acknowledge each other's presence.

I debriefed my tour as squadron scheduling officer with the skipper. He said I was doing great, but at the same time, I feel there is something "not quite right" about this group and how I fit in it. I think it's institutional as much as a personality thing. I can't quite put my finger on it, but I'm not going to dwell on it, either.

The phones on our ship have been down over thirty-six hours. Keep the faith. Dreaming about you.

Love,
Harry

19 May: Not That Kind of Tired

Hong Kong and Singapore were a drunken, sleep-deprived blur.

I volunteered for permanent shore patrol in Hong Kong. It sounded like a good deal because those of us on duty got to stay at the J. W. Marriott Hotel for free, and we collected some additional pay. We worked in shifts, twelve hours on, then twenty-four hours off. I wore my polyester "summer whites" uniform and spent most of my duty time at shore patrol headquarters by the pier.

As soon as my duty period was over the first day, I rushed back to the hotel, got out of my uniform, and went out with Jana and a bunch of the guys from our squadron. We started drinking at the hotel bar, then staggered upstairs to a hotel room that had become the unofficial meeting place for our squadron. All of us chipped in for the cost of the room, and we kept food and drinks there and took turns sleeping there when we wanted to avoid going back to the boat.

After more drinking and insulting each other in the hotel room, Jana and I decided around 2 A.M. to go dancing. Most of the guys were fading, so we tried to shame them into coming along by telling them they were losers if they couldn't keep up with the so-called weaker sex. Most of the guys caught their second wind then. A few others just passed out.

Our next stop was a club called the Pussycat Lounge. Normally a name like that would send me away, but we checked it out anyway and found the place almost empty. There was a huge dance floor and a great sound system, so we all danced and drank for hours. I kept my buzz going with Bloody Marys that were so strong they made my eyes water.

I got propositioned by an F-14 RIO that night. Everyone gets lonely away from home, myself included, and drinking lessens everyone's inhibitions. But I had come to regard the men on the ship—and particularly other aviators—almost like brothers. I didn't view them as handsome or sexy; they were shipmates, and that made them family. And even though most of them were great guys, the thought of sleeping with one of them seemed incestuous and repulsive. So I told the RIO to buzz off. Later I found out that he had also put the moves on Jana and Sue.

I finally made it back to the hotel around 5 A.M. and snoozed for eight hours before going out on a shopping excursion. Then I went back to the shore patrol headquarters and stayed on duty all night from 7 P.M. until 7 A.M. It wasn't easy to stay up all night after the previous day's activities, but I managed. Then I returned to the hotel and crashed until midafternoon.

Harry's ship, the USS *Constellation,* got back to California that day. And knowing that he had returned home safe lifted my spirits tremendously. I spoke to him from the hotel, and he sounded great. He said Stoney was doing fine and the house in Lemoore was in good shape.

I celebrated Harry's safe return from cruise by going out again with a group of female friends from our air wing. We started out with an amazing five-course dinner at the posh American Club. It's located at the top of the Hong Kong exchange building, and it caters to business types. The food was expensive but worth every penny after the industrial chow we had become accustomed to on the ship.

After dinner we caught a cab into town and stopped at a bar called Yeltsin's. I started drinking Malibu Oranges, one after another. The drinks didn't seem to be having much effect, though, so I switched to Johnny Walker Red. That did the trick. Soon I was slam-dancing and singing at the top of my lungs along with everyone else. I called it quits around 2 A.M. and went back to the hotel. I was scheduled to begin my next duty period in five hours. When my alarm clock sounded, I was still woozy, but I made it through the twelve-hour duty period on my feet.

After a couple of days in port it actually felt good to get back to the ship. I needed some rest; it takes a while to recover from all the craziness in port. But as much partying as I did in Hong Kong, it was nothing compared with what some of the sailors and other aviators did. Those animals could carry on for days without rest. One sailor I encountered had literally passed out in the gutter. He was sprawled in the street like roadkill. No one could find an ID card on him, so the shore patrol picked him up and tried to revive him with cold water and smelling salts.

One of the guys asked the sailor his name, and I could see the wheels start turning behind those bloodshot eyes. He muttered something incomprehensible, so the shore patrol asked him again: "Your name, stupid. What's your name?"

"Abraham Lincoln," the poor guy muttered. "Abraham Lincoln."

That same night two of the female sailors from the ship were hauled into the shore patrol office for getting involved in an altercation of some kind with the local prostitutes. We had the sailors sit in our office while we tried to settle the matter with the local law enforcement agencies. I was responsible for getting them back to the ship. I convinced the police that if there was to be any disciplinary action, it would be best to let the navy handle it. The two enlisted gals sat in my office, and their chief petty officer told them to be calm and stay quiet. Neither of them followed those instructions, though.

One was a loudmouthed New Yorker who had consumed so much "liquid courage" that she didn't care who she offended. The other was terrified at the thought of being thrown into the brig, and all she could do was cry. And each time the New Yorker spouted off, she made matters worse because her bravado made the other girl cry even harder. Before long the one sailor was challenging everyone in the room to a fight while the other just wailed.

Finally the shore patrol security officer came over to talk to the two gals. He sternly told the New Yorker to shut the hell up or he would personally make sure she was sent back to the ship in handcuffs. The girl just sneered back at him and stuck her wrists in his face.

"Just cuff me, man!" she goaded. "Just cuff me!"

At that the other girl sobbed uncontrollably.

It was a pathetic if somewhat comical scene.

§

Four days after we left Hong Kong, the *Lincoln* arrived in Singapore.

We stayed in the Sheraton Towers. Our suite was small by hotel standards and shared among several officers. But compared with our staterooms on the ship, it felt like a mansion. The hotel manager was a big navy fan, and he offered free drinks and food every evening starting at six.

Unlike polluted Hong Kong, Singapore was clean and sparkling. Both were oppressively hot and muggy. In Singapore I spent most of each day shopping, and I took it easy on the drinking. After my excesses in Hong Kong, alcohol just didn't seem appealing. The only late night came when a bunch of people from our squadron picked on our commanding officer and executive officer by buying them shots of Scotch. I had never seen Commander Smith out enjoying himself on a port call. Usually he stayed on the ship and got ahead on his paperwork. Seeing him kick back put everyone in a festive mood, and early in the morning we stumbled into a Denny's restaurant for breakfast. (Who would have thought there would be a Denny's in Singapore?)

Denny's brought on a "food coma," and we went back to the hotel to crash.

The commander of our air wing had prohibited men and women from sharing rooms on shore. Since Jana was on the boat doing duty that night, this meant that I got one room by myself and ten guys had to share the other one. We considered bending the rules by using "Fridge," a hulking naval flight officer, as a human room divider. Eventually, though, I took all the mattresses from my room and gave them to the guys. With the floor covered with mattresses and other bedding, their place looked like a pre-school romper room.

I slept on a box spring in the other room.

§

We hosted a group of foreign dignitaries in Singapore one evening. We displayed a variety of airplanes and equipment on the *Lincoln*'s flight deck, and some of us were assigned to stand there and answer questions from the visitors. It was fun to meet new people and show them around. They were usually in awe of what they saw.

I'll never forget one of the comments from a Pakistani government official, though. He asked Heidi, a female flight officer from one of the EA-6B Prowler squadrons, what she did on the ship, and she explained that she operated the electrical, radar, and weapons systems on combat jets. Prowlers are used for electronic warfare, and their powerful systems can jam enemy radar and fire antiradar missiles.

The visitor's eyebrows arched up, and he seemed pretty impressed. Then he asked how many men were on the ship and how many women. She quickly gave him the answer: about five thousand men and five hundred women. He looked at her sympathetically and in all seriousness said, "You women must get very tired."

Heidi kind of shrugged and said, "Everyone works hard on the ship, so everyone gets tired. But the women don't get any more exhausted than the men."

"But you must be more tired because you service all of the men," he explained.

This guy thought our collateral duty was to provide sexual services for the men on board! My jaw dropped, but Heidi did a remarkably good job of calmly explaining to the gentleman from Pakistan that we were not for hire and we didn't get tired—at least not that kind of tired.

§

The *Lincoln* and its battle group soon entered the Indian Ocean and steamed west, a few hundred miles south of Sri Lanka.

I took off just before sunset for a three-hour flight, and the sight of the stars emerging from the purple sky was spectacular. It was amazing how many stars were visible on a clear night in the middle of the ocean. The sun had long since dropped below the horizon when I approached the ship to land that night. But the diffuse starlight made the *Lincoln*'s silhouette almost as crisp and clear as day, and I could see the outline of the ship several miles away.

Because of the lack of satellite coverage in this part of the world, we weren't able to make telephone calls from the ship. But even without phones, navy rumor continued to operate at full speed. The last time we spoke, Harry said that he had heard all the way back in Lemoore that the female pilots on the *Lincoln* were flying poorly. People who thought women shouldn't be serving on combat ships or flying front-line jets were quick to believe what they wanted to believe.

§

Now and then I visited Lt. Brenda Scheufele, one of the F/A-18 Hornet pilots, and we talked about our significant others. Her boyfriend, Chuck, was a former A-7 and F/A-18 pilot. Chuck had left the navy a year before the *Lincoln* left on this cruise, and he used his severance bonus to buy a single-engine Cessna. He is a free spirit and an adventurer who has flown everything from helicopters to jets, and he is deeply interested in everything that relates to the ocean. He sails, scuba dives, fishes, and surfs.

Chuck has curly blond hair and a restless, slightly rebellious nature. As soon as he left the navy, he let his hair grow and flew his little airplane all over North America and Mexico. Brenda once joined him for a marathon trip from California to the East Coast, then all the way across Canada and into the remote northernmost portions of Alaska. Chuck had recently taken a job flying old military transport planes that had been converted to water bombers, and he was planning to spend the following summer fighting wildfires with the U.S. Forest Service.

In Lemoore, Chuck and Harry had quickly become friends, and they spent much of their free time together. Brenda and I enjoyed talking about our loved ones back home and comparing notes on what they were doing. It somehow made us feel closer to them.

§

Our battle group turned north, toward the Persian Gulf, and we all knew we would be there soon. I had total confidence in our ability to handle any military threat that came our way. We had trained so much, we knew our jobs, and we had great equipment.

All those annoying drills had clearly paid off. Within five minutes of the call to battle stations, sailors on the *Lincoln* could close every watertight hatch, send firefighters in protective suits throughout the ship, and get all of us covered from head to toe in flashgear designed to protect us from fires.

But I could tell that the Persian Gulf—or the Arabian Gulf, as we in the military called it—was going to be a challenging place to operate. The weather was already stiflingly hot, and it was only going to get more hellish throughout the summer.

Weather forecasts for the gulf seldom changed. We had been told to expect hazy, turbulent air with such poor visibility that we would probably have to make instrument approaches to the ship day and night, all summer long. The only positive was that the water surface in the gulf was absolutely flat, and that calm, glassy surface made the deck a stable target.

29 May: Postcard from Harry

(This postcard has a picture of Elvis Presley riding a motorcycle and came with a care package of gag gifts purchased in Memphis, Tennessee.)

Hey Babe,

Been putting together this care package all weekend. Had lots of fun doing it, as you can probably tell. Sure would have been better shopping for this stuff with you.

Wow. You know I'm missing you badly if I want to go shopping with you! Sorry for such a short note, but I'm in the car and don't have much time. I'm getting crazy excited about the trip out to the Middle East to see you. I'm a little nervous about whether all the travel arrangements will work out—but then they always do.

I can't wait to see, hear, and touch you again.

Love,
Harry

31 May: Letter from Harry

I made a low-level flight from Nellis Air Force Base in Nevada back to Lemoore today. I had that Hornet streaking through the canyons and between mountain peaks. You would have loved it. Now I'm back at the house. It sure will be nice when both of us are living in the same place.

Tonight Chuck stopped by, and we went to the store for food. We were cruising around the market and couldn't help think about the irony of changing times that has us pushing shopping carts through the aisles while you and Brenda are at sea in a combat zone. (Please tell Brenda hello from me.)

Now that I'm home, I'm looking at a few pictures of us laying on the beach in San Diego. I can't wait to walk on an Arabian beach with you. Or take you into the water and lose your bathing suit! I hope it floats!

Have you received my latest care packages? If not, they're on the way. So am I.

I haven't been this excited for a long, long time. I'm gonna see the woman I love, and I can't wait. . . .

Love you,
Harry

four

§

The Gulf

8 June 1995: A Resilient Guy

The commanding officer of our squadron called me at 1 A.M. and told me to come to his stateroom at once. I had no idea why Commander Smith would be calling me at that late hour. He had sought to talk to me alone on only two previous occasions: once to vent about the controversy surrounding the pregnancy tests, and another time to give me a pep talk about my marginal landing grades during workups.

This time I could hear the urgency in his voice, and I rolled out of bed, threw a flight suit on, and jogged down the passageway to meet him. When I got to his room, I knocked on the door. Usually he would shout "Enter," but this time he opened the door himself. He was wearing a T-shirt and running shorts, and he motioned for me to come in and sit down at the metal chair by his desk. His stateroom was slightly larger than ours, but it was barren and austere. There were no posters on the wall, no decorations. It was plain and orderly and reflected the skipper's Spartan, self-disciplined manner.

"The first thing you have to know is that Harry's OK," the skipper began, looking tired and worried. "He's been in an aircraft accident, but he's going to be all right."

I was speechless, so the skipper went on to say that Harry was in an intensive care ward at a hospital in California. He had some teeth knocked out, several broken ribs, multiple internal injuries, and deep facial lacerations. I assumed that the injuries had been caused by an ejection from an F/A-18 Hornet, but I soon learned that Harry had been flying with Chuck (Brenda Scheufele's boyfriend) in Chuck's Cessna on a weekend camping trip near Mount Whitney when their plane crashed at a very high elevation. Somehow Harry had been rescued and transported out of the mountains and down to a hospital.

Strangely, I knew all about the camping trip Harry and Chuck had planned to take. Harry had described it to me in his most recent e-mail. He said he and Chuck were going to fly to a sulfur hot springs on the east slope of the mountains, spend the night, and head back to Lemoore the next morning. I had received the electronic message the day before I got the news of the crash.

After the skipper told me about Harry, I pretty much stopped worrying about him. He had been banged up, but he was a resilient guy, and I knew he would bounce back. The scary thing was that the skipper had no information about Chuck. He had no idea whether Chuck was alive or not.

I tried to remain outwardly calm as I evaluated the news. I didn't cry or show much emotion other than relief that Harry was going to be all right. But I noticed later that my hands were trembling and my mouth was parched. Then the skipper accompanied me to the wardroom for a cup of hot chocolate, and I used the ship's phone to call Harry's parents at their home in Ojai. I was able to speak with both John and Wilma, and they said they had already been to the hospital to see Harry.

They also gave me the information I wanted about Chuck. It turned out that he had been injured too and was in worse shape than Harry. Chuck had a broken jaw, a broken arm, and some deep facial cuts from his head being slammed against the Cessna's instrument panel. But John and Wilma assured me that Chuck was going to be all right, too. He and Harry were expected to remain in intensive care for several days at least. There was some blood in their urine from internal injuries, and the doctors wanted to be sure that the hemorrhaging had stopped before releasing them.

Meanwhile Harry and Chuck had been stitched up, and their broken bones set, wired, or put in casts. They planned to recuperate in Ojai for a while after getting out of the hospital. Then they would go back to Lemoore once John and Wilma were convinced that they could take care of themselves. When I hung up the phone at about 3:30 A.M. local time, I was greatly relieved.

John and Wilma were very calm, and their tranquillity reassured me. When Harry was two years old, he fell into a pool and almost drowned. Wilma restarted his heart and got him breathing again. She revived him then, and I knew she would make sure that Harry and Chuck got everything they needed to recover from their injuries now.

Skipper told me that I could leave the ship and go home to help Harry recuperate if I wanted. In cases of family hardship, it's not unheard of for someone to leave the ship during a cruise. The offer was momentarily tempting, but I dismissed it. Harry was going to recover—I was totally confident of that. He had all the help he needed right there in California. He knew how important this cruise was to me, and I felt sure he would want me to finish. He would hate for me to fail to complete my mission because of him. There was no choice for me but to stay on the Lincoln.

I have to confess, however, that my relief and thankfulness that Harry and Chuck had both survived a potentially fatal crash quickly gave way to not-so-subtle flashes of anger at my husband. It was totally selfish, but I kept asking myself how Harry could have been so stupid as to go and get himself hurt right before he was supposed to fly to the Middle East to see me. We were about to pull into port, and Harry had planned to fly commercially out here to meet me. But now, because of this ridiculous Cessna accident, my chance to be with Harry was gone, and I didn't know when we would have another opportunity.

Our last rendezvous had taken place six months earlier when his ship, the USS *Constellation,* pulled into Hong Kong and I flew across the Pacific to see him. That was around Christmas, and now, as I sat in my crowded stateroom with the air conditioner rattling in its futile fight against the summer heat, it seemed like a lifetime ago.

I missed Harry all the time, but picturing him banged up in a hospital bed somewhere made me long for his company even more. I was his wife, and I wanted to take care of him. But I couldn't, and that made me feel helpless and inadequate.

Thank goodness Harry was still alive.

The jerk.

9 June: Pain and Uncertainty

I crawled back into my rack around 4 A.M., tossed and turned for a few hours, then fell into a groggy sleep. I was still in a haze when the ship's intercom blared, "Emergency breakaway, emergency breakaway!" I remember thinking that this was a little strange, since under normal conditions those announcements are preceded by the words "This is a drill. This is a drill."

Such drills usually took place following "replenishments at sea," in which supply ships steamed alongside the *Lincoln* and transferred provisions on heavy pallets. Instead of just slowly separating, the two ships practiced disengaging quickly to simulate actions they would have taken before an imminent collision. A steering failure on the part of either ship, or operator error, could cause such an accident.

The next thing I remember was the sound of the collision alarm, then a soft rumble passed through the ship. In my mental fog it didn't seem real, so I just turned over and went back to sleep. If there was a real emergency, I figured they'd call for general quarters.

When I finally awoke a few hours later, I learned that the *Lincoln* had collided with the USS *Sacramento,* and the *Sacramento* had sustained some pretty serious damage. Aboard the *Lincoln,* a couple of catwalks had been crushed, some lifeboats were shattered, and there were a few dents and a hole punched into the starboard side. Fortunately no one on either ship was seriously injured.

I brushed my teeth and had my flight suit halfway on when Brenda Scheufele knocked on my stateroom door. She was visibly shaken and desperate for information about Chuck. I had considered waking her up hours earlier to pass along the news of Chuck and Harry. But when I got off the phone with Harry's parents in Ojai, it had been 3:30 A.M. in the Arabian Gulf. I figured Brenda's commanding officer was waiting until later to inform her that Chuck had been injured but was going to be all right—just as Commander Smith had given me that same message about Harry.

As it turned out, Brenda's skipper had told her only that Chuck had been involved in a serious aircraft accident—that was it. Then he advised her to see me for details. Had my skipper not taken the time to investigate for himself and find out that Harry was going to be OK before informing me of the accident, I would have been a basket case. I was disappointed in Brenda's skipper for showing such callousness.

Brenda and I sat down in my stateroom, and I reviewed for her every detail of my conversation with Harry's parents. They had visited with Chuck in the hospital and had spoken at length with him, his doctors, and his parents. John and Wilma knew just as much about Chuck and his condition as they did about Harry. As soon as Brenda knew the extent of her boyfriend's injuries, and that he was going to recover, she calmed down. I felt awful for having unwittingly prolonged her pain and uncertainty.

12 June: A Different World

The first two weeks of flying in the Arabian Gulf gave me a hint of how difficult our summer was going to be. The heat was so intense that every aviator was drenched in sweat before even boarding the aircraft.

Air conditioners in the S-3s don't work until the engines are running, and temperatures inside the sun-baked cabins commonly exceeded 110 degrees. Haze clung to the horizon; it was like flying in a bowl of milk.

Each night catapult launch propelled us into a wall of total darkness. The horizon was nonexistent, and we had no references except for our instruments as to which way was up. If we were lucky, the ship would be pointed toward an oil platform and the orange flames would hint at the horizon. Even that could be disorienting, however, and I made it my practice not to look up from my instruments until we were a few thousand feet into the air. Then I could usually see the stars above. The haze would accumulate only around the horizon, so I could pick out constellations and see whatever portion of the moon was in phase. Each approach to the carrier at night was a vertigo-inducing blur.

On daytime flights we scanned the sea for ships, submarines, and sea life. I had heard that the gulf was full of poisonous sea snakes, and I saw plenty of them from the cockpit. Sometimes there were just a few, but occasionally I would see hundreds of them swirling together in giant, frenzied balls.

Lt. Larry "Jedi" Anderson sensed that the snakes made me uncomfortable, so he regaled me with imaginary tales of the snakes' ferocity. He said they could unlock their jaws and bite people on the eyes. And he told me they were known to jump six feet out of the water and come down in aviators' life rafts. He said he wanted to fly with me as often as possible while we were in the gulf because sea snakes preferred women; if we ever bailed out, he said, the snakes would chew me up but leave him alone. Jedi was only displaying his twisted sense of humor, but the snakes were definitely creepy.

After each flight I tried to cool off with a cold shower, but water demand on the ship was so high that they frequently cut off the flow entirely. Or they eliminated the cold water and left only steaming hot water, so it was common for us to go to bed tired and sticky.

I got to fly an S-3 over Kuwait on a refueling mission, and it seemed like the first time in months that I had flown over land. The terrain itself was so barren and featureless that it was hard to imagine why so many wars had been fought for control of it.

I looked down on miles of blackened oil fields that the Iraqis had set afire during the Persian Gulf War three years before. It was an amazing sight. There's a term in warfare—*scorched-earth policy*—for the practice whereby a retreating army ruins everything in its wake in an attempt to deny its opponents any resources. *Scorched earth* had always seemed to me a figurative term, but this land was literally blackened. Every inch of it was charred and lifeless, and the desolation extended for miles in all directions.

I thought about my dad when I saw the tortured desert. He had been in the same general area with the First Marine Division during operations Desert Shield and Desert Storm, and he had been one of the first generals in liberated Kuwait City. As I looked from my S-3 cockpit at the desolate panorama below, I tried to picture him and his marines lunging forward through obstacles and mine fields in armored columns that stretched for miles. What a challenge that must have been, and what an accomplishment.

I remembered receiving letters from him while he was preparing for war. As usual, his words were positive and upbeat. But I sensed he had a strong premonition that he was going to be killed. When I asked him about it later, he said that his sense of his own mortality was stronger during the Persian Gulf War than at any time during his previous tours of duty in Vietnam. As it turned out, his intuition was wrong. Months of ceaseless bombardment had decimated the entrenched Iraqi armies, and the allied ground forces overwhelmed them. But there was no way that my dad and the allied ground forces he commanded could have known that when they crossed the line. They charged forward despite their uncertainty. They faced their fears together—and I'll always admire them for it.

§

A few days before planes from our ship began patrolling the "no-fly zone" over Iraq, Lt. Carey Lohrenz, a female F-14 pilot, was grounded and ordered to go before an evaluation board composed of senior pilots. Her landing grades were poor, and her performance was inconsistent. Two F-14s had been lost because of pilot error so far, and the landing signal officers and others believed that Carey was an accident waiting to happen.

I didn't know Carey well. We had met in Kingsville when I was finishing jet training and she was just starting. I had offered her my assistance if she ever needed it, but she never did; she did extremely well in training.

I sympathized now with her plight on the ship. As the sole surviving female F-14 pilot, she was under incredible pressure. Back in the United States, one of her former instructors released her training grades and other confidential information to a group opposed to the policy of allowing women to fly combat jets. That group issued a "report" claiming that Kara Hultgreen and Carey, whom they referred to as "Pilot B," were unqualified to fly F-14s. The report made it back to the *Lincoln,* where some people began referring to Carey as Pilot B.

I was hearing both sides of the story of Carey's landing grade situation, and it was difficult to know whom to believe. Many people felt that no one could have stood up to the pressure she was under and she deserved a break. Others felt that she was not responsive to the LSOs and her stubbornness would get her killed. I was glad that I wasn't in her position. I thought back to my bad experience at Lemoore and tried to empathize with what she was going through.

The evaluation board was made up of four aviators and a flight surgeon, and they had the authority to recommend anything from reinstating Carey immediately to removing her wings and never allowing her to fly again. Her skipper and the air wing commander would review the board's recommendation. An admiral would make the final decision.

The board recommended that Carey be allowed to fly—but only in aircraft based on land. Then, to almost everyone's surprise, her skipper and the air wing commander ignored that recommendation and decided that Carey shouldn't be allowed to fly at all. Eventually the admiral backed that harsh judgment.

I saw Carey in the passageway after the board and asked her how she was doing. She angrily recounted a long litany of events that convinced her that the CAG LSOs were trying to get her. She warned me that they were trying to ground all of the female pilots one by one. Some of the other women believed this, and I could understand why. But I had seen the LSOs give dozens of debriefings, and I couldn't help but notice that they were curt and rude with everyone. The guys in my squadron called them equal-opportunity assholes.

The LSOs zeroed in on pilots and criticized the slightest imperfections in their approaches and landings. They were brutally frank, and their style seemed insulting and abrasive. When I asked some of them about it, they seemed genuinely surprised that they came across that way. As they saw it, they were being succinct and businesslike.

One afternoon I cornered Joe "Flojo" Keith, an S-3 pilot and LSO whom I trusted, and I asked him to tell me the truth about the LSOs and whether I should worry about how they were grading female pilots. I had heard that a few other women agreed with Carey that the CAG LSOs were letting personal prejudices interfere with their professional judgment and were abusing their power because CAG allowed it. Flojo assured me that there was no conspiracy. All the women on the ship were nuggets, and as a group we were doing about the same as the male pilots on their first cruise. A lot of pilots were struggling; a lot of nuggets had marginal landing grades. The women were conspicuous, he said, because all of us were rookies at the boat.

Flojo told me to ignore the controversy and concentrate on flying precise, consistent approaches and landings. If I ever got a landing grade that I didn't agree with, he volunteered to get the videotape from the platform camera, review it with me, and explain what the LSOs were seeing. There's an old navy truism that says the farther a pilot taxies from the landing area, the better his approach becomes in his own mind.

After the results of Carey's evaluation became known, the air wing commander, Capt. Gary "Dizzy" Gillespie, called all the female pilots on the ship together for a meeting. We met in the Prowler squadron's ready room, where we were greeted with cookies and Kool-Aid. The atmosphere felt weird, like we were being buttered up. Gillespie tried to convince us that we were being treated just like everyone else and that no one up the food chain was going out of his way to hinder us.

I wanted to believe him, but I was extremely wary.

Gillespie was a tall guy with a broad mustache and thick black hair that was rather long for a military officer. Contrary to protocol, he often wore his flight suit unzipped to the waist. Gillespie seemed completely at ease dealing with male pilots, but around female aviators he appeared tense and evasive. Whenever he spoke to the air wing, he seemed to find ways to remind everyone that our group was composed of "men . . . and women." It seemed like a subtle way of singling us out. We weren't a unified team; we were a group of men . . . and women.

At the meeting in the Prowler ready room, Gillespie's words sounded rehearsed, and I wasn't completely convinced that he was sincere. When someone asked him if he was in favor of having female sailors and officers on the *Lincoln,* he tried to introduce a little levity. He said that at first he had been opposed to allowing women to fly combat aircraft, but later he changed his mind and thought it was a "fine idea."

"Yes," he announced enthusiastically, "in fact I think the ship smells a lot better."

He seemed to expect laughter, but his joke was greeted with skeptical silence.

It was clear to me at that point that my best strategy was to fly well, keep doing my job, and avoid giving anyone the chance to lower the boom on me. I didn't want to believe that CAG and the LSOs were setting us up for failure, but I wasn't positive that they weren't. They hadn't earned the benefit of the doubt.

I spoke with Harry on the phone while he was still in the hospital. From the cheerful sound of his voice, I would never have known how badly he had been injured. He said that his four front teeth had been knocked out, and we joked about the slight lisp that resulted. He also gave me a summary of his other injuries: a deep gash in the center of his forehead, a couple of broken ribs, and a multicolored collection of bruises and scrapes covering the rest of his body.

We didn't get into the details of what had caused the crash. I let Harry know I was disappointed that we weren't going to be able to see each other during my next port call. But he assured me he would be ready to travel soon, and he was determined to get to the Middle East to meet me as soon as he was well enough. Hearing all this revived my hopes that we would indeed get to be together before too long. My anger at him for having been in the accident at all was probably a little irrational, but since when do emotions have to make sense? Anyway, I told him that I forgave him. I just wanted to see him and touch him and comfort him as soon as we could arrange it.

We were scheduled to pull into port at Jebel Ali in the United Arab Emirates, and I had no idea what visiting in an Arab country for the first time was going to be like. All of us on the ship—especially the women— were briefed on Islamic laws and on how we were expected to behave. Women were not allowed to drive cars or bare their shoulders, and we were supposed to wear long-sleeved shirts and long pants at all times. Fortunately we wouldn't have to wear veils. We could go out in public with groups of guys but were told that it was not uncommon for Western women to be harassed if they went out alone or in small groups.

There were cautionary tales for the guys, too. One story that circulated around the ship told of an American sailor who had tried to lift up an Islamic woman's veil to get a look at her face. Supposedly the sailor got his hand cut off right there on the spot. We didn't know if the story was true, but we were encouraged to believe that bad things would happen to us if we stepped out of line.

It sounded like a different world.

16 June: Good Thing I'm Not Blond

At first glance, Dubai seemed like any other modern, prosperous city.

The place was full of nice hotels, late-model cars, and great places to shop. It was sometimes easy to forget that it was an Islamic country. Then I would notice a man walking down the street looking around and peering at the displays in the store windows, and I would realize that the veiled women trailing a few steps behind were his wives. The women typically pushed baby strollers or carried things, and they were covered from head to toe with loose-fitting black garments.

On shore, I stayed with groups of guys from our air wing. I got plenty of stares and strange looks from the locals, but no one gave me any trouble. Good thing I'm not blond. A couple of the fair-haired women from the air wing went out together without male escorts, and they drew huge unwanted crowds everywhere they went. I'm sure they couldn't understand what the gesturing locals were shouting at them, but it's pretty safe to assume it wasn't complimentary.

There were lots of jewelry stores, and I shopped extensively but didn't buy much—just a couple of knickknacks. For me the highlight of the port call was a massage at the health club. Everyday life on the ship was so stressful that tension had begun to feel normal. Then something like a massage would relax me, and I would suddenly realize how stressed I had been.

§

One of the other female pilots on the ship told of an encounter she had with a young Arab woman in port. The woman spoke good English and asked what it was like to attend college in America, something she hoped to do if her father would allow it. The pilot told her about U.S. colleges and how education had prepared her for her current job, flying combat aircraft in the navy. There was no way a woman would be allowed to do anything like that in this society. They continued to talk until the young woman's father came into the room. When he learned that his daughter was talking to an American, he angrily ordered her to get away from what he must have regarded as a threatening, horribly corrupting Western influence.

I tried not to dwell on the big-picture geopolitical aspects of what we as a nation were trying to accomplish in the gulf. Obviously our economy depends on the smooth flow of oil, and this region was critical from that standpoint. But some of the ironies were hard to overlook. Harry, who is ethnically Jewish, was defending Arab countries that were sworn enemies of Israel. And American military women were risking their lives to protect societies that denied women the most basic rights. When I saw the hostility that many of the locals had for us, it made me want to let them fend for themselves.

§

The highlight of the port call was a scavenger hunt that Harry had set up for me when he was in the same region six months earlier. He sent a cryptic note via e-mail telling me to "go to a place where navy aviators are no longer welcome and look under the counter in the ladies' room."

I took a cab to the Hilton—whose management had kicked the navy out after the 1991 Tailhook debacle—and went directly to the bathroom in the lobby. It was fun walking around the hotel lobby realizing that Harry had been thinking of me when he was in this same place half a year before. There was a long counter in the bathroom, and I searched every drawer. There was plenty of soap and toilet paper, but no note. Then I got down on my hands and knees and searched underneath. Sure enough, taped to the underside of the counter was an envelope with my name on it.

I felt a little self-conscious sitting on the tile bathroom floor under the row of sinks, but I couldn't wait to read the note. I just sat there and howled with laughter as I opened the envelope and found some pictures of us that had been taken with Harry's camera in Hong Kong the previous year. There was also a handwritten letter and a receipt. The letter said, among other things, that I should take the receipt to the hotel jewelry store, where a little present was waiting for me.

I trotted off to the jewelry boutique and showed the clerk my receipt and told her why I had come. She looked at me quizzically for a moment, then her face lit up with recollection. Sure, she said; she remembered Harry. She disappeared into a back room, then returned with a gorgeous pair of gold hoop earrings. Harry had bought them when he was there and told the clerk to hang on to them until I showed up to collect my gift.

Harry's note also instructed me to go to a place that "Bob Hope likes to visit." I figured that meant the USO where the comedian traditionally entertains troops. So I went there and found a woman who had helped Harry make travel arrangements when he was there. She said Harry had given her an envelope for me, but she began to doubt that I would ever show up, so she had sent it out to the *Lincoln.*

Sure enough, when I returned to the ship that night, there was an envelope from Harry in my mailbox. Inside was another letter, more pictures of us, and a coupon for a free telephone call back home. I called right away and felt closer to Harry at that moment than I had in many months.

§

During our approach to the Arabian Gulf, I had been thinking more and more about trying to become a landing signal officer. It was an extremely demanding job, but I thought I would be good at it and would find the work enjoyable.

LSOs stand on a platform at the very back of the ship and direct arriving pilots to the deck. In the old days LSOs used a pair of orange flags or "paddles" to give hand signals to pilots during the critical moments before touchdown, and to this day LSOs are nicknamed "Paddles." In more recent years the lighted "meatball" has replaced the old paddles, but the LSO's job remains just as crucial. The LSOs are in radio contact with arriving pilots during the most sensitive stages of their approach. When an LSO tells a pilot to "come left," turn "right for lineup," add "power," or "wave off" to abort an approach, the pilot has to respond immediately. All LSOs are pilots themselves, and they must show consistently solid landing grades in order to qualify for the job. Grades are important because LSOs have to have the confidence of the pilots with whom they work. If a pilot doesn't implicitly trust the LSO, the results can be fatal.

I stood on the LSO platform many times during our long trip across two oceans. At first I came to watch pilots fly their approaches. I wanted to learn from them and try to improve my own performance. As time went on, though, I began paying more attention to the work of the LSOs. I studied their jobs and the way they went about them, and I came to believe that I could perform those complicated tasks, too. I also believed that I could earn the trust of my fellow pilots and in time could become a teacher.

I sought advice from some of the LSOs myself, and they helped me focus on the most important aspects of flying consistent approaches. I listened and tried hard to act on their recommendations. When I went to bed, I would picture myself guiding my S-3 through perfect approaches and landings. But while my landing grades were good (3.33), they were not spectacular. I knew that I would have to improve my own flying to qualify for LSO training.

In the gulf, the black LSO platform was like a furnace. Daytime temperatures on the flight deck commonly reached 117 degrees, and the jet exhaust from the airplanes was even hotter. The sky was cloudless every day, and the sun beat down constantly. The only relief came from the steady breeze created by the forward movement of the ship.

At night the LSO platform was still uncomfortably hot, but the view was unforgettable. My favorite planes to watch were F-14 Tomcats on night catapult launches. They taxied up to the catapults, and then large rectangular pieces of steel known as jet blast deflectors (JBDs) were raised on the deck behind them. From the LSO platform all I could see of the F-14s were the tall twin stabilators on the vertical tail sticking up above the JBDs. Then the Tomcats would go into tension on the catapults, revving their twin engines to 100 percent "military" power. The sound was deafening, even with the earplugs I always wore on deck. When the engines fired their afterburners, the tailpipes glowed, and orange fire, sparks, and smoke shot high overhead. It looked and sounded surreal, like some sort of mad scientist's experiment gone haywire. Two seconds later the Tomcat taillights would come on, and then the plane screamed down the catapult track with two white-hot burners launching it forward. As the Tomcat climbed into the night sky, the howling, glowing engines looked like a pair of otherworldly eyes retreating into the blackness.

Nothing else looked or sounded quite like a Tomcat.

16 June: Letter from Harry

(This letter was written in March and was included in the final portion of the scavenger hunt.)

Dear Love of My Life,

You've found the final item on my little scavenger hunt. Congratulations! You are entitled to a collect phone call to yours truly! Of course you must call immediately, regardless of the time of day or the length of the line to use the telephone. I know after having your butt run all over town, you've got some choice words for me.

And I've got some for you, too. Such as: I am the luckiest guy in the world to be married to you. And you are, hands down, the better spouse. And I long for the days when we've been living together for so many years that we'll barely be able to remember these difficult times apart.

I hope you had fun on my little hunt. I had a great time putting it together. I left more cards out than I ended up including because I wanted to take it easy on you. I know time in port is precious.

I love you, and I can't wait to hear your voice.

Love,
Harry

23 June: Industrial-Sized Cheerios

Meals on the USS *Abraham Lincoln* varied as we made our way around the world.

We got three square meals a day—breakfast, lunch, and dinner—plus midnight rations, or "mid rats," for those on the late shift. Most meals included fruit, vegetables, a salad bar, bacon, eggs, doughnuts, sandwiches, and fresh milk, and every meal was an all-you-can-eat buffet. But after a few weeks everything began to taste the same. The entrees on the hot line started repeating themselves, and none was very appetizing. Lunch brought "gristle-wiches," and dinner offered "Nairobi trail markers" (advertised as Salisbury steak). More and more people adopted a diet of breakfast cereal. And whereas the galley staff seemed to knock themselves out right after we left port, they soon became bored with their jobs—and it showed. One of the guys in my squadron ate nothing but turkey sandwiches for three months.

Each officer on the ship paid a mess bill that averaged about $150 a month during cruise.

Breakfast was served from 6 until 8:30 A.M. The cooks could whip up omelets or eggs any way you wanted them. Artery-clogging breakfast sandwiches were especially popular. They consisted of fried eggs with ham and cheese between two slices of bread, the entire thing being grilled in butter. Oatmeal, pancakes, and waffles were available most days, as were doughnuts—a breakfast staple. It was rare to make it through the breakfast line without hearing someone imitate Homer Simpson: "Mmm. Doughnuts!"

When the ship went through the tropics, there had been a wonderful selection of fruit. Each meal I would fill my plate with fruits that I didn't recognize and couldn't name. Such food was highly perishable, however, and it quickly became a memory. My standard breakfast consisted of cereal with fruit and grits and a glass or two of orange juice.

Food was a constant topic of discussion and a major source of irritation. One of the few times I lost my temper was a morning I woke up late and scurried to the wardroom at 8:34. All of the cereal had been put away, so I asked one of the enlisted men on duty to please grab a box of Cheerios for me. He answered that he had been ordered not to distribute cereal after 8:30; since I was four minutes late, he told me, I was out of luck. I went to the next person in the chain of command and was informed that the wardroom officer had recently reamed out her staff for giving food away after hours. She claimed that cereal was too expensive to be made available twenty-four hours a day, and cereal hours would be strictly limited from then on.

I became furious, fired off an angry note, and stuffed it into the wardroom suggestion box. I also wrote a letter to Harry that day in which I vented my frustrations at this nonsensical rule.

A few weeks later a large, dented box arrived for me in the mail. I unwrapped the brown paper cover and was delighted to find the biggest box of Cheerios I had ever seen. After receiving my letter, Harry had gone straight to the store, bought an industrial-sized cereal box, and sent it to me on the ship. I felt like Scarlett O'Hara: I would never be without cereal again!

Later our wardroom officer saw the light. After clamping down on cereal for a few weeks, she discovered that there was in fact a massive surplus. The wasteful practice of making it available around the clock was reinstated.

For most aviators lunch was the first meal of the day. Most of the flying took place from about 11 A.M. until midnight, so it was rare to see many fliers in the wardroom for breakfast. At lunch there was usually a long line as many aviators finished their briefings for their first flights of the day and the night crews awakened.

I usually ate a sandwich for lunch. The bakery's fresh bread was hard to pass up, and the salad bar was good, too. The hot food usually consisted of unappetizing greasy or fried fare, and it was easy to ignore. At dinner they listed the number of calories in each entree, and that usually played a role in determining what I ate. My customary hunting ground was the "potato bar," which served spaghetti, rice, chili, chips, and baked potatoes.

Mealtime was a relaxed and social period in which aviators from the different squadrons could meet and talk informally. Aviators seemed to spend their free time with other aviators, and members of the ship's company did the same.

Even though both groups, aviators and the ship's company, had been on board the same ship together for months, our lives were quite different, and we seemed to have little in common. Nonaviators worked long but regular shifts from day to day and week to week, and their schedules stayed pretty consistent. Aviators constantly bounced between day and night flying, and briefings, preflight inspections, and debriefings often straddled mealtimes. As a result, aviators commonly ended up rushing to the wardroom, begging for scraps, and becoming furious when they didn't get fed. The ship's company was generally unsympathetic. They figured that if we wanted to eat lunch, we should show up at lunchtime like everyone else.

Before the deployment, the wardroom officer implemented a Total Quality Management program. She had a system whereby we were encouraged to write our comments and suggestions in a green logbook that was kept in the wardroom. After a few weeks of increasingly nasty comments and biting criticisms from cranky aviators, the logbook was replaced with a suggestion box. As the months at sea wore on, even the suggestion box disappeared.

8 July: Getting Reacquainted

Just as he had promised, Harry mended quickly and hobbled halfway around the world to spend time with me. We spent six relaxing days and five nights getting reacquainted.

Getting to the Middle East was quite an odyssey for Harry. He drove from his home in Lemoore to Travis Air Force Base near Sacramento, California. There he got to ride standby on an air force transport plane to Andrews Air Force Base in Washington. Then he caught a bus to the air force base in Dover, Delaware, where he found a ride across the Atlantic to Germany. And from Germany he hopped onto another air force transport plane that took him to Saudi Arabia. There he caught up with the USS *Abraham Lincoln*'s liaison officer and arranged a flight to Bahrain.

The liaison officer got me a seat on a COD bound for Bahrain the day before the *Lincoln* pulled into port, and Harry and I spent our first night together in many months. It was so great to see him, even though he was still pretty beat up from his injuries and wiped out from jet lag. He had an impressive scar in the middle of his forehead that looked like a giant Nike swoosh. There were numerous smaller wounds on his hands, arms, legs, and midsection. His ribs were sore, too. I could hardly believe that as mangled as he was, he had decided to embark on such a long journey. But I was glad that he had.

After Bahrain we rode the COD to Fiyaira, then split a $90 cab ride with two other air wing folks to Jebel Ali. We stayed at a plush hotel right on the beach called the Forte Grande. After all that traveling and so much time apart, all Harry and I wanted to do was relax and be with each other every moment. We sat around the pool in the afternoons, did a lot of reading, and went to the gym. We slept late each morning, neither of us even beginning to stir until ten or later.

He listened to me talk in great detail about flying, the possibility of becoming a landing signal officer, and all the little things that have such a dramatic impact on the quality of life aboard ship. Since he had so recently been on cruise himself, he understood my concerns and was able to offer meaningful advice. Such conversations must be rare among navy spouses, because those who haven't spent long periods of time on warships can't quite comprehend what aviators and sailors go through during their time away from home. Harry could empathize.

He could also appreciate the minor milestone I had reached during this most recent period at sea by surpassing one hundred aircraft carrier landings. That entitled me to sew an oval "centurion" patch on my flight suit to show the designation. By the time the cruise ended, if all went well, I expected to have about 150 landings to my credit.

Harry also told me more about the details of his aircraft accident. He, Chuck, and Chuck's Labrador retriever Kato had gone for an overnight camping trip to a natural hot springs on the east slope of the Sierras. On their way home the next morning they decided to take a look at a remote airstrip in a mountain pass just south of Mount Whitney. No one was at the dirt runway in a flat meadow, and they flew over it about five hundred feet above the ground. Everything looked good, so they decided to make a closer inspection. They were talking about maybe coming back and landing there during a future camping trip.

Chuck lowered the flaps and slowed the airplane down in preparation for a low pass or even a touch and go. But the thin air at that high altitude decreased the plane's performance and reduced the amount of power the engine was able to produce. They were about two hundred feet above the ground when Chuck noticed that their descent rate was excessive, and he added full power to abort the approach. Under normal conditions that would have given them plenty of room. But since the airplane was slow, the flaps were out, and the engine wasn't producing much power, the Cessna just kept on descending.

Chuck was in a tough spot. He couldn't raise the flaps, or the plane would drop like a stone. And he had already added full power, but there just wasn't enough horsepower in that engine to make the airplane climb. They were headed toward jagged, rocky terrain, and Chuck started a gentle left turn to steer the plane around some of the biggest rock outcroppings. There was a meadow to their left, and if they could get there, they thought they could reverse their course and get more distance between themselves and the ground. But just as they were about to enter the meadow, the right wing of the airplane clipped the top of a tall pine tree.

From that moment forward, they were just holding on. The poor Cessna spun around, hit the ground, and cartwheeled. It came to rest upside down in the open grassy meadow that Chuck had been aiming for. Amazingly, miraculously, there was no fire.

Harry climbed out the passenger door and stood on the bottom side of the crumpled wing. Then he came around the other side of the plane and helped Chuck get out. Poor Chuck had a badly broken jaw, a broken wrist, and deep facial lacerations. He was losing a significant amount of blood, too; he was dazed and going into shock. Harry laid him down on the wing and covered him with sleeping bags and blankets to keep him warm.

Kato, the Labrador retriever, jumped out and explored the meadow. Evidently the pooch was fine. Harry said he himself felt pretty good physically at the time, too.

Chuck had brought along a hand-held radio and an emergency locator beacon, and Harry removed them from the baggage compartment. He used the radio and the beacon to broadcast distress signals while he unpacked the plane and prepared to spend the night on the mountain if necessary. It was a little bit before noon, so he was optimistic that they would be rescued before nightfall.

About thirty minutes after their first radio broadcast, another single-engine Cessna homed in on the distress signal and flew overhead. The plane rocked its wings and circled them. The other pilot wisely elected not to try to land at the nearby airstrip. By this time Harry was starting to feel pretty weak, and his injuries were making him so stiff that it was difficult for him to move.

The other Cessna pilot described the accident scene on the radio, and air-traffic controllers put him in touch with a nearby navy helicopter on a cross-country flight. The navy helicopter flew to the crash site, landed in the meadow, and picked up Harry, Chuck, and Kato. Over Harry's objections, they flew to the nearest hospital, in Lone Pine. Harry kept saying they should go a few miles farther to a real hospital where he and Chuck could get some meaningful assistance. But the helicopter pilot had been instructed to take them to the "nearest" medical facility—not the best medical facility.

Harry and Chuck reluctantly got out at Lone Pine, and the helicopter flew away. But the tiny emergency room in Lone Pine could do little for them. The technicians there called two airborne medical ambulances—one for Harry and one for Chuck—and the two airplanes flew them all the way to southern California for treatment. It was late at night before they finally made it to the intensive care ward, where they spent the next week.

It sure was lucky that they were able to make it out of the mountains that day. If they had been forced to spend the night, they would have been in far worse shape. As it was, fortune was on their side. Harry got some character-building scars that he hoped to use as props someday while he bored our grandchildren with tales of his heroism.

§

During port call we had a "hail-and-farewell" party for Skipper Smith. Hail-and-farewells are an opportunity to welcome new officers and say good-bye to those departing. Smith had been selected to become executive officer of an aircraft carrier, and he would soon be on his way to nuclear power school. We held the party on the roof of the Marriott and presented the skipper with some farewell gifts, such as a Playskool aircraft carrier for him to practice with before he got to his real ship. By the end of the night we had thrown him into the pool and enjoyed a fun evening. Cdr. Mark Boensel, our next skipper, hadn't arrived yet, but he planned to meet us on the carrier a few days later.

§

It was particularly sad for Harry and me to go our separate ways at the end of our visit. It seemed like every time we started settling into our roles as newlyweds, it was time for another long separation. He dropped me off at the pier and watched me walk up the brow onto the gray *Lincoln*. Then he headed back to Bahrain.

Harry had no idea how long his return trip was going to take. He was flying on a "space available" or standby basis the entire way—and military flying schedules are notoriously unreliable. But he was moving around a little better at the end of each day. I gave him enough backrubs during our time together to last a while. Since he had made it to the Middle East in one piece, I figured he could make it home, too.

The *Lincoln* was scheduled to make at least two port calls in Australia on the way home from the gulf—and Harry and I planned to rendezvous there. I knew there would be much more to see and do in Perth and Sydney than in the gulf. Harry had been in Australia briefly when the *Connie* stopped there, but his duties kept him so busy that he barely got off the ship. I had never been Down Under, and I looked forward to discovering the island continent with my husband. The Arab countries disdain the U.S. military presence, but Australia has a long history of welcoming our soldiers and sailors.

I looked forward to Australia and felt certain that it would be the highlight of the cruise. I read as much as I could about the place and—true to my organized nature—made lists of things to do and places to go when we got there. After being cooped up on the ship for so long, I longed to explore a real continent.

Australia would be like a second honeymoon for Harry and me.

Loree, at age two, with her father.

courtesy of Thomas V. Draude

Lt.(jg) Loree Draude at her "winging" ceremony, which marks the transition from student to full-fledged naval aviator. She is with her parents, Brig. Gen. Tom Draude, USMC, and Mrs. Sandi Draude, and her future husband, Lt.(jg) Harry Hirschman.

The author celebrates earning her navy "Wings of Gold" with her executive officer, Cdr. Charles Nesby, *right,* and fellow student, Lt.(jg) Jim Howe. *courtesy of Harry Hirschman*

Loree and Harry at their wedding reception in 1994. Note the miniature wings that adorn Loree's wedding dress.
courtesy of Faith Ramirez

Lt. Loree Hirschman in front of the engine intake of one of her
squadron (Torpedo Bomber Squadron 29) aircraft.

courtesy of Jana Raymond

Lt. Hirschman during the centuries old "crossing-the-line" ceremony. During this day-long rite of passage, traditional ranks are
abandoned in favor of a simpler seniority system—those who have
crossed the equator on a ship and those who have not.
courtesy of Duke Dietz

An S-3B Viking unfolds its wings in preparation for a catapult launch from the USS *Abraham Lincoln* in the Persian Gulf.

The author next to the Fresnel lens, or "Meatball," which tells pilots whether they are high, low, or on glidepath. The USS *Independence* is in the background.

The female officers of the USS *Abraham Lincoln* during its first gender-integrated deployment. Loree is standing, fourth from the right.

Lt. Loree Hirschman, *right,* and Lt. Cdr. Luther "Meat" Hook, *center,* on the "platform." Landing Signal Officers (LSOs) are responsible for the safe and expeditious recovery of all aircraft. When there is inclement weather, the LSOs are often the difference between an uneventful recovery and a fatal mishap. *courtesy of Chris Hagan*

Lt. Loree Hirschman and her husband, Lt. Harry Hirschman, with their aircraft. *courtesy of Kathleen Spane*

The author with her father, Brig. Gen. Tom Draude, USMC (Ret.), in the cockpit of a VS-41 simulator. *courtesy of Kathy Clark*

five

§

Pressure Cooker

10 July 1995: Change of Command

Our new squadron skipper came aboard, and my first impression was that he was quite different from Commander Smith. Unlike his predecessor, Commander Boensel had a reputation for making the most of port calls and almost running over junior officers on the way off the ship.

Skipper Smith broke from tradition with the change-of-command ceremony. Instead of wearing dress uniforms and standing in formation listening to speeches, we met in the ready room and he thanked all of us for having made his tour so rewarding. He packed his stuff, mailed it home, hopped into an S-3 jet with his garment bag, and did an in-flight lead change with Commander Boensel in another jet. Thus the change of command in VS-29 was complete. Commander Boensel returned to the carrier, and Commander Smith flew his plane to Bahrain, then boarded an airliner bound for the United States.

Smith had worked hard behind the scenes to help me and the other female aviators during our first few months at sea. He had done his best to make the integration of women work in his squadron—and when he left, I had the sense that I would miss his quiet support.

13 July: Power! Waveoff!

I messed up an approach to landing soon after the *Lincoln* steamed back out into the gulf, and I was extremely disappointed in myself. The conditions were fine, and I had no excuses. I just got complacent, and the result was a "no grade" landing that I feared would hurt my chances of becoming a landing signal officer.

The chain of errors began when I allowed myself to get distracted by a "wing unlocked" light that came on a few minutes before our approach. Obviously, if the folding wings of an S-3 had come unlocked during flight, it would have created an extremely dangerous situation. But the hydraulic pressure in our airplane was steady, so we concluded that there must have been a loose switch somewhere and the warning light was giving us an incorrect indication.

We were cleared for a straight-in approach and landing, and everything started out just fine. Then I allowed the plane to drift slowly off the centerline as we neared the ship. When I recognized that I was too far left, I lowered the right wing as I should have. But I let the wing stay down too long, then had to correct back to the left at the last minute—and I still touched down right of center. It was frustrating and disheartening to screw up like that. On my next flight, a night refueling mission, I made an OK trap, and that made me feel a little better.

I wasn't alone in my troubles among the female pilots on the ship, though.

Lt. Pam Lyons, a female F/A-18 Hornet pilot, scared the shit out of me during one night landing. I wasn't grading her pass, but I was up on the platform watching. She lined up a little too far right. The LSO told her, and she dipped a wing to correct for it. But when she dipped the left wing, she didn't add enough power. With the wings banked and the throttles near idle, Pam's Hornet wasn't creating enough lift, and it started dropping out of the humid night sky like an anvil.

The tension in the LSO's voice became noticeable as he called for Pam to add power, but there was no immediate response. A second later, the LSO was screaming, "Power! Power! Waveoff!"

Pam's plane was headed straight toward the stern of the ship, and it looked like a sure disaster. Then she reacted to the LSO's desperate calls and kicked in the afterburners. But the plane was coming down so fast that the two powerful jet engines couldn't keep the Hornet from slamming against the steel deck short of the wires and right next to the LSO platform. The Hornet's tailhook scraped along the deck until it caught the number one arresting wire and dragged the plane to a stop.

Pam got a "cut pass" for a grade, which is the worst anyone can do and still be alive.

If an indecisive or less experienced LSO had been monitoring her approach that night, Pam might have crashed her jet into the back end of the ship. The poor LSO who saved her looked as though he was about to have a heart attack right there on the deck. Another LSO had to take over that night because the first guy was so shaken.

I had no idea what would happen to Pam after her close call. She had been flying well up to this point, but everyone assumed she would have to go before an evaluation board to decide whether she should keep flying, move to a different type of aircraft, or, like Carey Lohrenz, lose her wings. I had heard the LSOs complain that Pam was hard to debrief because she got defensive and refused to accept criticism. Other women admired her for standing up for herself under the wilting antagonism she faced from her squadron leaders. I knew she was encountering difficulty in her squadron, but it was hard to point the finger. There were many strong personalities in her squadron, and Pam was one of them. Sometimes it seemed to me as though she didn't want to fit in. She wore bright red fingernail polish and let her long hair stick out from underneath her helmet and blow in the wind. I didn't know the details of Pam's situation, but I was disappointed that we seemed to be on the verge of losing another female aviator.

I tried to focus on improving my own performance while avoiding the myriad potential dangers on the flight deck. Once when I was taxiing an S-3 to a catapult for departure, I stopped and waited for an E-2C Hawkeye to take off. As the E-2 gunned its engines, the propeller blast started making our plane jump around. Our S-3 was big and heavy, so I didn't expect it to move very much. But the hurricane of prop wash from the Hawkeye began shaking our plane violently, and I felt it beginning to slide forward. The nose wheel was headed for a giant hole behind the raised jet blast deflector. I stomped on the brakes as hard as I could and dropped the tailhook to indicate to the flight deck crew that my brakes weren't holding the plane. I tried to turn right, away from the hole, but the plane kept lurching forward. It was a horrible feeling to be just sitting there, unable to control my plane. A few seconds later the E-2 was airborne, the air around us settled down, and my plane was still again. I continued the pretakeoff checklist as though nothing unusual had happened.

An essential part of a naval aviator's training—as important as memorizing information—is learning to forget, or to banish certain thoughts from the conscious mind. I couldn't allow the unnerving loss of control on deck to make me overlook an essential item on the checklist. We had narrowly avoided crunching our airplane. In the blink of an eye, we were back in business preparing to fly.

17 July: The Most Destructive Couple on Earth

Harry and I celebrated our first wedding anniversary by e-mail and telephone.

Harry had sent me the telephone number of a restaurant in Sacramento where he and my parents planned to eat dinner that night, and he told me to call at exactly 8 p.m. California time. The plan worked great. I got through on the first try, and it was fantastic to hear everyone's voice and to know they were together enjoying such a happy time. I only wished I could have been there.

My dad was totally surprised to hear from me. Harry has always had a real talent for setting up inventive surprises. Dad described their situation to me in great detail. He said they were having a fancy seafood dinner at his favorite restaurant downtown, and they were sitting around a circular table on a wooden patio overlooking the tree-lined Sacramento River. Harry's parents had known that my parents were going to be in the area, and they had set the dinner up a couple of weeks in advance.

After we hung up, I got to thinking yet again about Harry and how little we had been able to see each other. We had been married for three months when his ship, the USS *Constellation,* left for a six-month deployment to Korea and the Persian Gulf. My ship left port a few weeks before the *Connie* came home. Our two battle groups passed somewhere west of Hawaii.

In the last twelve months, my husband and I had been together three or four weeks at most. I knew that eventually we would be together more —probably when one or both of us left the navy. But we had no idea when that would be. Harry talked about going to graduate school in business when his ten-year commitment to the navy was up, but that was still four years away. I was going to be eligible to leave the navy in four years too, but I wasn't convinced that I wanted to do that. Military life was all I had ever known.

Harry liked to joke that it was the navy that brought us together, and it was the navy that kept us apart. His family laughingly called us the "most potentially destructive couple on earth," a reference to the bomb-dropping nature of our jobs. But on special occasions like anniversaries, it was sometimes hard to maintain a sense of humor.

A normal couple would have been settling into familiar, comfortable routines at this point in their marriage. Maybe they would have been considering starting a family. Harry and I were scheming to meet up for a few days in Asia here, a couple of weeks in Australia there. Managing one military career is hard, and two is just about impossible—especially for two aviators. Still, I had known what I was getting into from the beginning.

I was totally confident that our marriage would survive, but at what cost? I hoped that someday we would look back on this trying period with decades of perspective and be able to smile, knowing that the benefits had been worth all the shared experiences we had given up. In the meantime, occasional long-distance telephone calls, care packages, and e-mail had to suffice.

6 August: Added Pressure

Lt. Sue McNally, one of my roommates, turned in her wings a few nights ago.

The news came as a complete surprise to me, since Sue had never given any indication that she was thinking about quitting. But evidently she had been contemplating it for some time. She told me she felt unsafe flying E-2C Hawkeyes, the stress of being on cruise was gnawing at her, and then a frightening night landing convinced her to give up her wings. I was told by another female pilot that one of the senior officers in Sue's squadron had been giving her a rough time, but Sue never talked about that with me.

Sue's plane had touched down that night far right of centerline and completely missed the arresting wires. It was lucky that no planes were parked on the deck at the time, because with the E-2's long wingspan, she would have collided with them. She boltered that approach, then landed successfully on the next attempt. But the horrific images of the bungled approach stuck with her, and Sue told her commanding officer she didn't want to fly anymore. She quit rather than face an evaluation board.

Sue was matter-of-fact when she informed us of her decision. She seemed relieved, as though a tremendous burden had been lifted from her shoulders. She had many friends in her squadron and on the ship, and even when she was feeling down she usually managed to smile or crack a joke. Her landing grades had been good up until her most recent bolter, and I was disappointed that she would be leaving us.

Sue asked to continue flying land-based planes, but that request was denied. Her second choice was a transfer to the Naval Intelligence branch. I hoped she would get to do that. She was a good officer and a fine, honest person. With all the military cutbacks, changing career paths in the navy wasn't easy. I respected Sue for having made a tough choice. She tried her hardest, but she felt unsafe and didn't want to endanger anyone else.

Yet it was sobering and a little discouraging to realize that with what were likely going to be the toughest months of our cruise still ahead, one-fourth of the female pilots originally assigned to the *Lincoln* were gone. And with each female pilot who went home, those of us who remained felt added pressure.

Personally I wanted to be part of this historic cruise. I had asked for the assignment and was glad that I had gotten it. I felt I could play an important role as part of a pioneering group, and I believed I could perform my duties well and make things better for the women who would follow us. Even in my darkest times on the ship, I wouldn't have traded places with anyone.

For me the novelty of being one of the first women to fly combat planes had worn off long ago. I hadn't chosen to go into aviation to draw attention to myself or break down social barriers; I just wanted to serve my country in a challenging, meaningful assignment. And once I began flying airplanes, I found that I wanted to go as far as my ability could take me.

I also truly believed that my seeing the *Lincoln*'s cruise through to a successful conclusion would benefit many others in the navy. Being around competent, mission-oriented female pilots would increase men's confidence in their female shipmates and smooth the transition for everyone. That was one of the thoughts that kept me going.

If I ever thought I was unsafe in the cockpit, I would have turned in my wings just like Sue. It would be selfish and crazy to put lives at risk just to gratify my own ego. I have made some below-average landings during my aviation career, but I learned from them, and I believe that the experience made me a better pilot.

Another thought that kept me motivated was knowing how humiliated I would feel if I had to go home early, whatever the reason. It would give too much satisfaction to Pug, the F/A-18 instructors who had hassled me at Lemoore, and all the naysayers who believed women shouldn't have been allowed to fly combat jets.

I had boarded the *Lincoln* to do a job, and that job wasn't going to be finished until our ship steamed under the Golden Gate Bridge and into the San Francisco Bay. I tried to picture myself at that moment, standing on deck with my shipmates, our coats flapping in the cool autumn breeze.

I had to make it that far. Giving up was not an option.

7 August: A Good Cry

Another lousy approach dropped my landing grade point average to the point that I felt sure I would miss the chance to become an LSO. Failure to meet my own goals, combined with heat, exhaustion, stress, and loneliness, made me more depressed and miserable than I had ever been.

I made a poor approach on a daytime landing attempt and got waved off. I had hoped that the waveoff was due to a fouled deck or something beyond my control, but no such luck. Just like my last below-average landing, this series of missteps began with something that should have been easy. I was approaching the ship in broad daylight, but when I reached the point at which I planned to begin my descent, I made a misjudgment: my S-3 was particularly light that day because we weren't carrying any bombs or buoys, and when I pulled back the throttles to initiate a descent, the plane just seemed to soar like a hawk on the rising air currents. I chopped the power back to idle, but too late to get the plane on the proper glide-path. The LSO had already waved me off for being too high.

The next approach was fine, but by then the damage was done. I knew that a big red "WO" by my name was going to be sticking out like a sore thumb on our squadron greenie board. VS-29's greenie board was the biggest, most ostentatious one on the entire ship, and I dreaded having to face that red mark every time I went to the ready room.

I tried to keep a positive attitude and avoid getting down, but that waveoff pushed me over the edge. I found it impossible to maintain a sense of humor. We still had two months remaining on our cruise, and to me that sounded like an eternity. A spiral of negative thinking set in, and I pulled the curtains on the bunk in my hot, noisy, crowded room and wondered why no one had sent mail recently. I thought about how crappy my landings were, and how much I missed my husband.

Real life was passing me by at home, and my existence on the ship revolved around landing grades, breakfast cereal, faulty air conditioners, and navy showers. I was surrounded by people but isolated from my loved ones. I could feel myself coming down with a cold. My ears were stuffy, my throat hurt, and my nose was running. Being sick on the ship was especially miserable when it was 120 degrees outside and the air conditioning was sporadic. I was so sick of living on the ship that I wanted to scream.

Instead I climbed into my rack, closed the curtains, and had a good long cry.

11 August: A Well-Deserved Shower

My long cry seemed to do some good. I had been so stressed out and exhausted that after hitting rock bottom, my spirits started to rebound. I slept soundly straight through the night—my first full night's sleep in more than a week—and woke up refreshed. I had a cold and was off flying status because of the potential damage that changes in pressure could do to my ears. But the crying had released a lot of pent-up tension.

I don't think any of my roommates heard me, but I wouldn't have cared if they had. It was the first time I had cried since that terrible night off the California coast when I boltered three times, and I had to get it out of my system. But I refused to cry in public; I allowed it to happen only when I was alone.

§

One of my sailors in the avionics shop accidentally called me sir instead of ma'am, and the poor guy blushed and apologized profusely when he realized his mistake. I assured him that it was no big deal and that it happened regularly. It was totally understandable, since the vast majority of the officers on the *Lincoln* were men. Whenever it happened, I tried to laugh it off by telling the sailor that titles on our ship should be like those on *Star Trek,* where everyone was called sir regardless of gender. I would have found it even more amusing, however, if after talking to me for a while one of the sailors had called a male officer ma'am.

Despite the few blunders in landing pattern, my landing grades were solid and improving, and my application to become an LSO was accepted. My discussion with Commander Boensel was hardly a moment of celebration, however. He gave me a speech in which he more or less said, "I've got some reservations about doing this, but I'm approving your request anyway—just don't fuck up."

It wasn't the resounding vote of confidence I had been hoping for.

I put in an order for a white jersey and the "float coat" with an inflatable lifejacket that I would be required to wear on the LSO platform. Even though I hadn't been feeling well, I went up to the platform every time an aircraft landed. One day I was up there for six different sets of arrivals. The temperature wasn't too unpleasant at night, but during daylight the heat was oppressive, and each time a jet would turn away from us and blast us with hot exhaust, the raw skin on my runny nose felt like it was on fire.

I was on the platform another afternoon when the LSO team leader pointed to me and told me to wave my first series of aircraft recoveries. I stepped forward and grabbed the "pickle," which controlled the light signals, and the radio. There were two S-3s approaching the ship, and I looked behind me to make sure the deck was clear. The weather was cloudless and the surface of the ocean was calm, but when that first airplane rolled into the groove for landing, I felt nervous and very much alone.

I tried to lower the pitch of my voice, but it was obvious to everyone that, yes, that really was a gal making those radio calls to the arriving planes. Darcy, one of the COD pilots, was an LSO, so hearing a woman on the LSO radio wasn't a big shock. We kept the planes coming aboard at forty-five-second intervals, and everything went smoothly. I stayed on the platform throughout the day and into the night. We finally recovered the last plane at 1 A.M., and I was debriefing pilots and doing paperwork until after 3 A.M.

After being on that frying pan of a flight deck all day, all night, and into the morning, it felt wonderful to go below decks into the air conditioning and take a long shower. Gritty nonskid material from the deck had been blasted into every pore of exposed skin. It was a rare pleasure to lather up and wash all the grime out of my skin and hair. After my well-deserved shower, I slept late the next morning, so weary that the noisy catapults, elevators, and other usual sounds didn't bother me at all.

My ears were clearing, so I planned to return to flight status quickly. With a couple of shots of Afrin, I figured my sinuses would compensate for the changes in atmospheric pressure as planes climbed and descended.

So far I had really enjoyed working on the LSO platform. Waving the planes was demanding, and everything had to be done quickly and precisely. It required teamwork between the people on the platform and the pilots in the air. As soon as the last plane from each recovery landed, we scurried off the flight deck and gathered on the O3 level. A team usually consisted of six LSOs—one for each aircraft type. The most senior was normally the team leader, and one of the CAG LSOs supervised. (In addition to its squadron LSOs, an air wing has two or three CAG LSOs assigned to it—former squadron LSOs who return to the land-based training squadron for their aircraft, spend about two years training new pilots to land on carriers, then are reassigned to a CAG as CAG LSOs.) The team reviewed the passes for administrative errors and ensured that we all agreed on the way the passes were recorded. We always wrote in pencil in case there were any changes later. The CAG LSO or the team leader got the last look and then led the debriefings in the ready rooms.

Normally the CAG LSO, the team leader, and the LSO who was controlling the recovery (i.e., manning the pickle and talking to the pilots) walked to all the ready rooms. When I first started training to be an LSO, I followed along like a kid sister. It was good for me to watch how the debriefs were conducted and to listen to the pilots' responses. Debriefing the pilots could be tough—especially when they were unhappy about their grades. Sometimes they wanted to argue, and the situation could become quite tense.

We started at the aft ready room, VFA-22, and worked our way forward through VF-213, VAW-117, VA-95, VS-29, VFA-94, and then all the way toward the bow to VAQ-135. The Prowler ready room was right next to the wardroom, so we often stopped in for a glass of ice water or soda and then returned to the CAG office, where we typed all the passes into a computer data base. By the time that was done, we had about twenty minutes to relax or swing by our respective squadrons before it was time to return to the flight deck for the next recovery.

One day on the platform I was the controlling LSO when a familiar voice came through on the radio as an F/A-18 made its approach to the ship. It was Pug, the F/A-18 officer who had caused so much trouble for me while I was in Hornet training in Lemoore.

"Roger, ball," I responded after he announced he had the "meatball" lighting device in sight.

I watched his pass closely, and in truth I would have been glad to have an excuse to downgrade him. But he flew a solid pass, and I wrote down OK on the sheet, the equivalent of an A grade. Although I believed he had unfairly pushed me out of Hornets, I vowed to treat him fairly.

Later, when I went to the VFA-94 ready room to debrief him, I felt a little uncomfortable. It was going to be the first time I had spoken to him during the months we had been on the ship. Pug saw me walk into the orange and black "Mighty Shrikes" ready room with my grade book in hand, and he smiled and shook his head.

"Oh no," he laughed. "Here comes my worst nightmare."

I wasn't sure how to take the comment, so I just ignored it and launched into my review of his approach and landing. I told him that I graded it as an OK pass. He nodded and agreed, and I promptly left. So far I hadn't had any problems debriefing pilots, but the senior LSOs were usually there to back me up. I had no idea if people's demeanor would change when I started doing the job alone.

15 August: False Intimacy

Saddam Hussein's sons-in-law unexpectedly complicated our lives.

They defected to Jordan a few weeks before the review period for United Nations sanctions against Iraq was scheduled to begin. Then Iraq's "Republican Guard" armored divisions increased their activity along the borders, and life on the *Lincoln* began to get a little more intense. Several Arab linguists who were supposed to have left stayed on the ship. Then some of the military brass in the region flew aboard for a conference. The rumor mill started going full tilt, and everyone speculated that our tour in the gulf was about to be extended.

The rumor turned out to be true.

As I was in my stateroom getting ready for a flight, the long whistle sounded that always preceded an address from the captain. He rarely spoke to the entire ship, so I knew the announcement was likely to be important. I sat down and continued lacing my boots as he told us over the intercom that we were going to stick around in this part of the world for another two weeks at least. In order to arrive home on schedule, we were going to skip port calls in Australia. Harry and I wouldn't get to rendezvous Down Under after all.

The news was disappointing, but people took it in stride. Everyone knew we had come to the gulf to perform an important mission, and protecting the free world could mess up the most carefully planned vacations. In order to make the extended assignment more palatable, our next three-day port call in Jebel Ali was increased to five days. Plus, we would get to have another short stop in the gulf to pick up provisions before heading home.

§

I conducted a reenlistment ceremony for two sailors in my division and had a great time doing it. The three of us boarded a Seahawk helicopter and strapped into the seats on the port side. It was 120 degrees outside, but the air conditioning inside the helicopter worked great, even with the engines off. Then the crew started the engines, and the massive blades atop the helicopter slowly began turning. I watched them until they were spinning so fast that they became a blur.

The helo lifted off the deck, then slid out over the port side of the ship. The nose dipped as we gained forward speed, and we stayed off the port side of the carrier as I read the sailors their oath of reenlistment over the intercom. The microphones on their helmets didn't pick up every word, but I watched their lips move. The guys did a great job of keeping up.

When the oath was finished, we stayed off the port side of the ship and watched several jets shoot off the catapults on the bow. It was like an out-of-body experience watching the launch from that unusual perspective. We hovered alongside the ship as it clipped along into the breeze. It was an unforgettable sight, and the sailors and I just sat there in a state of awe and wonderment.

Whenever I'm part of the spectacle, I'm so focused on performing my own little role that I can't just look around and appreciate the enormity of what's going on around me. Watching from the helicopter was like seeing a magnificent parade from the reviewing stand instead of marching in it.

When the helicopter landed, I took a few snapshots of the sailors proudly wearing their flight suits by the helicopter's open side door. They said they enjoyed wearing the flight suits because of the extra respect the drab green garments commanded.

§

Several nights ago we had a "ladies night" of sorts in which a number of female officers got together to watch the movie *A League of Their Own*. Eleven gals piled into a two-person stateroom. Some of us were on the floor, others on beds and chairs. We passed around small bags of micro-wave popcorn.

The movie was about a league of women baseball players during the 1940s, and the parallels between their situation and ours were obvious. In both groups the women had to endure long separations from their loved ones, and they had to rely on each other. The baseball players were doing something they enjoyed—just like us—and it was something that had never been tried before.

As I watched the movie, I couldn't help thinking about our differences, too. Female pilots weren't the novelty that female baseball players must have been more than fifty years before. At least no one was buying tickets to watch us fly airplanes and helicopters. And whereas the women's baseball league eventually folded, I was convinced that women would be involved in military combat roles far into the future. I believed we would keep our place as long as there were competent, qualified, motivated women willing to accept the challenges, risks, and sacrifices that go with the job.

There's a scene in the movie in which the Geena Davis character is going home with her husband after deciding not to play in the championship game. She tells the manager, played by Tom Hanks, that "it's too hard," or something like that. And he replies, "It's the hard part that makes it so great."

I'm not sure I have the line exactly right, but it conveyed the same sentiment that I felt when I thought about why I wanted to be on the *Lincoln*. I loved flying on and off aircraft carriers. Every day presented new challenges, new emergencies, things that were different and difficult. I loved being on the LSO platform and being responsible for bringing pilots, crew members, and multi-million-dollar airplanes onto the ship safely. I wanted to be on the *Lincoln*, I want to excel—and I knew I had the ability to support those desires.

It really was the hard part that made it worthwhile.

§

During our last port call in Jebel Ali (our fifth!), Jana and I split a room at the Marriott Hotel with two other gals from the air wing. It was great to sleep in a real bed with a soft mattress and clean sheets, and it was a luxury to shower using a hot-water supply that flowed continuously. I worked out each afternoon in an air-conditioned gym, and on the last day I had a long massage. We went to the market and loaded up on fresh fruit and large stashes of candy that would supposedly last until Hawaii. That was unrealistic, of course; I knew the chocolate would disappear in a week.

Jana and I went up to the pool on top of the Marriott to relax. On one side of the pool were guys from the F/A-18 squadrons—tan, muscular, wearing their cool sunglasses and posing for the visiting flight attendants. On the other side were guys from our S-3 squadron—some slightly balding, many with an extra tire around the middle, laughing and drinking beer. Jana and I looked at each other and decided we were very happy to be in the S-3 squadron. We might not be as pretty as those Hornet guys, but we sure had a lot of fun together.

The first night in Jebel Ali, we all went to Cyclones, the bar of choice for most of the air wing. I danced for a while. But some of the things I saw there were disturbing, and the images stuck with me.

One of the male pilots met up with a female sailor from his squadron at the bar. There was nothing wrong with either of them being there; Cyclones hadn't been designated an "officers' bar," so if an enlisted woman wanted to have a drink, that was her prerogative. But after a while the distance between these two started shrinking, and soon they were groping each other on the dance floor. It was quite a spectacle.

The pilot was married; I didn't know about the enlisted woman. But whatever arrangements they might have made with their spouses back home, fraternization between officers and enlisted troops was against military law. It destroys the effectiveness of combat units, and it's a crime. Those who are found guilty of it can get some pretty severe punishment, part of which is being kicked out of the navy. But the commanding officer of the pilot's squadron was there at the bar, too. He just laughed and shook his head as he watched their escapades as if to say, "What can I do? Boys will be boys."

I know how lonely people become. I've seen how horny people get. But I wouldn't be able to live with myself if I ever cheated on Harry. I don't mean to sound like one of the nuns back at St. Francis High School, but even just flirting with someone and giving him the impression that I want him sexually—to me, that would be cheating.

Every time the *Lincoln* was in port, it seemed, the same people would get falling-down drunk and start groping each other. Female officers lived in such a fishbowl that the irresponsible actions of a few would inevitably come back to haunt the rest.

I was disheartened every time I saw one of these same few female officers getting drunk, flirting with the guys, and then blaming their behavior on alcohol. When the hangovers wore off, these women went back to the ship where they were required to work with the same men for months on end in extremely close quarters.

Women hurt themselves, and they damage our ability to be effective, when they behave so recklessly and selfishly. Their actions encourage the guys to believe that all they have to do is get us drunk and we turn into raging nymphomaniacs.

With a couple of exceptions, I was very proud of the women on the *Lincoln*. As a group we had performed extremely well under tremendous pressure. That's why it hurt to see those legitimate, hard-won gains that all of us had contributed to at sea being squandered on shore for a few fleeting moments of false intimacy.

28 August: Letter from Tom Draude

Dearest Loree,

Great to hear from you this week. I enjoyed the pictures of you and your "Hoover."

Harry sounded good when I talked to him on the phone. We have a surprise for you on October 14 in Sacramento: I have tickets to Les Mis for the four of us. I'll even spring for dinner!

Your comments in your last letter about some of the other pilots were tough but honest—just like you. Your objectivity is always going to be an asset. (I think they call it fairness, but it's a rare quality.) Keep your head clear of any extraneous issues that don't bear on your performance as a carrier pilot. You are obviously doing a superb job. Keep it up. I continue to be proud and delighted beyond words. Congrats on the LSO designation—you earned that honor by performance.

In a previous letter, you touched on the way you were raised. It really hit me that you sense how well you are received in a tough community. As you were growing up, I had those same feelings—you were going to be a great officer and a real asset to some lucky commander's wardroom. You continued to display the combination of fairness, sense of humor, pragmatism/idealism, and teamwork that we all strive for but seldom achieve. It thrills me that you are a good officer as well as a good aviator. Not everyone is both.

We saw the movie Babe Friday night. It's about a pig that wants to be a sheepdog. You'll love it.

Hang in there. If Saddam causes any problems, tell him "Sage" is coming back! (That should bring him in line.)

Love,
Dad

28 August: Letter from Sandi Draude

Wow—you mailed your letter on the fourteenth of August and we got it on the eighteenth! Talk about making great plane connections. The photos were absolutely terrific—thank you, thank you. I like the "Hoover." It looks like such a reliable aircraft, unlike the F/A-18, which reminds me of a nervous mosquito!

Dad and I were delighted at your designation as LSO. What a wonderful indication of the great job you're doing as a pilot: they let you grade other pilots. Way to go. Your comments on pilots not listening to advice from LSOs was sadly familiar to me. I would often give my students advice on better study skills, writing, etc., which they disregarded. At least my students didn't kill or injure themselves and others by misplacing a comma!

I sure hope your ship remains on schedule so that it arrives in Alameda on the ninth!

I can't tell you how often I think of you every day. I am so proud of your life and how you're living it. Michael, Tobias, Raphael, and Gabriel (the great archangels) cringe when they see me coming via my many prayers for you and Harry. They look forward to the day you and Harry enter a less perilous line of work.

Sweetheart, take good care of yourself, keep that angel I gave you in the pocket of your flight suit, and stay happy!

Angels bear you up in joy and land you down softly!
Love,
Mom

4 September: I Just Can't Listen to This

It's amazing how lonely a person can feel on a ship carrying more than five thousand people.

I stopped by Brenda and Pam's room to drop off a video I had borrowed, and when I came in they were talking about landing grades. There was a new F/A-18 pilot in VFA-94, Paul, and he wasn't doing very well. Brenda remarked that if Paul had been a woman, he would have been sent to a review board already.

I thought Brenda seemed to be alluding to Carey Lohrenz, the female F-14 pilot who had been sent home by a field evaluation board for poor landing grades. Carey had done well in jet training, but she was mediocre in F-14 training and below average on the ship. I wish it hadn't been that way, but it was. Paul had been outstanding in Hornet training—good enough to go directly to an operational squadron at sea. Only the best pilots in training are given such difficult assignments; new pilots usually go through a whole series of short warmup cruises before they go to sea for real. I thought Paul deserved the extra latitude he was apparently being given.

Later in our conversation Brenda and Pam brought up "the list," which divides all pilots into three categories—A, B, and C—based on their ability to fly in poor weather conditions. They thought the list was just another tool that LSOs and senior officers could use as punishment. I strongly disagreed, but I was physically and mentally exhausted and didn't want to get into a long emotional debate. Instead I just said I had to go and walked out. Brenda called after me, so I poked my head back in and said, "Look, I'm sorry, but I just can't listen to this."

I tried to do it nicely; I didn't storm off and slam the door or anything. I hoped that I hadn't offended them. But it was a waste of my energy to think about conspiracies that no one could prove or disprove. I was on my way to becoming an LSO when some female pilots believed that the LSOs were out to get them. At the same time, the LSOs were under pressure to grade all pilots the same and not give women any slack. I understood the tension between pilots and LSOs; I certainly didn't agree with every grade I had received so far. But repeating the same complaints over and over seemed counterproductive.

Fortunately my flying had been steadily improving. My last night trap resulted in an awesome OK 3-wire. It was a great way to end the most recent grading period. I finished with a 3.2 landing grade point average, about average for nugget pilots in the air wing. My grade should have been better, but a couple of waveoffs had really killed my scores. Both waveoffs were for being too high, and they were totally deserved.

Despite my less-than-stellar landing grades, my confidence in my ability to do my job had never been higher. Even though I had screwed up a few approaches, I felt that my actual skills were better than they had been several months before when my landing grades were at 3.5. Bringing an airplane aboard a ship was an art that took time to master. In recent weeks I had begun recognizing subtle changes in the arrival pattern that I hadn't noticed before. My anticipation was better, and because of that my corrections were smoother and smaller. Instead of just reacting to the meatball during those final, critical seconds before touchdown, I was placing the airplane where I wanted it to be. I was consciously initiating actions instead of passively responding to external forces.

Spending so much time on the LSO platform also helped my performance in the cockpit. I had been up there during hundreds of landings, and it demystified the process. I gained a deeper understanding of the entire system and became more comfortable with my role in it.

I also enjoyed the camaraderie of being part of the LSO team. A few days earlier I had showed up on the platform wearing my brand-new white float coat. Paco, one of the F-14 LSOs, noticed it and grabbed the front of the float coat, pushed me down onto the flight deck, and started rubbing the back of my nice new coat across the oily deck.

"There," he said happily. "Now you look salty."

On a recent morning recovery I waved about twenty landings—and each one was a blast. I even waved CAG Gillespie's fifteen hundredth trap. I graded it as an (OK) 4-wire because he was high the whole way. But a higher-ranking LSO changed it to an OK because it was such a major milestone. Very few navy pilots make half that many aircraft carrier landings during their entire careers. Pilots traditionally get an OK when they fly their last pass at the boat, so the grade inflation wasn't unusual.

The one aspect of the milestone that troubled me, though, was the fact that CAG Gillespie had been putting himself on the schedule to fly twice a day in order to reach his goal. Meanwhile, several new pilots who had recently joined us in the gulf had been having trouble getting enough flight time. All of them were nuggets, and some of them had fewer than thirty fleet traps. It bothered me that instead of making sure the junior guys were getting enough practice, our leader seemed fixated on a personal goal.

10 September: A Homecoming Queen

Jana and I had been getting along extremely well in recent weeks, but that came to an abrupt halt when her alarm clock started going off at 7:30 A.M. and she kept hitting the snooze button.

I had gone to sleep at 2 A.M. after a long day and night on the LSO platform. Her alarm kept going off every five minutes, and each time I got more irritated. Finally Jana got up and went to the bathroom, but her alarm clock kept going off while she was gone. I pulled myself out of my rack, turned the alarm off, and—just as I had done the other two times this had happened—put the clock by her desk hoping she would take the hint. When Jana came back into our room I asked her as nicely as I could to please make sure and turn off her alarm when she left the room.

She snapped back at me, "Like I meant to leave it on."

I really didn't want to get into an argument, especially since I was half-comatose at the time. But I told her that it wasn't the first time she had left her alarm on, and it was absurd to keep repeating this annoying situation.

She had demonstrated as a naval flight officer that she was capable of operating complicated electronic equipment; she should have been able to turn off an alarm clock.

"Well, you don't have to be snotty about it," she said.

I know it was a stupid argument, but I was in it already, so I told Jana that I wasn't being snotty, I was making a reasonable request, and she really ought to be more considerate of her roommates. After that I put on some shorts and shower shoes and left to go to the bathroom. When I came back I crawled back into bed without speaking to Jana. We pretty much ignored each other for the rest of the morning. Then when I went to the ready room in the afternoon, she was being nice to me again. I was tempted to hold a grudge, but I didn't really want to keep feuding. I figured she was just not a morning person, either.

As much as I argued with Jana, my relationship with A. J., our other roommate, was far worse. She had been running around with one of the guys in VFA-94 like a homecoming queen. The two of them said they thought it would be cute and funny to start rumors about themselves being an item and spread gossip around the air wing. Then, when the rumors were everywhere, A. J. insisted that it was all a big show, that she and this guy were only real good friends. The whole charade was embarrassing to witness.

There was more space in our room since Sue turned in her wings and left the ship. A week after she quit, a COD took her to Bahrain. She rode an air force plane to Italy and then home. After she left, our stateroom had an extra bunk, a spare desk, and some more locker space. But her resignation was a little like having a death in the family. There was a certain emptiness and sadness, even before she left the ship.

Sue's departure had been upsetting. When one of your contemporaries throws in the towel and says, "This isn't worth it," it's hard not to get rattled. Such actions force a kind of mental reappraisal among those who stay behind, and I just didn't want to go through that wrenching process on the ship. I had committed myself to finishing the *Lincoln*'s mission a long time ago; there would be plenty of time for soul-searching later. For the time being, I had to concentrate, keep learning, and keep looking forward.

On a social level, I was afraid that Sue's absence would complicate the dynamics in our stateroom. Sue had had a pleasant, calming personality that smoothed over the conflicts among Jana, A. J., and me. With three of us left, I was concerned that one person would feel like an outsider. It always seemed easier for two or four people to get along than three.

§

The hardest part of our cruise was supposedly behind us, but we had to guard against psychological letdowns. It would be a shame to endure all the loneliness, stress, and heartache of an entire cruise and then get killed toward the end.

I kept catching myself envisioning what life would be like when the cruise finally ended. I fantasized about how great it would be to get away from the people I hadn't been able to avoid for all these months. At sea the only place to escape was the airplane, and there the hazards never seemed to end.

I was doing the preflight inspection on an S-3 at the very rear of the flight deck one morning when I literally got roasted by a pair of taxiing F/A-18 Hornets. I had my helmet and earplugs on, and I was looking at my plane and not paying attention to the Hornets when they turned their tails toward me and scorched me from head to toe with hot exhaust. By the time I realized what was happening, there was nowhere to go. I turned my back to them, crouched down, and tucked my hands into my armpits as their engines roared and the searing heat poured over me like the breath of a dragon. The roar of their engines reverberated through my chest, and it felt like every cell in my body was melting.

A few seconds later the Hornets mercifully turned away. I shouted and swore at them even though I knew the furnace blast was my fault, not theirs; I should have been paying attention. When I looked at my hands, they were red from the intense, fiery wind. The Nomex flight suit had done a great job of protecting the skin on the rest of my body.

Inside the airplanes, pilots are protected from the noise, heat, and fumes that permeate the chaotic aircraft carrier deck. Once we get out of the cockpit, though, we step into a confusing, dangerous world. After my very first night landing in an S-3, I hopped out of the plane onto the flight deck and was instantly warmed up all over by hot exhaust from another jet. My eyes burned and watered profusely, and the fumes made breathing difficult.

Fortunately the instructor NFO I flew with was nearby, and I reached out and grabbed hold of his survival vest. I could still see, but it hurt to open my eyes, and I was afraid of stumbling into a place I didn't belong. At night, planes on deck leave their lights off until they are ready to be launched from the catapults. Until then, it is difficult to tell which jet engines are turning.

I held on to the other pilot's vest, and we wove around airplanes and equipment and dodged jet blast until we came to the "island," the tall structure on the right side of the ship that towers above the flight deck. We found a ladder and went down to a safe place below. That first experience certainly reinforced the idea that the less time I spent on the flight deck, the better.

11 September: A Very Strange Scene

Jana and I had quickly put ourselves back on speaking terms. Unfortunately, we had some hard things to tell A. J.

A. J. and her "boyfriend" were sitting close together in our stateroom when I came back from dinner. We weren't supposed to have men in our staterooms at all. Besides, I had planned to lie around in my underwear all night and work on my computer; with him there, my evening was shot. I quickly turned around and left the room, then walked around the ship for a while and tried to simmer down. I was still angry when I bumped into Jana, though, and we both decided that the situation was intolerable.

We went back to our room, and it was a very strange scene. The ship's crew was doing some tests on the nuclear reactor, so virtually all the lights in the ship were off. I stood in our pitch-black stateroom with a flashlight and asked the guy to leave; he went and stood right outside our closed door. Then, trying not to shine the flashlight into A. J.'s face, Jana and I told her that we were uncomfortable having guys in our room, and that we didn't want her tying up our telephone. People from my squadron had said they had tried to call and couldn't get through for hours. We told A. J. that these irritating habits had to end right away. She just nodded and left. I was disappointed with A. J. because she was a great pilot and could have set a positive example for female officers. Instead she was only seen as someone's girlfriend.

Despite the roommate dramas, work and flying continued to go well. I wrote an LSO reference guide to define barricade/eject parameters for "blue water" operations far from land. I went outside briefly, and it was such a beautiful day that I promised myself to come out later and go running or walking when flight operations were over. It was clear and cool, and the calm ocean surface made it was easy to exercise on the stable deck. Later I alternated running and walking for about forty minutes.

Before dinner we decorated the wardroom in a Hawaiian theme, since our next port call was going to be in the islands. People were in a festive mood now that the end of our time in the gulf was in sight. The aircraft carrier USS *Independence* and its battle group were nearing the Persian Gulf to relieve us.

It was going to be a long trip home, but we intended to be on our way soon.

six

§

The *Independence*

13 September 1995: Miniature Rainbows

A wave of relief swept over me when I saw with my own eyes that the USS *Independence* had truly arrived to take our place.

Everyone knew that the *Indy* was on its way to the Persian Gulf, and we could chart its progress on the tactical maps that showed the positions of our two battle groups as we came progressively closer. But I hadn't allowed myself to really believe that the *Indy* and its escorts would get here until I stood on the flight deck and saw that they had actually arrived. The magnificent gray aircraft carrier was visible about two miles off our port side, and helicopters were shuttling VIPs back and forth.

We cleared off the USS *Abraham Lincoln*'s flight deck while helicopters hovered nearby and photographers made aerial pictures of our combined battle groups. When the photographers were done, the captain invited everyone to come outside onto the expansive flight deck and gaze at all of the ships steaming together in formation. It was an awesome sight— the turquoise sea filled with slate-gray American warships, all of them slicing deep, foamy V-shaped wakes in the calm ocean surface. I handed my little point-and-click camera to one of the other officers, and he snapped a picture of my smiling, wind-blown face with the *Indy* in the background. Late that afternoon, with the turnover complete, the *Lincoln* turned east, and we began our long journey home.

I knew it was all psychological, but the water in the shower felt cooler and the air conditioners seemed to be working better. Everyone was relaxed and congenial. We steamed through the Straits of Hormuz into the Gulf of Oman and south into the vast expanses of the Indian Ocean. We planned to turn left around Sri Lanka and a day or two later pass through the narrow Straits of Malaca.

I had recently been on the LSO platform during an afternoon recovery when the sun angle made it difficult for arriving pilots to see the lighted meatball on the side of the ship. It was a trial by fire for me, because I had to talk the pilots down as they approached the ship. I goofed up by telling the first pilot he was "on glidescope" instead of "on glidepath." The glidescope is the picture air-traffic controllers see on their TV monitors; the glidepath is the slope that arriving aircraft are supposed to follow. It wasn't a big deal, but the guys in my squadron had a good laugh about my faux pas.

Also on the platform that day I was writing down the LSO's grades and comments when someone noticed that I was using a brightly colored, oversized pencil with polka dots and jazzy splashes of paint all over it. I had purchased it at a tourist shop in Dubai and thought it would be cool to bring a little pizzazz to the platform. The guys were traditionalists, though, and they disagreed. Someone started laughing at my girlie pencil, and soon all of them were joking about it. Finally Paco couldn't stand it anymore. He yanked the pencil out of my hand, threw it overboard, and handed me a standard yellow pencil so that I could keep on taking down the grades and comments.

Working with the LSOs was turning out to be the unexpected highlight of the cruise for me. We joked around and had fun on the platform, and I liked the informality of our casual dress and interaction. But when an airplane was in the groove, we were all business. We worked as a team.

§

Once we left the gulf I seemed to view my surroundings with a greater detachment, and at times that brought a new sense of appreciation. Even the ungainly S-3s evoked feelings of fondness. The trusty planes had taken me and my crews halfway around the world, and into harm's way. Now we had met the challenge and were on our way home together. To me the stubby old airplanes were wonderful works of art.

During the previous five months, all of my preflight "walk-around" inspections of the aircraft had seemed the same. I did them all by rote. After we left the gulf, however, I tried to look at each step more closely.

Starting on the right side of the aircraft, I peer into the jet engine and make sure that none of the fan blades is chipped or cracked. Then I spin the fan clockwise to see that it turns freely. I run my gloved hand over the inside of the engine cowling and try to feel if any of the rivets or screws is loose or missing. I check the engine oil and generator fluid levels and make sure no wires or mechanical parts are broken or disconnected.

Next I take a few steps toward the right wing tip and put both hands on the metal drop tanks that our planes use to carry extra fuel. I pull and push on the streamlined tank to make sure it's attached securely. The fuel caps in the drop tank are closed tight, as they should be, and the rods and hinges that hold the ailerons and spoilers on the wings seem secure. The undersides of the wings are streaked with clear jet fuel, but such minor leaks don't concern me.

At the rear of the aircraft, the forged steel tailhook seems firmly in place. And the magnetic anomaly detector boom is stowed properly. Moving to the left side of the aircraft, I climb up into the port wheel well and inspect the emergency hydraulic pump and flight control cables, then measure the hydraulic fluid levels. After stepping back out, I look at the auxiliary power unit on the left side of the aircraft, then peer into the position lights to make sure none of the bulbs is missing or broken.

The entire procedure takes less than five minutes, but it brings home my responsibility: I am entrusted with this aircraft and the lives of every-one in it—and I have to know that the aircraft and I are ready.

All three of the other crew members are already in the plane when I climb the four steps that lead to the cockpit. The cockpit itself is roomy and wide enough that I can reach out with my right arm and touch the naval flight officer sitting beside me. But getting in requires stepping gingerly over the radio console in the center of the cockpit and sliding into the pilot's seat on the left side.

§

Away from the gulf, the weather became increasingly mild and the scenery spectacular. The gulf's listless haze disappeared, and the sky was crystal clear for miles in all directions. The horizon looked razor sharp and flat as a carpenter's level. There were small, isolated clouds, and the sunlight shining through them cast the world in shades of pink and blue-gray.

On a recent daytime flight our ship passed through a rain squall just before we launched, and the glistening black deck was so hot that steam rose up along the entire length of its surface. Everywhere I looked, miniature rainbows were rising from the deck of the *Lincoln*.

The light at the end of the tunnel was approaching, and it grew larger and brighter all the time.

13 September: Letter from Harry to Flojo

Dear Flojo,

You might think it strange for me to send all my wife's birthday presents to you. But the truth is she'd open them all the day she got them, and I want to string this gag out as long as possible. This is a golden opportunity for you to torment and extort Loree.

Please give her a present every day or so until her actual birthday on the seventeenth. Then she can have the rest. But make her work for her presents! You'll be surprised what she'll do for something that's gift-wrapped!

The more public the humiliation, the better. I know I'm going to pay dearly for this stunt when Loree and I see each other again, so make it worth my while. . . .

Take pictures, too!
Thanks,
Harry
P. S.: She does some mean barnyard noises!

16 September: High Expectations

The executive officer of the USS *Abraham Lincoln* invited everyone up on deck today to catch a glimpse of land as we passed through the Straits of Malaca.

The weather was sunny but hazy, and we could see the jagged islands of Malaysia on the gray southern horizon. I made my way to the starboard side of the bow and found a group of aviators sunning themselves in lawn chairs and taking in the view from the "steel beach." The air had a tropical feel to it—warm, breezy, and comfortable. I stopped on the catwalk on my way down from the deck and just stood there, mesmerized by the rushing water. The air had a sweet, flowery smell to it that reminded me of Hawaii. I had been on the ship more than five months, but during that time I had been so harried that I seldom stopped to appreciate the impressive scenes around me. I decided to be a better sightseer the rest of the way home.

For a year before the cruise began, I had known I wanted to be part of it. I knew that VS-29 would be the first West Coast ship to deploy with female pilots, and I felt drawn to play a role in that historic event. Since then the women who boarded the *Lincoln* with me had had spectacular successes and heartbreaking failures. My biggest single disappointment was the gradual realization during the cruise that there were going to be good and bad female officers, good and bad female pilots—just the same as men.

I don't know why I ever thought we would be different, or better.

A few months before our cruise began, I had naively thought that all the women on the *Lincoln* would realize what a rare opportunity we had been given, and how important it was to set a positive example. I sincerely believed that all of us would find the strength and character to rise to the occasion. I expected the female officers, and especially the female pilots, to be the utmost professionals. I wanted us to strive and reach higher standards than the men. I believed we owed it to our predecessors and the women who would follow us.

Sadly, we hadn't achieved all of my lofty goals. Most of the women performed their jobs extremely well and represented their country admirably. There were a few who were unprofessional. I used to think that they had done a disservice to themselves and their shipmates, but I realize now that we are all human and deal with stress in different ways, some better than others. I used to get furious about it. I wanted to scream at the offending women or turn them in, for their behavior compromised all of us. The men weren't in the same fishbowl environment. But the more I thought about it, the more I realized that I could set standards of personal conduct only for myself. Others were going to do what they were going to do; I couldn't control them.

Despite the shortcomings of a few, I still believed that the integration of women into combat units had gone well, and that women would contribute to the navy's success in the future.

Being part of this group of female officers also deepened my understanding of the women who had served in the military before us. They paved the way for women of my generation, and my appreciation and admiration for them was heartfelt. But whereas I used to think of the female officers who served before me as trailblazers and crusaders, I have since come to regard them in a more realistic light. Surely they had shortcomings and weaknesses, just like us. That seemed so obvious in retrospect, but it took time for the realization to sink in.

Some will think I'm a hypocrite for criticizing the behavior of other women on the *Lincoln*. After all, Harry and I met in the navy, and we had a relationship while we were in flight training together. But we were of equal rank, living off the military base at the time, we were never going to serve on the same ship, and we never advertised the fact that we were together or asked for special treatment because of it. I think those differences are significant.

I admit that during my time on the *Lincoln,* my performance was not perfect. In the plane, on the ship, and during port calls, I made errors that I regret. I accepted responsibility for those mistakes, I learned from them, and I know I'd never repeat them.

§

I reached my twenty-eighth birthday aboard the *Lincoln,* and Harry sent a huge box full of presents. Instead of addressing the box to me, however, he made sure that it was delivered to Flojo. Harry knew that I would open my gifts early if I had access to them, so he and Flojo went to elaborate lengths to tease me with them. Each day they set up little obstacles for me to overcome in order to receive a gift. Harry knew how boring life on a ship could be, especially during the long transit home from the gulf, so he wanted to stretch out the birthday games as long as possible. That was fine with me, and I tried to be a good sport.

Flojo was quite creative when it came to inventing embarrassing gimmicks. First, he made me compose a poem on why he was the best LSO in the world. I had to read it to him in the ready room with dozens of people watching. At the conclusion, he reluctantly handed over my daily present from Harry: a *Batman Forever* compact disk.

Another time I got a telephone call in my stateroom and was told to see Commander Boensel immediately; the caller said the skipper was really upset about something. I tried to remember all the things I had done, or not done, as I ran to the ready room. When I got there, the skipper just smiled and laughed and handed over another gift: a pair of Minnie Mouse shorts from Harry. Other practical jokes and humiliations earned me a pair of boxers, earrings, and books by Dave Barry and Winston Groom.

§

The deck crews too were relaxed and playful after leaving the gulf. On one particularly gorgeous afternoon I was assigned to operate a backup S-3 for a refueling mission. My crew and I knew before we got into our plane and started the engines that we weren't going to fly unless the other Viking had to abort the mission.

Using our customary hand signals to communicate with the ground crew, we got our plane ready for departure, and the ground crew indicated that they had finished their inspections. The plane captain formed a triangle with his hands, the standby signal. But instead of acknowledging that I understood by repeating the sign, I grinned and gave him the "go fly" signal. It was such a gorgeous day that I would have loved to get airborne.

The plane captain laughed and rubbed his fingers together as if to say, "Give me money." I reached into the pocket of my flight suit and pulled out my wallet, then held my Visa card against the windshield. He responded with an enthusiastic "go fly" signal. The flight deck controller saw that signal and ran over to see what the heck was going on with us. When he realized it was all a game, he pointed to himself, then made a motion like he was running a credit card through an imprinting machine.

I didn't get to take off, but I had enjoyed our playful improvisation.

Then, as the *Lincoln* neared the equator, the message came over the intercom that everyone on our ship would soon be subject to Neptune's Law, an ancient seafaring rite of passage. "Shellbacks," experienced sailors who had crossed the equator aboard ship before, would be allowed to haze all of the "pollywogs" who hadn't. It promised to be a strenuous day. Jana and I tried to persuade some of our fellow pollywogs to rise up and resist by launching a preemptive strike, but most of them were too afraid.

What a bunch of losers.

17 September: Letter from Sandi Draude

(This birthday card has a picture of Amelia Earhart on the cover.)

Dearest Loree,

> *Many women have taken to the skies*
> *Lured by a singular rhythm that set them*
> > *to dancing on the clouds.*
>
> *Entranced by the stately glissad between*
> > *towering thunderheads,*
> > *the jolly gavotte up and down air currents,*
> > *and the arrested tango of a carrier landing.*
>
> *Poor kiwi that I am, I have still given life to*
> > *a daughter in whose eyes rest the falcon*
> > *and the dove.*

One soars with infinite grace and power, strength
and the courage to ride the tumbling waves of air.
One softly settles to the earth, gentle in her love,
quiet collector and trustee of many hearts.

Amelia would have been proud of you as I am and loved you as I do.
Mom

18 September: I'm a Shellback!

All of us pollywogs had heard stories about "crossing-the-line" ceremonies and how they had become infamous for their excesses. Several years earlier the navy had actually issued a broad set of rules spelling out exactly what sorts of abuse shellbacks could dispense.

Fortunately some of the more grotesque and sadistic rituals such as beating pollywogs with fire hoses, forcing them to dress as drag queens, and rubbing their faces into the greased belly of the fattest person on ship had been prohibited. Before the equatorial crossing, I was a little concerned that with female pilots aboard, hypersensitive officers might regulate this ceremony right out of existence. As it turned out, I needn't have worried.

I awoke at 4 A.M., and Jana and I began our preemptive pollywog strike against the shellbacks. We donned our bathing suits and pollywog T-shirts under our flight suits, then rounded up some fellow wogs. As quietly as possible, we went to the staterooms of some of the more senior shellbacks, and using a long roll of silver-colored duct tape, we fastened their doorknobs together. We spread Vaseline on other doorknobs, just to make the shellbacks even madder.

Then we hurried back to our squadron ready room around 5 A.M. and gave the secret pollywog knock for quick entry. No sooner had we arrived than the captain of the ship announced over the intercom that King Neptune had arrived aboard our ship. The battle between shellbacks and pollywogs was on, but it wasn't much of a contest. We could hear the wogs outside getting routed.

There were two tiny holes on the bottom of our metal ready-room door, and about ten of us pollywogs took turns getting down on our hands and knees to watch the bedlam outside. Cruel shellbacks were marching the wogs through the passageways making them sing idiotic songs. I took off my flight suit and put on khaki trousers—inside out and backwards, according to tradition. We put a Guns 'n Roses CD into the stereo and cranked it up full blast for inspiration. Then we took a group pollywog photo.

By this time the shellbacks were banging furiously at our door, screaming for us to come out. We slid a request chit under the door telling them to have their commanding officer sign it and ask for an audience with the mighty pollywog chief. Written exchanges followed, with short-tempered threats and demands from the shellbacks and smart-ass replies from us. Around 6:10, one of the wogs suggested that we open the door and reap the whirlwind we had sown. But the rest of us were still enjoying our resistance and voted him down.

Five minutes later the vote became moot. One of the sailors outside had managed to pick the lock, and the door came flying open. The shellbacks stormed in and ordered us to lie on our backs while they berated us. Didn't we know they had a full agenda of activities scheduled for us this morning? Weren't we concerned about pissing them off? Too late, they yelled; now they were mad, and we were going to be made to regret having upset them.

The shellbacks cleared all the chairs from our squadron ready room and created a wide open space for us. Whenever any of them yelled "Dead bug!" all of us pollywogs had to lie on our backs with our hands and feet in the air and yell back "Raid!" They made us practice over and over until we could do it in perfect unison.

Then they handed out song sheets. They conducted as we sang "Anchors Aweigh," "Feelings," the *Brady Bunch* and *Gilligan's Island* theme songs, "I'm a Little Teapot," and "Baby Got Back"—a rap tune extolling the virtues of big butts. I was designated song leader. Every now and then one of our choruses would be interrupted by a Dead Bug call, and we would have to halt our renditions and hit the floor.

This went on until the shellbacks determined that we had practiced enough to take our show on the road. At that point we all lined up with our hands on the shoulders of the pollywog in front and sang as we marched through the ship's narrow passageways. Our booming voices echoed through the long metal corridors. After months of walking these same passageways in total seriousness, dressed in full flight gear prepared to give up my life defending my country, it made me laugh to tromp along with my clothes inside out singing "I like big butts" at the top of my lungs.

Finally, around 8:30, we sang our way to the cavernous hangar bay. The floor was covered with dirty water from previous groups of wogs being doused there. We were ordered to lie down and start rolling. After a thorough soaking in filthy, foul-smelling salt water, we were told to line up at the elevator that carried aircraft and heavy equipment up to the flight deck. We sang our silly songs during the ride up the elevator, and the shellbacks poured water on us the entire way.

Once on the deck we were ordered to get down and start rolling again. The steel deck was covered with shredded paper and bits of food —remnants of the "continental breakfast" we had been told to expect— and we were blasted continuously with more nasty liquid. Then we were herded back onto the elevator, down through the hangar bay, and into the ready room. The ready room was air-conditioned, and since we were all soaking wet, we got cold and started shivering. We sat there for about thirty minutes with our teeth chattering before the shellbacks had mercy and marched us up on deck again. By this time the sun was out, and we sat for about forty-five minutes enjoying the respite and the warmth that dried our clothes.

But the wog antics weren't quite over. We were marched back to the ready room again and each of us had to perform a "wog audition": a solo rendition of "Feelings." After that embarrassment, each of us was given a condom and commanded to race to see who could blow it up the fastest; the first to pop their condom would be the winner. I fumbled with my condom at first, but once I figured out how to blow it up, it got huge.

Mine wasn't the first to break, but I got kudos for enlarging it to such ridiculous proportions.

Next each pollywog received a Letter of Condemnation (not Commendation). My denunciation read as follows:

> For miserably failing in your responsibility as a Naval Officer and a human being; For enraging the Executive Officer by failing to pay her mess bill on time; Her Marine-like demeanor and drill instructor mouth make her a standout on the LSO platform; Her uncanny ability to produce chocolate chip cookies at a moment's notice truly validates that her freckles are actually chocolate chips rising to the surface of her skin; She is a constant source of embarrassment to the squadron and lowers the traditions of a once-proud navy.

All pollywogs now had to go before the skipper in a sort of mock trial. Each of us wore a mask, because the skipper refused to set eyes on the miserable faces of lowly pollywogs. Our commanding officer read the charges, and each of us pled guilty, or at least we were supposed to plead guilty. A few guys threw themselves on the mercy of the court or offered some bogus excuse for their behavior. Each of them was branded a "special-case wog" and got a big red *S* painted on his back. The letter was meant to attract extra attention from the shellbacks who would dole out more punishment for them on the flight deck.

We were shepherded back to an elevator and sang Harry Belafonte's "Day-O" as we were hauled back up to the flight deck. Even though I wasn't a special-case wog, I got yanked out of line and was told to lie on my back and throw a tantrum. I pitched a pretty good fit, which resulted in plenty of foul water splashing into my mouth, nose, and eyes.

On deck we were separated into three lines. Everyone in my line had to squat down and duck-walk to one of four doorways in a huge cardboard apparatus. It was painted to look like a storefront, and each of the doorways was only about eighteen inches high. We duck-walked halfway, then were told to roll the rest of the way to the doors. Once there, a couple of shellbacks ordered me to quack like a duck, and I quickly complied. Then I crawled through the entrance and into a cardboard tunnel. The entire structure was shaking from shellbacks pounding on the outside, and water dripped from the saturated ceiling. I had to duck-walk to the "Royal Court," where I joined another group of wogs. A dais had been constructed on the fantail, and members of the Royal Court stood there looking down at their lowly subjects.

Somebody dressed as King Neptune with a long robe and flowing white hair scowled at us. Next to him stood several court members covered from head to toe in bright green body paint; to this day I have no idea who they were. They screamed at us for being such pitiful pollywogs, then commanded us to wave our hands overhead and sing "Hey Hey, Good-bye." I was pulled out of the group and told to "swim" in the inch-deep muck that covered the deck. I did the backstroke for a while, then the crawl. Then I was ordered to beg Flipper for forgiveness as I blew the salt water out of a shallow "padeye," a concave area used to tie airplanes down on deck. I had no idea what I might have done to offend the TV dolphin, but I was a good sport and went along with the spirit of the event.

"Forgive me, Flipper!"

I quickly discovered that the water I blew out of the padeye came straight back into my face. Then I was ordered to do the butterfly stroke, which I did until being told by another to stand. I thought my punishment was over, but then I was ordered to waltz by myself. Finally I was excused and told to join the "Trough of Truth" line.

My khaki pants marked me as an officer, and the enlisted shellbacks seemed to savor the opportunity to punish those of us who outranked them. To my chagrin, I got yanked out of line again. This time I was placed with Jana and a female petty officer. We had to sing "Row, Row, Row Your Boat" as loud as we could. Finally we approached the trough—a huge, cylindrical metal container used on the ship to store jet engines. The trough was about eight feet long and two feet deep, and it was filled with dark, disgusting fluid; more than a thousand people had already swum or waded through it. As we waited in line, Flojo, a shellback, came by to check on us. He told us that if we were asked what we were, we should yell, "I'm a pollywog!" He grinned and then ran off. I saw a pollywog ahead of me stand up at the end of the trough. One of the shellbacks said something to him, and he responded, "I'm a pollywog!" The shellbacks groaned and sent him back to the end of the line. I vowed to put Flojo at the top of my practical-joke victim list.

When my turn came, I stepped in and submerged myself. Then I pushed off and glided to the other side. Two sets of arms grabbed me and hauled me to a standing position on the deck.

"What are you?" somebody asked.

"I'm a shellback!" I answered proudly.

They gave me a paper cup of what looked like apple juice; actually it was warm nonalcoholic beer. I slugged it down and was welcomed into the world of the shellbacks by the ship's command master chief.

The ceremony was over for me, and my mouth tasted like seawater, rubber, and grease. I went to get a soda, or anything else that would get rid of the foul taste. On deck, the new shellbacks were in line for hamburgers and chips. The wind had started to freshen, and empty burger boxes were blowing all over the place. Since we were in the middle of the ocean, no one seemed to care.

Back in our stateroom, I peeled off my wet, grimy shirt. The shower felt great, but I really had to scrub to get off all the grit and grease. Afterward I crawled into bed and started reading a novel, but I quickly fell asleep and didn't awaken for five hours. When I got up at 8 P.M., my thighs were sore from duck-walking, and my palms were scratched and bruised from rolling and doing pushups on the steel deck. My tailbone was bruised, I'm not sure from what—maybe from sitting on the zipper of my turned-around pants. My quadriceps were so sore from duck-walking that it was painful to move. I did my best not to limp, though, because it would have made the veteran shellbacks even more proud of themselves.

Jana was awake too, and we decided to watch the movie *Raising Arizona;* it's a cruise classic. Later I went to the ready room to see if anything was going on. In one of the passageways I saw Lt. Sarah Morley from VAQ-135, and I stopped and chatted. A couple of the other gals stopped by, and we all laughed and compared notes on Wog Day.

Lt. Peggy Stephan, one of the C-2 pilots, had gone through it a few years before, and she said it had been pretty much the same. The only difference was that instead of having grungy water in their Trough of Truth, they had to wade through sour, curdled milk. But I was glad to hear that the ceremony itself wasn't much different. I didn't want people blaming the presence of women for the loss of a sacred sailor ritual.

19 September: I Wish I Hadn't Called

One night I couldn't resist the urge to call Harry on the phone. I had written to him almost every day, yet there were times when I just needed to hear his voice. I thought it was 6:30 A.M. in California when I dialed his Lemoore number, but I had miscalculated the time change, and it was actually 4:30 A.M.—and Harry was sound asleep. We talked for a few minutes, but he was tired and groggy and not real enthusiastic about being awakened from his slumber.

Our brief conversation was extremely frustrating to me. I was so happy to hear Harry's voice and so excited to talk to him, but he was dead to the world and didn't seem very interested in talking back. It made me mad that he seemed unwilling to make an effort to wake up enough to chat. It had been about a month since we had spoken. It didn't matter so much what he said; I just wanted to feel close to him.

A few times during our long voyage I had called Harry when no one was home. Even though no one picked up the phone, it made me smile just to hear my husband's irreverent voice on the answering machine. Now, this one-sided conversation was making me wish I had gotten the recorded message. The long periods of silence on the other end of the line made me feel ignored. Even though I had him on the phone with me, Harry seemed more distant and out of reach than ever. I wished I hadn't called.

After we hung up, I went back to my room and vented my frustrations in a letter that I never sent. I just needed to get it out of my system. I worked on a cross-stitch for a while, then studied some Chinese and made a banner on the computer printer for Flojo's birthday on the twenty-first.

Flojo and his roommate, Jedi, had become trusted advisers to me during our time at sea. They were like the big brothers I had never had, and they helped level my emotional ups and downs. Both of them had been enlisted air crewmen before they became officers. Flojo became an S-3 pilot, and Jedi was a limited duty officer who flew in the TACCO position.

Jedi got that call sign because he was a wizard at operating the complex tactical systems in our jets. He was from Boston, and I liked to give him grief about his accent and the way he pronounced certain names; Jana, for example, became "Janner."

I expected Flojo and Jedi, as former enlisted men, to be navy traditionalists hostile to the idea of having women on combat ships. I never spoke with them about the policy in broad, political terms. But they seemed extremely accepting, and their vast experience with S-3s, undersea warfare, and the navy in general was tremendously helpful to me.

Both of them had been on several cruises before, and they had grown up in the navy. They were extremely adept at seeing people and procedures for who and what they were. Flojo and Jedi didn't get wrapped up in ideology. They knew their jobs backwards and forwards, and they were excellent teachers. They recognize good leaders—and they could spot a bullshitter a mile away.

I felt that they came to regard me as their shipmate, not their "female shipmate." They teased me mercilessly, like older brothers interacting with a younger sister. They were excellent sounding boards, and their knowledge and humor were lifesavers. I was proud to count them as friends.

§

In an effort to keep everyone from going crazy in the middle of the ocean, the Lincoln's leaders held frequent drills. On a typical day we had a general quarters drill, and less frequently we held abandon-ship drills. One afternoon I went up to the flight deck and watched some of the Philippine Islands pass by just seven miles off our port side. It is great to see that we were making such rapid progress.

23 September: Pizza Night

My last flight aboard the *Lincoln* was among the most enjoyable.

It was an absolutely gorgeous afternoon in the central Pacific, with a deep blue sky and scattered puffy white cumulus cloud formations. I maneuvered my S-3 gracefully around some clouds, then rolled the plane onto its back and dove through some others. It was a pleasure just to look around and zoom freely about the sky.

I did barrel rolls, aileron rolls, half Cuban-eights, and Immelmanns until I thought the crew would get airsick—but they kept asking for more. My landing was pretty average—an (OK) 3-wire—but I'd had so much fun buzzing around that I wasn't upset about it.

We were only three days away from Hawaii and within easy COD range. I received a birthday package from a friend back home, Kathleen, which contained cookies and plastic sunflowers. The yellow flowers went straight to my desk, and the cookies quickly disappeared with help from my roommates. Kathleen was engaged to be married to one of the pilots in Harry's F/A-18 squadron, and she had been a cheerful friend and correspondent throughout my months at sea.

As the end of our cruise drew nearer, I felt calmer and more relaxed. But I was tired of being around the same people all the time, and it was sometimes difficult to suppress my irritation at a few of them. For example, I had been talking with one of the flight officers in our squadron when the subject of a recent F-14 accident came up. Both crew members ejected safely after one of the plane's engines exploded in flight. I made the comment that the RIO was probably being treated for burns at Brooks Air Force Base in Texas. It turned out that the injured RIO had been sent to Guam, and the guy who corrected me added a snide "little Miss Know-it-all" to his remark.

A few months earlier I might not have responded to such a remark. But this time I laid into the guy and told him I didn't like his prissy attitude and he had better just shut the fuck up. He seemed a little taken aback, but I didn't care; he was a spoiled, immature brat, and I wasn't going to put up with his attitude anymore.

§

We had our last "pizza night" on the *Lincoln* before arriving in Hawaii. Pizza night had become a Friday tradition, a fun, informal way to end the week and enjoy a little social time. Everyone would hang out in the wardroom eating homemade pizza and drinking nonalcoholic beer. Actually the Sharps beer had about 0.5 percent alcohol, and we joked that a person would need to down about fifty of them to get a proper buzz—or have their blood drawn beforehand. During the previous six months the cooks on the ship had baked more than fifty-seven thousand pizzas. That's a record that Domino's would have found hard to beat.

I visited with Waylon, the F-14 pilot who had recently ejected from his Tomcat when an engine exploded. He looked and sounded great. His eyebrows had been singed off, and he had a few minor facial burns, but his spirits were high, and he said he looked forward to getting back into the cockpit right away.

A lot of airplanes were scheduled to fly off the ship the next day and land in Hawaii. They planned to be there for a couple of days before the ship arrived. Most of the aviators flying the planes had family waiting for them in Hawaii, and the prospect of a few extra days on shore with their loved ones was a great bonus.

I planned to stay on the ship, though. My parents were scheduled to meet the ship in Hawaii after the *Lincoln* pulled into port. Then Dad was going to fly back to California while Mom and several hundred other members of the crew's families stayed aboard. The five-day "Tiger Cruise" would take them on the final leg of the trip home to San Francisco. It was designed to be a way for navy families to get a taste of the lives their loved ones experienced at sea. They would get to tour the *Lincoln* from bow to stern, and different activities were planned for every day. I knew Mom was going to have a great time on the Tiger Cruise. She could ask as many questions as she wanted and satisfy her curiosity.

I had already begun putting my things into boxes and sending them back to San Diego via the CODs. I could hardly wait to return to shore and reality. A few nights before, the members of my squadron had been watching a training film that happened to include some aerial pictures of our base at the naval air station at North Island. The runways, the city, and the harbor looked so sparkling and beautiful from the air. Everyone in the room cheered wildly at those familiar sights.

The first thing I planned to do when I got there was take Stoney for a long run on the white sand beach at Coronado. I intended to throw the tennis ball for him until my arm wore out.

25 September: Burnable, Sinkable, and Plastic

In preparation for reentering the real world, everyone on the ship had to sit through a lecture entitled "Returning to Intimacy."

It seemed like a good idea to try to prepare us for the changes we would face on shore, but the presentation itself was a superficial waste of time. The sexist stereotypes about the little wives waiting at home for their warriors to return from the sea were laughable. And the lecture just belabored the obvious. Of *course* we all needed to think about how much things had changed since we left San Diego the previous spring. We needed to be sensitive and take time getting reacquainted with family members and friends we hadn't seen in a long time. Certainly they had adjusted to our absence and had developed their own routines. We couldn't expect everyone to drop everything and turn back the clock just to accommodate us.

All of this was certainly true, but I had hoped for more than a simplistic examination of relationships and some real information from the hundreds of people on the *Lincoln* who had been through the process so many times before. After the lecture I went to the ready room and watched *Pulp Fiction* for about the twentieth time.

§

On the last full day before the *Lincoln* pulled into Hawaii, I lost my temper with a sailor for a stupid reason. I noticed that the trash in our room had not been emptied, so I went to the sailor in charge of that task and asked why it had not been done. She explained that the trash hadn't been emptied because we weren't sorting it correctly.

Trash on the ship was divided into three categories: burnable, sinkable, and plastic. I thought I had been pretty strict about making sure that the right kind of trash went into each receptacle, but I guess not; this unfortunate sailor came back with me to our stateroom, and she showed me that there was burnable trash in the sinkable basket and vice versa. I was pissed, and I started yelling at her. Our trash hadn't been picked up on previous occasions; why hadn't she told us that this was the reason? When she tried to argue with me, I wrote down her name and stormed off to see her supervisor.

I was still fuming when I got there, but the supervisor was really calm and reasonable. I realized that I was mostly mad at myself and my roommates for not separating the trash, and instead of going to the source of the problem and confronting them, I was taking out my frustrations on this poor sailor. After a while I went in search of her, and when I found her, I apologized. She gave me some new trash bags, and I took them back to the room so that we could re-sort our trash. Jana and I took care of the job.

When A. J. showed up, we explained what we were doing, and she started complaining. We let her complain for a few minutes, then told her it was fine to feel that way, but in the future she would have to make sure her trash went into the proper container.

The next day we crossed the International Date Line and got to relive 26 September.

26 September: Love Boat

I stepped out of the bathroom next to our stateroom that night and saw something that didn't look right.

A male petty officer whom I recognized from some of the shore parties walked by me in the passageway. It struck me as odd that an enlisted guy was in "officer country," but I didn't ask him what he was doing; I just continued on the way to my room. When I got to the door, though, I was curious, so I turned around expecting to see the guy walking on past the female officers' staterooms. But he was out of sight. And the only place he could have gone was into one of the women's staterooms.

I stepped into my own room and seethed.

Fraternization between officers and enlisted sailors was illegal. I could think of few things more ruinous to military organizations than unduly familiar relationships between officers and enlisted people. Officers and enlisted troops have to remain separate because in times of war, officers are the ones who give the orders to fight and die. The troops they command shouldn't have to wonder whether these orders are colored by favoritism for particular individuals.

But here was one of our female officers fraternizing with an enlisted man, and doing it on the ship. It was bad enough to see her dirty-dancing with this guy in port, but now she seemed to be going for new records in unprofessional conduct. I was astonished and not sure quite how to react.

Back in my room I told Jana what I had seen, and she got interested, too. Jana decided to go to this woman's room under the pretense of picking up a pair of slacks that she had borrowed. Sure enough, when Jana knocked on the door, the enlisted guy was inside.

I could have reported the woman's behavior to her superiors. The matter would have surely gone up the chain of command, but the results would have been unpredictable.

I couldn't sleep, so I went to the wardroom for a bowl of cereal. When I got there, A. J. was sitting there all giggly and cozy with her "boyfriend." They left together a few minutes later.

What any of these people wanted to do with each other on their own time was their business; I couldn't have cared less. But their unprofessional behavior on the ship was an insult to those who worked hard and upheld professional standards. It felt like the *Lincoln* was turning into the Love Boat, and I couldn't wait to leave.

30 September: Idyllic Vision

I met my folks at the airport in Honolulu, and we spent the next three days together.

In accordance with Hawaiian tradition, I brought a pair of sweet-smelling plumeria leis to give them, and we hugged and kissed as soon as we saw each other in the terminal. They both looked great and seemed to be getting younger, not older. Dad was fit and relaxed, and Mom was thin, tan, and as exuberant as ever.

They rented a car, and we drove to the Royal Hawaiian Hotel, a luxurious historic place right on the beach at Waikiki. Just driving up to the hotel made a lasting impression. There was a lush pathway that led to an open-air lobby. We were greeted there with more beautiful, fragrant leis made of orchids and other native tropical flowers. All the rooms had hand-carved antique furniture and balconies that faced the ocean. At night the maids turned down the beds and placed little chocolate mints on each pillow.

The place had to be expensive, but Dad said my safe return had put him in a mood to celebrate. Just being near my parents made me giddy, too. I had missed them so much over the past six months and had thought about them every day. Finally they were close enough to touch, to embrace. I laughed with them and felt warmed by their company.

On our first night together we went out for a steak dinner at a fancy restaurant. I had vowed not to eat chicken on shore since it had been served so frequently on the ship. The cooks on the USS *Abraham Lincoln* were masters at finding new ways to cook chicken. They made chicken Alfredo, chicken à la king, chicken fajitas, chicken nuggets, chicken pot pie, Szechwan chicken, grilled chicken, chicken sandwiches, chicken soup, chicken Adolfo, chicken and dumplings. The list went on and on like the scene in *Forrest Gump* where they review the many ways there are to cook shrimp.

My parents arrived on a Saturday, and Sunday we drove to our old neighborhood in Hawaii Kai and attended mass at Holy Trinity, our former church; we had lived in Hawaii ten years earlier, when I was in high school. It was strange being in church with my parents again. They had always been devout believers, but I had come to have serious doubts about the Catholic church. I tried to be respectful, but I didn't recite any of the prayers, sing the hymns, or take communion. My parents didn't say anything about it, but I was sure they noticed, and I hoped my behavior hadn't hurt or offended them.

Growing up, I always attended Catholic schools and went to church every Sunday and on Holy Days, and I believe those practices gave me a good moral foundation. But most of the lessons I learned came from my parents—not from the religion. During college, when I began studying religious history, I came to have doubts about organized religion. So many wars had been fought and so many innocent people had suffered over religious differences that I began to regard organized religion as a hindrance rather than a channel to human spirituality. I believed in God as much as ever, but I was still trying to sort out my feelings about Catholicism.

After church my parents and I drove to Pearl Harbor, and the pleasantness of our first few hours together seemed to disappear all at once. Dad was driving, and he missed the freeway exit because he didn't move over into the right lane soon enough. Mom got on his case, and then he blew up at her. I was stunned and hurt; Mom shouldn't have nagged, and Dad shouldn't have lost his temper. Under normal conditions it wouldn't have been a big deal, but this tiff had an unusually powerful effect on me.

During all that time at sea, I always thought about the happy times with my parents. I had developed this idyllic vision in my mind of what they were like, and how our time together would be spent when my cruise was over. Instead of the love and togetherness I had fantasized about for all those months, I was suddenly confronted with the unpleasant reality of them snapping at each other and bickering over something as trivial as a missed freeway exit. It was a rude jolt that yanked me back to a reality I was unprepared to confront.

We got out of the car at the military exchange on base, and I told my parents I would meet them in thirty minutes or so; I needed to get away for a time. I shopped at the sprawling tax-free stores and bought a few

Hawaiian shirts and a stack of magazines to read during the rest of our Pacific crossing.

The car ride back to the hotel was icy and silent. My folks were still feuding. Maybe the tension was my fault; maybe my not participating at mass had bothered them more than any of us knew. But whatever had brought it on, the situation was becoming awfully depressing. We were supposed to meet for dinner that night with a few of the other female officers from the ship and their parents. I told Mom and Dad that we could make other plans if they weren't going to be on speaking terms by then. They just shrugged and went their separate ways.

Mom put on her bathing suit and went out to lie by the pool, Dad went for a run on the beach, and I took a walk. When I got back to the room, I called Harry and cried on his shoulder long distance. He had always been a good listener, and he understood my parents implicitly. It made me feel better just to talk to him and to hear his voice. We had an exceptionally clear telephone connection, and it didn't have the one- or two-second delays that we had become accustomed to during the times I called him from the Middle East or from on board the Lincoln. That fact alone was a pleasant reminder that we were actually getting closer and would soon be together again.

My parents came back, and we all cleaned up and got ready to go out to dinner. We stopped at the Mai Tai bar for a drink, and I excused myself temporarily; I wanted to give my folks a chance to start talking to each other. I stayed in the bathroom several minutes longer than usual, and my ruse worked. When I came back to the bar, my parents were talking away just fine. They both explained what they had been feeling and why they had acted the way they did. We all vowed to get along better. Then we finished our drinks and went on to dinner at Keo's.

Linda Heid (an NFO from VAQ-135) and her dad, Alex, arrived with Pam and Brenda; Jana came with her mom, Shirley, and a buddy from an ES-3 squadron; and Heidi brought her dad, Jeff, and brother Bill. It was great to see them all in a relaxed social setting and to meet their loved ones. Those of us who had been on the ship had lived through so much together; we got on each other's nerves, but at least we could leave our disagreements behind when we went ashore. And while we were away, our families had endured their own trials separately. As soon as we met, it seemed as though all of us had been friends for a long time.

2 October: Memory Lane

Mom and I drove to St. Francis High School for a trip down memory lane.

She had taught there, and I had attended the Catholic girls' school as a student. We saw many of Mom's friends—my former teachers, administrators, and nuns. They all looked and sounded very much the way I remembered them. But the school itself was nicer and more spacious and the campus was more picturesque than I recalled. Many of my friends who went to the U.S. Naval Academy said that when they returned to visit Annapolis years later they were struck by how beautiful the place was; all they remembered was stress and chaos.

We met Dad a few hours later, then Mom and I packed up our belongings and we all headed to Pearl Harbor and the USS *Abraham Lincoln*. When we got there, I slyly let the ship's crew know that my dad was a retired brigadier general, so they piped him aboard with formal whistles when we walked onto the ship. Dad never liked drawing attention to himself, but he got a kick out of the official welcome.

We dropped our stuff off in my stateroom, then went for a quick tour of the ship. Several aircraft were on display in the hangar bays, and I showed my parents the ready room and our squadron's dreaded greenie board. Then we said good-bye as Dad went back to the hotel for another night. Mom and I went back down to my stateroom and unpacked.

We left Pearl Harbor early the next morning to begin our five-day trip home.

All of the "Tigers" went up on deck for a group photo. A helicopter with a photographer at the door hovered overhead while the eleven hundred guests stood in line spelling out "Tiger 95" on the flight deck. As the ship entered international waters, we were treated to a spectacular air show. At least one of each type of plane based on the ship flew by overhead. And unlike land-based air shows, at sea there were no restrictions on how fast the planes could fly or how close they could get to the spectators. An F-14 Tomcat came streaking overhead at about four hundred feet, then broke the sound barrier with an ear-splitting sonic boom. Mom just about jumped out of her skin!

We watched the landings on TV in the ready room, and I explained to Mom the details of what she was seeing. She saw the pilots, the LSOs, and the deck crews in action, and it was good to give her and the rest of the visitors a glimpse of what we had been doing all those months at sea. Later we had a bowl of Chef Boyardee ravioli, talked, and read magazines.

Mom was up early the next morning while I was still tossing and turning in my usual morning stupor. I remember dreaming that I was at a perfume counter in some huge department store trying on samples. It was very peculiar because the sensations were so lifelike. Then I awoke and realized that Mom had been putting on her Obsession perfume, and the scent had taken hold of my dreamy mind. I went back to sleep while she went out to the fantail for the skeet shoot. She said later that she had fired a twelve-gauge shotgun and a .45-caliber pistol.

That evening at sunset everyone was invited onto the flight deck to watch the marines perform their silent drill routine. I had watched marines put on these intricate dances of silent synchronized movements since I was a little girl, and they always give me goose bumps. The marines are so precise, so mechanical in their movements, that it is hard to believe that they are not of one mind.

Later that evening I was taking care of a few administrative matters in the ready room when a group of kids swarmed in to play. I had been getting sucked back into the detail-oriented aggravations of my military job, but these visitors elevated my mood. How could anyone be serious in the middle of a bunch of rambunctious kids chasing one another over and under tables and chairs, sucking on Otter Pops with their lips turning orange and blue? I put my pen down and laughed with them.

I looked forward to the time when Harry and I could start a family. He had three brothers growing up and wanted to have at least that many children. I didn't think that I could handle that many, but I was anxious to try for one or two. I hoped that when I finished my next cruise, Harry and I would be ready to embark on our parenthood adventure. By that time I figured we could coordinate our assignments so that at least we would be living in the same city.

I knew that if and when I did get pregnant, I would be prohibited from flying navy jets until after the child was born. Pregnant women weren't allowed to fly planes with ejection seats, but I could still be a ground-based instructor.

During my afternoon workout aboard the ship, I rode an exercise bike as hard as I could, as long as I could, to tire myself out and help me sleep. My quadriceps had recovered from the Wog Day abuse, and I put twenty-five miles on the bike's odometer in record time. The next morning the ship would be within striking distance of land, and once again every air-worthy jet, and every crew member they could carry, would fly off the ship for good.

8 October: Last Pizza Night

Mom and I got up early in the morning and watched as one plane after another revved its engines, then shot forward from the catapult on its way to naval air stations at Whidbey Island, Washington, and at Lemoore, Miramar, and North Island in California. One S-3 gave us a bit of a scare when it appeared to lose altitude right after takeoff, but then the plane began climbing normally. As soon as all the planes were gone, I started feeling slightly depressed, as though I had been left behind. It was sad and kind of anticlimactic to see so many of the people leave, especially since they were the ones I had worked with the closest.

There had been no official end to our historic cruise; people just went their separate ways. Our squadron was scheduled to regroup in San Diego a few days later, and by then everything would be different. I hoped that each of us would have gained some perspective on what we had been able to accomplish during our shared six months at sea. Then again, I realized that we would probably be overwhelmed trying to resume our former lives, and we would want to put the recent deployment behind us. Somehow, though, I didn't think that would be entirely possible, or desirable.

With the airplanes and so many of the pilots and crews gone, the ship was a different place. Absent the weight of the airplanes, jet fuel, and scores of aviators, the ship rode higher on the waves, and it rocked and swayed quite a bit more. We passed through a storm front, and the high winds and heavy seas tossed the *Lincoln* about more than normal. Inside, the ship's passageways weren't jammed with people anymore, and the hangar bays looked like vast empty caverns. It was hard to realize how massive the hangar bays were when they were packed to the rafters with airplanes and equipment.

I gave the Tiger briefings eight times in one day, and by the end of my last presentation, my voice was hoarse and weak. I'm sure I told the guests more than they ever wanted to know about S-3 Vikings, but they seemed interested and attentive.

Back in the stateroom, Mom, forever the organizer, helped me pack all my belongings into boxes for removal from the ship.

Our final pizza night convinced me beyond any doubt that I was ready to leave the ship for good: the thin, homemade pizzas we had been eating every week were actually beginning to look and taste normal. I wondered how I would react to a real deep dish pizza.

In a few hours we were scheduled to steam under the Golden Gate Bridge and into San Francisco Bay. That amazing sight was still etched in my memory from the exercises we had participated in the previous February. I planned to take my final "navy shower" aboard the *Lincoln* and smugly press the aggravating button on the shower nozzle for the last time. At breakfast I was going to eat all the cereal I wanted, remembering the absurd battles I had waged with the wardroom officer over Cheerios. Then I was going back to my stateroom to put on my dress blue uniform. It was ironed and pressed and wrapped in plastic.

But even though I was anxious to leave the ship, I kept finding little mementos that gave me pause. While packing my belongings, I came across an article by Michael Kilian of the *Chicago Tribune* that my parents had clipped and sent. It was about Lt. Kara Hultgreen. It had come at a hectic and tumultuous time in the middle of the cruise. I had glanced at it and filed it away to read later, and finally the time seemed right.

ARLINGTON, Va.—I think I may be the first to lay flowers on your grave, Kara, at least since the marble stone bearing your name has at last been set in place.

It says with military simplicity, "Kara Spears Hultgreen, Lt., U.S. Navy, Oct. 5, 1965–Oct. 25, 1994." I last came here to Arlington Cemetery the day you were buried, a day as gray and teary as this one. I came then to say goodbye. Now, I'm here again to say hello, and lay these pink blossoms by your head and touch this white marble, and bring you happy news.

Your sister Dagny just had the baby you knew was coming—a little girl, named Schuyler. I asked her earlier if she'd name it after you, and she said, "No. She can't be Kara. There's only one Kara."

I don't know which is the more peculiar: my talking to someone who is dead or talking like this to someone I never met. But, in the manner of so may others lingering alone by graves here this chill morning, I am speaking to you—quietly, in my thoughts, as intimately as I might to my own sister. And with as much affection.

I knew nothing at all about you, Kara, until the day you died. You were a news story, the navy's first female carrier fighter pilot—a woman who had gone to Congress to win the right to fly combat roles, who hoped to become an astronaut—killed in a landing accident in the Pacific off San Diego, just 29 years old.

Your picture showed such a fresh, pretty face, courage and spirit as evident as your uniform insignia. I wanted to learn all about you, to find out how you came to be in that seat, piloting those 25 tons of shuddering metal as that F-14 turned over and plunged into the sea. I wanted to know you. Very much.

And now I do.

I've looked at you and listened to you as well, Kara, sitting with your mother in her living room in San Antonio and watching videotape after videotape of you until her tears became too much.

"This beautiful girl, flying those airplanes," she said.

I thought about how different the last six months would have been if Kara had lived. Surely there wouldn't have been as much pressure on the female aviators, and perhaps the whole controversy about whether women were qualified to fly would have remained under wraps. No one seemed to recall that the USS *Eisenhower* had deployed a few months before the *Lincoln,* and no one had questioned the credentials of the female aviators on the *Ike.* The *Eisenhower*'s air wing had performed its mission well and had suffered no major aircraft accidents.

If Kara had survived, perhaps her squadron mate Carey Lohrenz could have avoided being grounded and sent home. She wouldn't have had to deal with the stress of losing a friend or having her training record published.

Kara's death had cast a shadow over the entire air wing, and we hadn't been able to shake it. The aftermath brought out the worst in a lot of people, and it strained relationships between the male and female aviators. Worst of all for our air wing, it deprived us of a strong leader who could have been successful as the navy's first female fighter pilot.

§

On my last night aboard the *Lincoln* Mom and I watched a sappy romantic movie that got me thinking even more about what it would be like to see Harry again. He was going to meet the ship in Alameda, and after that we planned to borrow his parents' motor home and take a two-week camping trip around northern California. We were going to drive through the wine country in the Napa Valley, then head to the mountains or the coast. The destination really didn't matter. Just being with Harry and our dogs—my Stoney and his Aiko—seemed like an ideal way to decompress and reenter reality.

The only scheduled stop on our Winnebago trip was in Sacramento to visit my parents and see *Les Misérables.* Victor Hugo's moving tribute to fallen comrades always reminded Dad of the friends he had lost in Vietnam and Iraq.

I tried to picture what it would be like, that first moment I saw Harry again. I had gone over the scene in my head a thousand times, but I really wasn't sure how I would respond. Would I cry? Would he? As many times as we had parted and been reunited, I really didn't have a clue.

9 October: A Majestic Floating Apparition

The northern California coast is shrouded in fog, and we scan the cool mist for the first sight of land. Rocky outcroppings jutting out from the coast provide our long-awaited first glimpses of the North American continent. Black-faced seals bob among the waves near the beaches. Then the shoreline comes sharply into view with steep, sandy hills behind. Finally the silhouette of the Golden Gate Bridge appears through the mist, and my mixed emotions pour out.

I try to hide my tears of joy. During six months of the most demanding flying and the greatest personal anxiety that I have ever known, I kept myself from crying many times. But even though these are tears of happiness and celebration, the feelings behind them are too personal to share.

There were so many dark night landings, so much isolation, so much fear. There was so much camaraderie among the people in my squadron, so many laughs, so many unforgettable moments. None of the five thousand people who took part in the *Lincoln*'s historic cruise will ever be quite the same. A defining chapter in our lives is coming to a sudden end.

I feel as though I am graduating from school or leaving home or passing another of life's major milestones. A confusing jumble of emotions comes to the surface all at once: depression and pride, loneliness and accomplishment, nervousness and gratitude. I am glad to have been one of the first female aviators to go to sea for a full deployment, and I am proud of the work we did.

Still, I wish we had done better.

I wish I had done better.

Yet I am thankful to be alive and uninjured. I am frequently reminded of Lt. Kara Hultgreen, killed almost exactly a year before—and I think about how easily our fates could have been reversed. I think of Lt. Glenn "K-9" Kersgieter and the cruel suddenness of his death. I wonder whether Kara or K-9 could have done anything to survive the aerial emergencies that confronted them, and I wonder whether a similar crisis awaits me someday.

Pilots have always had a habit of mentally putting themselves in emergency situations and imagining how they might respond to a given set of circumstances. The exercise can be a helpful learning experience, but it's also a defense mechanism. Those of us who are still alive can second-guess the dead and distance ourselves from their actions. We wonder out loud how our departed friends could have made such careless mistakes or failed to recognize minor anomalies before they became critical malfunctions. We assure ourselves that we would have made all the right moves, all the right calls. Some aviators seem to actively try to convince themselves of their own invincibility, their own immortality.

But the longer I fly on and off of aircraft carriers—the more accidents and mishaps I witness—the more I realize that a similar disaster could befall me someday. I haven't given in to fatalism; my knowledge and abilities are constantly expanding, and they are the tools that can keep me alive and benefit my team. But I don't try to deceive myself about the hazards or minimize the risks. My training, my instincts, are no better or worse than my fallen peers'.

Some pilots resort to a macho kind of denial ("That couldn't happen to me; I'm too damn good.") Some drink to quell their fears, or they isolate themselves through a subtle but very real kind of emotional detachment. My challenge is to recognize the inherent dangers of navy flying, accept them, and carry on. It's the only way for me to do this job and remain a whole person.

The Golden Gate Bridge comes clearly into view.

Alameda is only a few miles across the bay, and it warms my heart to think of all the families and loved ones waiting for us there. Most of the sailors on the *Lincoln* and their families have had to endure the entire six months with only letters and infrequent telephone calls to sustain them. I imagine the anticipation and delight they will feel when the *Lincoln* emerges from the morning fog like a majestic floating apparition.

The air-traffic controllers, mechanics, flight deck crews, and sailors who make up the ship's crew all have different backgrounds, and they joined the navy for various reasons. But we are united by service to our country, our shared experiences, and the unsinkable faith of the people who await us on shore.

The fog begins to lift as we enter San Francisco Bay, and the sun turns the windswept sea and sky matching shades of deep blue. Cars on the Golden Gate Bridge honk their horns, and spectators shout and wave in jubilation as the *Lincoln* passes under the magnificent red-painted span. An antique biplane circles noisily overhead towing a banner with a simple, heartfelt message: "Welcome Home!"

As strange as it is to hear myself think it, I know now that I will miss being on the *Lincoln*. I am accustomed to life aboard ship—the routines, the flying, the whole structured yet unpredictable nature of it. It is going to be quite a transition to jump back into my former life of shopping malls, traffic jams, and home-cooked meals—all the things I yearned for during my long absence.

I look forward to settling into the relative comfort of life in Coronado. I plan to get accustomed to spending days and nights with Harry, and playing catch and running on the beach with Stoney and Aiko.

But looking further forward, I know that next autumn I will step back into the peculiar shipboard life I have chosen. In twelve months VS-29 is scheduled to go back to sea aboard the USS *Kitty Hawk* for another six-month cruise. In all likelihood we will be heading back to the Arabian Gulf—and this whole rewarding, agonizing cycle will repeat itself.

I hope that by that time the novelty of having been one of the first female combat pilots to go to sea will be long forgotten. I expect male and female aviators and crew members to be more comfortable working together; there will be more confidence, more trust. On the next cruise I will be one of the more senior members of my squadron. I will be able to concentrate on my job without wondering whether I am regarded as a token or some kind of feminist social experiment. With luck, I will be a senior landing signal officer for my squadron.

But most important, I will be just another navy pilot—nothing more, nothing less.

If that is indeed how it turns out, then the *Lincoln*'s cruise will have accomplished its purpose. The dreams and aspirations of those who made it possible for women of my generation to advance so far in the military will have been realized.

It seems to take forever for the *Lincoln* to reach the navy pier on the eastern shore of San Francisco Bay. But finally, four growling tugboats position themselves around the ship's gray hull and nudge the mammoth aircraft carrier into its berth. Heavy lines secure the ship to the long pier. Below, family members and friends clap and cheer, whistle and wave. Many of them carry homemade signs to get the attention of their loved ones. Mom and I scan the thousands of beaming faces on the pier looking for our husbands. I see several of the spouses from VS-29, but Harry and Dad are nowhere to be seen.

Mom and I scurry down to the hangar bay, where a line has formed to exit the ship. When my turn comes, I salute the officer of the day and ask permission to go ashore. He returns my crisp salute with a boyish smile. Then I salute the American flag and step down the steep metal walkway that leads to the pier. Mom is right behind me. We look around nervously for our husbands. Maybe they got delayed in traffic somewhere; maybe Dad took a wrong turn like he did in Hawaii.

Then I see a towering arrangement of red roses making its way through the crowd. Harry's mischievous face peers out from behind the ornate bouquet, and Dad is striding briskly beside him. Harry wears faded blue jeans and a T-shirt with "MY WIFE WEARS COMBAT BOOTS" written across the front in block letters. He flashes me one of those crooked, winning grins, and I keep my eyes focused on the roses so as not to lose him in the boisterous, joyful crowd.

When we find each other, Harry and I hug for a long time.

"We did it!" I whisper into his ear. "We did it!"

Epilogue

A Change of Heart

The year after the *Lincoln*'s historic cruise was a whirlwind of activity.

Harry and I spent two glorious weeks driving around northern California in his family's motor home. We had no set schedule, and several times during our trip from the wine country to the ocean and back to Ojai, we completely lost track of the days.

A few weeks later, however, Air Wing 11 reassembled with a challenging task ahead. We had to get ready to go back to sea in eleven months on the USS *Kitty Hawk*. Most air wings got to spend eighteen months on shore between deployments, but not us. Early in 1996 we resumed flying with a vengeance. There were frequent "detachments" to the bombing ranges in Fallon, Nevada, and El Centro, California, where groups of different aircraft were sent to practice coordinated strikes. Sometimes those "dets" lasted several weeks or more.

The unrelenting pace was accompanied by more tragedy. Bill "BB" Braker, an F/A-18 pilot, was killed in a midair collision that took place in the night sky over Fallon. Less than a month later, John Stacy "Sprout"

Bates, an F-14 pilot, and Graham "Hobbes" Higgins, an RIO, were killed when their plane crashed in Nashville, Tennessee.

Sprout had been at the controls of an F-14 that crashed during our cruise on the *Lincoln,* and he had survived that accident without serious injury or repercussions for his role in the mishap. But in 1996 he flew to Tennessee to visit his parents, then lost control of his Tomcat shortly after takeoff from Nashville International Airport. Three people on the ground were also killed. Evidently Sprout made a maximum-performance takeoff and pulled up too steeply. He became disoriented in the clouds and lost control of his Tomcat. Sadly, his parents had come to the airport that morning to watch his departure. Since 1992 more than thirty Tomcats have been lost or severely damaged in aircraft accidents.

The memorial service for Sprout and Hobbes was held at Miramar, and it was packed with people from our air wing. The aviators from VF-213 seemed stunned. This was the Black Lions' fourth crash in fifteen months, and my heart ached for them. Hearing the muffled sobs of Sprout's mother affected me deeply. I had met her a few months earlier on the *Lincoln* when she took part in the Tiger cruise. She had been so proud of her son and so interested in learning all about his life on the aircraft carrier. Suddenly that joy and pride had turned to agony.

We aviators have it easy. When we make mistakes, we die—we're gone. If we're lucky, death is instantaneous and unanticipated. Our families have the burden of picking up the pieces and trying to carry on. As I listened to the lone bugler play taps for Sprout and Hobbes and felt a group of F-14s thunder overhead in the "missing man" formation, I prayed that this would be the last memorial service any of us would ever have to attend. Sadly, that wasn't to be.

Our air wing was back at sea for two weeks of exercises aboard the *Kitty Hawk* when, on our fourth day off the California coast, a four-seat EA-6B Prowler crashed. The two backseaters survived with serious injuries, but the pilot and flight officer in the front seats were killed. I watched with great trepidation as the rescue helicopter landed on deck and delivered its battered cargo: two soaking-wet aviators in great pain, and a lifeless corpse. The pilot's body was lost at sea.

In less than a month, five aviators had been killed, and our entire air wing was numb. Sea exercises were abruptly canceled, and the ship returned to port. It was time for a major self-assessment. Why were we having so much trouble? Was there a root cause to our spate of accidents? Each squadron, each pilot, each flight officer, had to scrutinize their practices and their state of mind. We had to do better. Everyone knew that. But there was no time to rest. We needed to get ready to deploy in October —and that date was cast in stone.

We were going to go back to the Arabian Gulf, and we would stay there throughout the winter of 1996 and spring of 1997. There our squadron would monitor Iran's Kilo-class submarines and provide critical fuel to other planes in flight. In fact, our refueling missions would increase because the navy's A-6 Intruder squadrons were being decommissioned and they were retiring their tankers, too.

§

In addition to flying, I was to be a landing signal officer and team leader during the *Kitty Hawk* cruise. I had attended LSO school in Virginia during the summer of 1996, and part of our training involved watching "crash and burn" videos of aerial mishaps. We studied every conceivable form of landing accident and looked for ways to avoid similar problems through better, more timely exchanges of information between pilots and LSOs.

In the darkened classroom at Oceana, all of the LSOs were confronted by stark images of Kara Hultgreen's fatal accident. The same footage had been broadcast nationally on CNN and other news networks at the time of the accident, but I had missed it at the time. It was wrenching for me to watch the grainy pictures on the black-and-white TV screen. Kara overshot the 180-degree turn at the beginning of her approach, and her F-14 decelerated rapidly as she tried to align it with the centerline of the ship. A small puff of black smoke trailed from one of her Tomcat's two engines as the plane descended with its landing gear and tailhook down in preparation for landing.

"Power, power," the LSO gently coaxed as Kara's plane began to drop below glidepath. When it continued descending, the LSO commanded her to abort the approach.

"Waveoff, waveoff," the LSO announced firmly. "Raise your [landing] gear."

Kara's plane yawed drastically to the left when she added full power. With the good right engine in afterburner and the faulty left engine producing no thrust at all, asymmetrical forces skewed her airplane violently sideways. I watched in horror with the other future LSOs as Kara struggled to keep her aircraft straight and level. I found myself willing her airplane to fly—even though all of us knew what came next. The stricken Tomcat suddenly rolled to the left, then the nose dropped and the plane began its fatal plunge to the sea.

"Eject, eject!" the LSO in the video shouted.

The radar intercept officer in the back seat of the F-14 barely got out in time. His parachute opened just before he hit the water. But it was too late for Kara. The plane was inverted when the rocket motor in her ejection seat fired, slamming her through the previously calm ocean surface. The jet fell down on top of her in a huge, sickening splash off the left side of the Lincoln.

It was hard for me to review that accident analytically. I kept thinking about the loss Kara's family and friends had endured since that horrible day, and all the controversy that had followed about the qualifications of female navy pilots. I kept wishing that by rewinding the tape and replaying it we might somehow be able to change the outcome. Why couldn't both engines have kept running? Why couldn't Kara have grabbed the ejection handle? Why couldn't she have lived to fulfill her goal of successfully completing the Lincoln's historic cruise?

We also discussed the near accident that had persuaded Lt. Sue McNally, my former roommate on the Lincoln, to give up flying on a carrier. Her E-2C Hawkeye was left of centerline as it approached the ship for a night landing. She began a shallow turn to correct the misalignment, but the backup LSO didn't notice and ordered her to turn even more. She complied with his instructions, and that made the problem worse. Luckily her plane was the first to return that night, so no other aircraft were parked on the fantail. The absence of obstacles at the rear of the ship saved Sue and her crew.

Sue boltered on that pass, then trapped successfully on the next one. I'm sure she was terrified by her close brush with disaster. Things can go so wrong so fast in aviation. But I was surprised to learn in LSO school that the mistake had been induced by someone else's bad call. When Sue turned in her wings, she never said anything about the erroneous information from the LSO; she just said she was too frazzled to continue flying. I felt bad that someone else's error had contributed to her decision to turn in her wings. But I respected her decision to get out of the cockpit when she knew she couldn't deal with the pressure anymore.

§

Lt. Pam Lyons, the F/A-18 pilot who flew a cut pass in the Persian Gulf, was allowed to keep flying Hornets. She was told that her landing grades had to improve immediately—and they did. She finished strongly and went on to become an instructor in two-seat T-45 jet aircraft used for advanced flight training. During our deployment three other pilots, all men, flew cut passes. One of them went to a review board.

§

Lt. Brenda Scheufele earned a prestigious assignment to the navy's test pilot school and went to begin training at Patuxent River, Maryland, before our air wing was sent back to sea on the *Kitty Hawk*. She returned to the fleet as a department head and will deploy in 2000. Brenda has a master's degree in physics from Tufts University, and I have no doubt that she will someday fulfill her goal of becoming an astronaut.

§

The distraught female sailor whom I counseled on the *Lincoln* made a success of herself.

Her spirits rebounded, and she rededicated herself to her job and the navy. By the time our cruise ended, I'm delighted to say, she was happy, popular, and performing her tasks extremely well. Her positive attitude was refreshing and gratifying.

I don't know whether my encouragement had anything to do with her turnaround. But I felt after talking to her that I had begun repaying the debt I owe to Lt. Kathryn Hobbs, now a captain, the ROTC instructor who had been there for me years before when I needed a boost.

§

Harry and I were driving on a remote road at the naval air station at North Island one summer afternoon when we came upon the wreckage of a Hornet. It was broken into two pieces and pushed off to the side of a road in a dusty, desolate part of the sprawling base. The plane's composite nose cone was smashed, and pieces of metal were peeled back around the cockpit. Other parts were damaged almost beyond recognition.

We stopped the car and got out to take a closer look at what had once been a fearsome aircraft.

On the Hornet's tail was the faded image of a jaunty red cock with a pair of dice showing eleven—the markings for VFA-22. We quickly realized that the wreckage was Lt. Glenn "K-9" Kersgieter's former airplane. It had been pulled from the bottom of the ocean so that navy investigators could determine the exact cause of the accident. Apparently a damaged Pitot static system had fed incorrect information to the plane's flight control computer. The computer overruled the pilot's control inputs and forced the Hornet's nose down just as it catapulted off the ship. There was nothing K-9 could have done to save his life except eject—and he simply didn't have enough time.

Harry was silent for a long time when we finally got back into the car.

§

The clock finally ran out on Saddam Hussein's sons-in-law.

Six months after Lt. Gen. Hussein Kamel al-Majid and his brother, Col. Saddam Kamel, defected to Jordan and blew the whistle on Iraq's secret nuclear, chemical, and biological warfare programs, they made a serious error in judgment: they went home.

In February 1996 the two brothers left Jordan for Baghdad. They had complained bitterly that they weren't treated as well in the West as they deserved, and they were upset that Iraqi opposition groups didn't want them as their leaders. As soon as their car crossed the Jordanian border and entered Iraq, the government-controlled Iraqi news agency announced that their wives—Saddam Hussein's daughters—had divorced them. When the two men arrived in Iraq's capital city, they were promptly murdered by their former family.

§

Harry and I attended a naval aviation symposium in San Diego, and I was interested to see that the Tailhook Association had sent a representative. The organization had nearly been disbanded after the debacle at its 1991 convention, but now it seemed to be making a comeback.

I had planned to join the organization a few years before and had even made out a membership check. Then I noticed that they had invited Elaine Donnelly to be the keynote speaker at one of their meetings, and I promptly tore up the check. Donnelly was the author of the infamous "Pilot B" report that had unfairly lambasted Kara Hultgreen and Carey Lohrenz, using illegally obtained training records.

At the symposium I stopped by the booth to take a fresh look at the organization. Leafing through its most recent *Hook* magazine, I was disappointed to find an article that blamed women for the navy's retention problems. I told the guy at the table that I endorsed Tailhook's goals of supporting carrier aviation, but I couldn't join because of the organization's hostile attitude toward women. To me, it still seemed like a women-haters' club.

The guy listened impatiently and dismissed me by saying something like, "Well, I'll pass that along to the other officers." I'm sure he did no such thing. I also spoke with a junior officer who advised the senior members of the Tailhook Association, and he said that the organization still believed that navy flying was a man's job. That frustrated me, because I had really enjoyed the professional aspects of the organization, and I felt that carrier aviators deserved a strong support group. But we needed an aviation forum, not a political forum.

I wrote letters to the president of the Tailhook Association and, through the chain of command, to the head aviator on the West Coast, the chief of naval air forces, Pacific (CNAP). CNAP, a three-star admiral, was interested and very responsive; he even called me on the phone. Tailhook, meanwhile, had sent me a form letter. The day after I spoke with CNAP, however, the president of Tailhook called me, and we had a great talk about the association's attitude. Many Tailhook members still blamed women for the debacle in Las Vegas. I tried to make the point that if the Tailhook Association wanted to change that perception and gain the navy's support, it had to support the navy's policies, including the integrated squadrons. The Tailhook's president seemed to agree. After speaking with him, I decided to give the organization another chance.

§

Cdr. Matthew "Pug" Boyne, the F/A-18 squadron commander who had tried so hard to get me kicked out of Hornets while I was in training at Lemoore, apparently had a change of heart after the *Lincoln* returned to port.

I bumped into him several months later when our air wing went on a detachment to Fallon. I was getting ready to go roller-blading when Pug saw me and said he wanted to talk. I had done my best to avoid him during our six months at sea, and I was a little apprehensive about meeting with him. But I was curious about what was on his mind. We sat down in the lobby of the visiting officers quarters, and Pug handed me a manila envelope. There was a letter and a cigar inside.

In the handwritten letter Pug apologized for mistreating me while I had been in his training squadron several years earlier. He said he had misjudged me then, and that he was sorry. He added that during our cruise on the *Lincoln,* he had been impressed with my flying, my professionalism, and the way I had become, in his words, "an asset to VS-29." If I wanted to return to Lemoore and fly Hornets again, he said, he would write a letter of recommendation and do whatever he could to get me back into those awesome airplanes. The cigar was a peace offering.

The thought of living with my husband again in Lemoore and returning to the cockpit of those magical supersonic jets was tempting, but I quickly rejected Pug's invitation. I just couldn't bring myself to trust him.

Besides, I *was* a valued member of VS-29, and I was immensely proud of that fact. It would have been disloyal of me to leave my squadron mates for the chance to fly a different type of plane.

My squadron mates in VS-29 had welcomed me with no preconceptions about what kind of pilot I would turn out to be. They had supported me when I needed them, and I would never forget them for it.

§

Lt. Carey Lohrenz, the F-14 pilot who was sent home from the *Lincoln* during the cruise for poor landing grades, subsequently sued the navy. The charges got widespread publicity when Carey appeared on a *Dateline NBC* broadcast in July 1996. During the program Carey called CAG Dennis Gillespie, our air wing commander on the *Lincoln,* a liar. I disagreed, and I was sorry that Carey had decided to use such a desperate tactic. Months later *Newsweek* took up her cause in an article entitled "Falling out of the Sky," which criticized our air wing and insinuated that the men had conspired to drive women out of navy planes.

The coverage was slanted, misleading, and flat-out wrong in places. I wrote an angry letter to *Newsweek,* which was printed in a subsequent issue. I think Carey had chosen to see conspiracies where none existed, and she was wasting her time and energy in a futile attempt to blame her failure on gender discrimination.

Members of Carey's former squadron were offended and insulted by her charges, and they responded angrily. Several times I heard the callous comment "The wrong one died," an oblique reference to Kara Hultgreen's fatal crash. Kara had been well liked and widely regarded as a superior pilot.

Carey's charges led to the formation of a Naval Investigator General Board of Inquiry, and I was called to testify along with other aviators, male and female, who had gone to sea on the *Lincoln*. The board investigated the accusations thoroughly, and the scope of their inquiry went far beyond Carey's landing grades. After many months the board issued a 276-page report that concluded that the integration of women into Air Wing 11 should have gone more smoothly, and that stronger leadership would have eliminated the perception that women were less qualified or received special treatment.

The board criticized CAG Gillespie for holding separate meetings for female aviators and ordering pregnancy tests after leaving port. The board also found that Carey's landings had been unsafe aboard the ship, but the members said that she should be allowed to fly land-based aircraft.

After my letter was published in *Newsweek,* I received this unexpected e-mail from Captain Gillespie:

> *God bless you for taking the time and exhibiting the type of courage that I see so little of these days. You are one of those unique pioneers who understood danger, faced difficulty with an immense positive attitude, and went on to achieve success in spite of those who would have enjoyed seeing you fail. As I watched you grow, with the other nuggets (male and female), it made me feel good to watch real warriors develop in the most dangerous occupation on earth. You are the singular point of truth I have seen from those involved in a great and successful cruise. I wish others felt compelled to stand up and be counted, and not be satisfied with a lie. Thank you from the bottom of my heart. I would be proud to fly with you again.*
>
> —*CAG "Dizzy" Gillespie*

Carey later settled her suit with the navy out of court. She received $150,000 and left active duty in early 1999.

Under Way

Harry got the orders we had been hoping for. After his cruise on the USS *Constellation,* he was sent to fly F/A-18s at North Island in San Diego. He rented a two-bedroom house near the beach in Coronado with a backyard for Stoney and Aiko. We planned to live there together for at least two years after I came home from my second cruise. The house was close enough to the navy base that we could meet there at lunchtime. The beach was only a few blocks away, so we could take Stoney there every day.

As the departure date for my second cruise drew near, I knew I would face challenges on the *Kitty Hawk* that I couldn't even begin to anticipate. The pressure of being a nugget and making the grade had been replaced by a larger sense of responsibility. On this cruise I would be in charge of training new pilots and crew members, and I didn't want to let them down. Just as Larry and Jedi had helped me with their sound advice and encouragement, now it was my turn to assist others. I had survived trials at sea before, and I knew that I could do it again.

In my new role, new pilots would look to me to help them overcome the same obstacles I had faced. They asked what it would be like to operate in the Arabian Gulf—and I could answer their questions with the accuracy and confidence of someone who had been there before. New pilots seemed to regard senior women like me as resources. We were experienced aviators, and we knew that the future of women in the military didn't depend on us alone.

On this cruise I wouldn't be concerned about my landing grades falling to the point where I would have to be called before a field evaluation board; I knew I could fly better than that. My goal was to set high standards for the new pilots to follow. I was fully qualified as an LSO, and I felt prepared to guide pilots toward the ship on dark nights, in high seas, and in bad weather. I trusted myself to do that critical job, and I believed that my fellow pilots trusted me, too.

§

Then, on a foggy, dreary autumn morning, Harry helped me stow the last of my belongings on the *Kitty Hawk*. There I would share a six-person stateroom with Jana and four new roommates. We were on the O3 level this time—right underneath catapult two—just like the rest of the junior officers. No more Sleepy Hollow, and no more appearance of special treatment. The noise level would be higher inside the room, but at least the chorus of complaints from the guys would be quieted.

As I made my final preparations for our long journey, I could only hope that it would pass as quickly as the first one. And I trusted that at the end, Harry would be there to hold me again along with the rest of my family.

Their courage and faith had made it possible for me to travel so far, and I felt sure that their love would bring me home again.

Harry left behind a small parting gift, a teddy bear–sized stuffed seal with a recorded message inside. Whenever I squeezed the furry little toy, it would play a recording of Harry comically singing "I love you, a bushel and a peck, a bushel and a peck and a hug around your neck. . . ."

He stuck around for a few minutes, then we hugged one last time before he left the ship.

It was indescribably sad to see him go. But I knew that the sooner my *Kitty Hawk* cruise began, the sooner our forced separations would end. A few minutes later I stepped outside and went to the side of the ship to get one final look at my husband. I scanned the parking lot below and spotted Harry leaning against his car—a rusty, weather-beaten gray BMW. A light rain was falling, but he seemed impervious to it as he sat on the hood munching a jelly doughnut and taking in the commotion that surrounded him. I closed my eyes and tried to create a lasting mental image of him that would sustain me during the months ahead. At last he looked up and waved to me. I waved frantically back and blew him a kiss. Then I retreated to the bustling, crowded hangar bay.

Back in my stateroom, I felt a quiet rumble and a slight shudder throughout the ship as several tugboats nuzzled against the massive aircraft carrier and began to push it away from the pier. The faint sensation of movement was followed by a short announcement over the intercom: "Under way."

Eagerness and Hope

The USS *Kitty Hawk* took my shipmates and me back to the troubled Arabian Gulf, but our air wing's performance was much better this second time around.

Air Wing 11 flew exceptionally well. We had no major aircraft accidents and no fatalities. The female "nuggets," on average, flew as well as their male peers—and there was far less tension between male and female pilots. The six rookie female pilots turned to veterans of the USS *Lincoln*'s cruise for guidance and encouragement. They concentrated on their jobs without the distractions or pressures of being among the first group of women on the West Coast to deploy at sea.

Also, since most of the male pilots on the *Kitty Hawk* were making their first cruise, it was hard for them to argue that more senior women shouldn't be there. After all, there were women on the ship who had been patrolling the "no-fly zone" over Iraq while these guys were still in flight training. We had proven ourselves, and no one in the fleet questioned our qualifications or motives.

Most of the junior pilots wanted to hear about our experiences and learn from them, just as I had tried to learn as much as possible from more seasoned aviators during my first cruise. Sometimes, however, I'm sure our sea stories got a little tiresome. Some senior pilots would denigrate their subordinates by beginning their lectures with comments like "Son, I've got more time in tension than you have in the navy," or "I've got more time on a saltwater shitter than you have away from your momma."

Once I found myself poking fun at a junior crew member and started repeating the line about having spent more time on a saltwater toilet than—

"Well, of course you have, Rowdy," this guy interrupted. "That's 'cause you've got to squat to pee."

Unfortunately I couldn't come up with a witty retort to that one.

Among the new female pilots on my second cruise, two flew F/A-18 Hornets, one piloted an ES-3 Viking, one flew a COD, and two flew helicopters. Their performance covered the full spectrum, but all of them completed the tour successfully. At the conclusion of six months at sea, one of the Hornet pilots, Beth "Gabby" Creighton, won the Top Nugget Award for having the best landing grade point average of any new flier. My own performance was consistent, too. I left the *Kitty Hawk* with a 3.83 GPA during the final grading period, good enough to be among the Top Ten pilots in the air wing.

The communications officer on the *Kitty Hawk* allowed virtually unlimited e-mail and telephone links. That small fact improved morale tremendously. In the future there's a chance that the video links that had proved so invaluable in allowing the sailor on board the *Lincoln* to communicate with his hospitalized young son will be used more widely.

§

Harry was flying F/A-18 Hornets at NAS North Island, and for a few months it seemed that we would finally succeed in advancing our navy flying careers while living together as husband and wife. Soon after I deployed on the *Kitty Hawk,* however, Harry was diagnosed with Crohn's disease, a chronic, degenerative intestinal disorder, and his military flying days came to an abrupt end.

Harry tackled this bleak, unanticipated development with his usual humor and optimism. "Does this mean I can get a handicapped sticker for my car?" he quipped to the doctor who made the diagnosis. "Will you prescribe some of that medical marijuana for me?"

Fortunately the medicine that the doctor did prescribe was effective, and most of Harry's symptoms soon disappeared. He lost some weight, and he got night sweats from time to time. But with proper care we figured he could keep the disease at bay for years; maybe he could even push it into long-term remission. Still, it was extremely difficult for me to be on the opposite side of the world once again when my husband was ill and needed me.

Harry had always been so healthy that we never anticipated that a medical condition might someday ground him. In the months after his disease was diagnosed, he spoke often about how he missed flying supersonic jets, performing aerobatics over the ocean and racing at low altitude through valleys and canyons. He also longed for the camaraderie that came from shared flying experiences with fellow aviators. But he told me many times that he was grateful to have had the opportunity to fly such fantastic aircraft, to work with such dedicated people, and to serve his country in such a fulfilling way.

After the *Kitty Hawk* returned home to San Diego, I became an S-3 Viking instructor at NAS North Island, just as I had expected. The work was challenging and rewarding, and I enjoyed helping the new arrivals improve their skills and gain confidence. Some pilots had more native ability than others; some had better attitudes. But I knew that all of them could become reliable navy pilots with the right coaching.

Whatever surprises may be in store for Harry and me, we look forward to our future together with eagerness and hope.

Appendix A: Other Voices

Lt. Jana Raymond, Naval Flight Officer, VS-29

Loree and I were the first female pilot and naval flight officer qualified to fly S-3 Vikings in combat when we joined VS-29 in San Diego. We got along well, but our personalities were very different—and the contrasts were evident from the start.

When we first arrived at VS-29, it seemed that Loree could do no wrong and that I could do no right. Loree fit in with the guys. She thrived on the give and take and constant one-upmanship in the ready room. The guys genuinely liked her, and if they wanted to watch *Pulp Fiction* six times in a row, Loree could sit right there with them and not be bothered.

I'm more of an introvert. It took me a long time to get comfortable in the ready-room environment, and it took the guys a while to get to know and accept me. I remember being somewhat jealous of the ease with which Loree seemed to gain the confidence of the men in our squadron, and I'm sure that I resented her for it—even though it wasn't right for me to feel that way.

Loree has always been an extremely professional officer. She could laugh and joke on the outside, but she kept her emotions to herself. If you asked her how she was feeling, she would tell you—but it was unusual for her to volunteer anything. She genuinely cared about the sailors who worked under her.

As a pilot, Loree worked hard and kept improving. I always felt she was safe in the cockpit, and no one I knew was ever reluctant to fly with her. She got the job done and brought her crews back safe.

Being roommates with Loree on the USS *Abraham Lincoln* was tough at times because we were in such close quarters and subject to such unrelenting pressure. Loree and I saw each other in the ready room, the wardroom, the stateroom, and occasionally in S-3 cockpits. We had a close relationship, but it was different from that of a family member. If you get angry at a brother or sister you can yell at them, and you know that when it's over they're still going to be your sibling; nothing really changes. With a shipmate, however, you have to try to let the little things go. Otherwise the tiniest annoyances will build up and drive you crazy. It's a difficult relationship under any circumstances, and it gets even more complicated when you are stuck in the middle of the ocean.

The day of Lt. Kara Hultgreen's accident stands out in my mind. It was literally my first day at sea. I was on the *Lincoln* when it left San Diego that morning, and I was directly below the flight deck when the call came over the ship's intercom that there was an aircraft in the water. The next minutes and hours were a frenzy of activity. I went to the ready room to watch the internal TV system. The search helicopters were up, the emergency crews were at their stations. There was nothing for the rest of the aviators to do except let the others perform their specialized tasks.

In such situations I always find myself hoping that the accident doesn't involve anyone in my squadron, or any of my friends. I know it's selfish to think that way, but those thoughts pass through the minds of most aviators during such moments. Then you put the crisis aside and go out and fly. I don't know if that kind of emotional distance is something that aviators are born with, or if tragedy is so much a part of our profession that we just come to accept it.

I compare aviation mishaps to bad traffic accidents. When cars crash and people are hurt or killed, all the witnesses get back into their automobiles and they drive away. Pilots do the same thing.

In Kara's case the loss was especially severe. I knew Kara well enough to be impressed that she was a good pilot. She was smart, witty, friendly, and an exceptionally hard worker. Her death was hard to take. But everyone around us continued flying and doing their jobs, and we knew that we had to do the same. That's the way it's always been in navy flying.

I didn't know that Loree had trouble with her approaches and landings after Kara's death. She kept a tight rein on her emotions. I seldom saw her angry; I never saw her cry.

I didn't really appreciate what the women on the *Lincoln* had accomplished until we went back to sea on the USS *Kitty Hawk*. During that second six-month deployment the atmosphere was vastly improved. Personally I felt much more at ease with the people in VS-29 and my role in our squadron. I was more relaxed, I had a lot more fun, and the time seemed to go by more quickly.

The new female aviators in our air wing were not subject to the pressure of being the first to serve in combat roles. In fact, most of the new women on the ship seemed to take for granted that combat assignments would always be open to them. They didn't seem to realize that those of us who had been on the *Lincoln* had been the first to hold such positions on the West Coast, and that historically those billets had been off limits to women.

Like Loree, I had been disappointed by the actions of some of my female colleagues during the first cruise. During the second, however, I realized that each female aviator was going to be evaluated as an individual. We weren't judged by the irresponsible behavior of a few other women. The guys knew what kind of morals and integrity each of us had, and we worked together extremely well.

Francesco "Paco" Chierici, F-14 Pilot, VF-213, LSO Team Leader

I've heard a lot of talk about conspiracy theories among the LSOs and accusations that we were out to ground the women—but they are absolutely untrue. Most junior officers like me wanted the integration of women to succeed. Some of us weren't convinced that the policy would ultimately work, but no one tried to hinder the women on the USS *Abraham Lincoln* or force them to fail.

As fellow aviators, we tried to find common ground with our female counterparts, but it wasn't always easy. For seventy-five years navy pilots had been men, and all the traditions and social customs were developed exclusively by and for males. For example, each squadron's ready room was the center of activity, and ready rooms could be pretty raunchy places. No one ever thought much about it; that's just the way the tradition had developed. But suddenly female officers were a part of the ready room, and no one was quite sure how to behave anymore.

Most nights we watched movies, and in the darkened room with thirty or forty people, the off-color comments would fly. Any time there was sex or nudity or violence in the movies, people would shout out jokes and comments. Some of the women tried to fit in. They did their best to be part of the crowd, but I'm sure it was difficult for them.

On the flight deck all of the women were rookies, and there were no really strong ball fliers among them. That's not unusual, since it typically takes at least one cruise before a pilot really finds the groove. Flying on and off aircraft carriers is so demanding and there's so much to learn that it's rare for someone to master all of it right away.

Let's face it, the women were put on the *Lincoln* by congressional decree. Right or wrong, they didn't have to go through the same selection process that the men did, and everyone on the ship knew it. Joining an operational squadron is kind of like being the new player on a baseball team. Everyone has roles, everyone knows each other, and new arrivals have to learn the subtle ways each individual communicates. Some rookies try too hard to be part of the team; some are too aloof. Every new person gets tested, and everything they do is scrutinized. That's the way it was with the women on the *Lincoln,* only more so.

Loree struggled with her landings at first. The most that could be said of her flying when the first cruise began was that she wasn't terrible. As time went on, however, she moved up. During her second cruise she evolved into a very capable ball flier and made the Top Ten on the *Kitty Hawk.* Her positive attitude and desire to keep learning were the characteristics that allowed her to make the most of her talent.

Loree blended in well with the other pilots, but she wasn't a follower. She definitely had her own personality. I remember the times she brought her frilly pencils onto the LSO platform. It seemed like she was trying to provoke a reaction, and she did. I grabbed her pencil, snapped it in two, and threw the pieces overboard. She laughed and seemed to think it was pretty funny. Then the next day she brought another one of those ridiculous pencils. It was her way of showing that she could take a joke—but she certainly wasn't intimidated or inclined to back down.

The women on the *Lincoln* seemed to fall into two categories: those who believed that the men were conspiring against them, and those who did not. In general, those who believed we were plotting against them didn't perform very well. They became bitter, they blamed others for their shortcomings, and they didn't progress. Those who concentrated on improving their skills, however, generally succeeded.

Loree was definitely part of the latter group.

I enjoyed working with her on the LSO platform because she wanted to learn, she wanted to be there, and she didn't take anything for granted. I never heard her ask for any favors, and she didn't believe she was entitled to special treatment. She was there to do an important job, and she quickly became a contributor.

The only female aviator on the *Lincoln* who surprised me was Lt. Sue McNally, an E-2 pilot. She was a very capable, genuine person, and everyone thought highly of her personally and professionally. She was nice and upbeat and fun to be around. She worked extremely hard and pulled her own weight. Then one day she turned in her wings.

I was very sorry to see Sue go. It never even occurred to me that she was frustrated or having difficulty. But you can't just take a good pilot and make that person a good carrier pilot. Flying the ball is unique. Being out there in the middle of the ocean at night with nowhere to go except the ship is lonely, and not many people can come to grips with the enormity of it. If Sue lost confidence in herself, she did the right thing, and I respect her decision.

Was the *Lincoln's* cruise a success? It depends on how you define the word. My squadron, VF-213, had serious problems. We had two female Tomcat pilots, Lts. Kara Hultgreen and Carey Lohrenz. Kara was killed in an accident, and Carey was sent home for poor landing grades. The only female aviator left in our squadron at the end of the cruise was Chris "Jolly" Taylor, an RIO. She was put in a very tough, very isolated position, and she handled it with great dignity and humor.

But to this day VF-213 hasn't had another female pilot or RIO. I'm not privy to the reasons why.

Lt. Joe "Flojo" Keith, S-3 Pilot, VS-29 Landing Signal Officer

Loree's reputation preceded her when she joined our S-3 squadron. The guys in the F/A-18 Hornet community told us they were glad to get rid of her because she had been a poor performer and a troublemaker. Fortunately we didn't pay much attention to what the Hornet guys said, and we judged Loree on her own merit.

From the first day she arrived, Loree made a real effort to fit in. She didn't try to be one of the guys; she just worked hard, pulled her weight, and didn't complain.

As our squadron's senior landing signal officer, I watched Loree's flying very closely and tried to be a good coach. It's absolutely vital for pilots to have confidence in their LSOs, and Loree was in a delicate position. The other female aviators on the ship—Loree's personal friends—kept telling her that the LSOs were actively working against them. They accused us of trying to sabotage them and make them fail. Even though none of it was true, I'm sure it was tempting for Loree to believe—especially at the beginning of the cruise, when she was really struggling with her landings.

I kept telling Loree that she wasn't doing any worse than I had done when I was a nugget; I struggled, too. And aboard the USS *Abraham Lincoln,* virtually all of the nuggets were having a hard time. I debriefed Loree extensively after her flights, and we reviewed videotapes of her landings. But even so there was a time when I was afraid that I would lose her. If she didn't trust me, if she didn't think her LSO was her biggest fan, she would do what some of the other women on the ship had already done: they got defensive, they blamed the LSOs for their problems, they blamed the airplanes, they blamed everything and everyone except themselves. In order to learn, pilots have to be willing to accept criticism—and they have to take total responsibility for everything that their aircraft does.

Finally I invited Loree to come up onto the LSO platform and watch us in action. During daytime arrivals we usually don't talk to the pilots on the radio, so the LSOs have no way of knowing who is in what airplane—and we don't care. We just grade the approaches and landings the way we see them. When Loree started coming up to the LSO platform, it marked the turning point for her. She saw that there was no secret agenda and that lots of new pilots were having difficulty. Since all of the women on the ship were new, it wasn't surprising that as a group they were below average. She began to appreciate the subtle, intangible things that good pilots do to fly precise, consistent passes.

From then on Loree made my job easy. She learned from her mistakes, she didn't sulk, and her landings steadily improved. In short, she broke through.

My experience in the navy is different from most pilots' in that I was enlisted for ten years before I started flying, and I think that gave me a slightly different perspective. I had been on four cruises before I became a pilot, and the first cruise with female aviators was my sixth. Being thirty-four years old during the *Lincoln* cruise, and having seen how changes were made in the military, I had no illusions of being a policy maker. Regardless of my personal opinions, women had been assigned to fly combat missions, and it was my job to do everything possible to make the new system work.

It was also kind of ironic that Cdr. Chuck Smith, the commanding officer of our squadron, was an old-fashioned officer who wasn't crazy about the idea of having women in his squadron. Still, there were several occasions at the beginning of the cruise when Commander Smith personally intervened to defended Loree and the other women. I heard him tell other senior officers that if they ever had a problem with one of his pilots, they had damn well better bring their concerns to him—not to the offending individual. That fact alone probably spared Loree from getting chewed out by the Air Boss more than once.

By the time Loree's first cruise ended, she didn't need anyone to stand up for her. Her landing grades had improved to the point that she was solidly in the middle of the pack. During her next cruise aboard the USS *Kitty Hawk,* she excelled. I wasn't there to share in Loree's triumph, but I always knew she had the ability to become a top-notch ball flier.

Because of all the media hype about Lt. Carey Lohrenz being grounded and Lt. Kara Hultgreen being killed, the navy got a black eye from the *Lincoln's* cruise. The truth was lost amid the false accusations, investigations, and uninformed debate. Women like Loree who worked hard and did their jobs well were overlooked or forgotten. Personally I still have serious doubts about policies that put women in combat roles in the first place, and I believe that the navy was more effective when it had an all-male fighting force.

But that doesn't detract from Loree's accomplishments. She was a pioneer and a success story—and I'm proud to have played a role in helping her realize her potential as a pilot.

Lt. Christina "Jolly" Taylor, VF-213, F-14 Radar Intercept Officer

Growing up in New Mexico, I had an uncle who used to fly his private airplane down from Arizona on family visits. He would take me for airplane rides and tell me stories about his flying experiences in navy A-4 Skyhawks. Those early influences convinced me to pursue a military flying career when I came of age.

During high school I applied to the navy and air force academies, but I chose Annapolis for a frivolous reason: I thought the air force uniforms were dorky, and I couldn't stand the thought of wearing them for four years. Since I had grown up in the Southwest, I was also intrigued by the idea of going away to college on the East Coast.

My eyesight wasn't good enough for me to become a pilot, but I knew that I wanted to fly, so I became a naval flight officer. At the time that I graduated, in 1989, females were still barred from combat assignments, and I was sent to VAQ-34, a composite squadron flying F/A-18s in Lemoore, California.

That's where I met Loree. She was in F/A-18 pilot training at Lemoore, and since VAQ-34 was the only possible place she could fly Hornets, she came over to our squadron to get acquainted with her future co-workers. My initial impression of Loree was that she was so nice and so sweet that I felt certain she wouldn't last long in the navy. I had heard that the guys were shunning her and giving her a rough time in training, and I figured those monsters would eventually drive her out. The thought that they were picking on Loree at all made me mad. I mean, here was this bright, enthusiastic, motivated person—the kind of person anyone would be thrilled to have as a friend or a co-worker or a sister—and the Hornet guys were treating her like dirt. I'm six feet two inches tall in my bare feet, and I get pissed off whenever I see people getting picked on. I wanted to help Loree, but at the time there was nothing I could do for her except offer encouragement and moral support.

A few months later I was pleased to learn that Loree had made it through Hornet training and joined VAQ-34. We didn't spend much of our spare time together in that assignment, though. She was getting engaged to Harry, and I was about to become engaged myself. Then the squadron was disbanded and all of us went our separate ways.

When the combat exclusion law was repealed, my skipper recommended that I transition to F-14 Tomcats. I've always been aggressive and focused, and I have a sort of twisted sense of humor. The skipper thought those personality traits—or personality defects, depending on how you look at them—would allow me to do well in the fighter community.

Even though I had logged quite a lot of time as a naval flight officer before going to RIO school, I had a tough time learning my combat role. Everything was totally new to me, and the atmosphere was openly hostile. The instructors made it clear that they didn't want me there, and they seemed to be just going through the motions of teaching. Also, I felt a lot of pressure to do well for other women. I hadn't joined the navy to strike a blow for womankind, but I felt a tremendous burden because I didn't want others to be denied opportunities if I failed. I had become a naval flight officer because flying was my dream—and right then I didn't give a rat's ass if any other women chose to follow me or not.

When I finished RIO school and started flying in F-14s at the naval air station in Miramar, California, two other women were being trained there as Tomcat pilots. Lt. Kara Hultgreen and Lt. Carey Lohrenz were both tall like me, but their personalities couldn't have contrasted with each other more starkly. Kara was outgoing and genuine, and people couldn't help but like her. She was extremely enthusiastic and grateful for the opportunity to fly Tomcats, and she really enjoyed firing up the jets, going supersonic, and chasing other fighters around the sky.

Carey had a different approach. She wore nail polish and makeup in the ready room, and she didn't seem to make an effort to fit in. She wanted people to like her, but she came across as manipulative and shallow. She didn't take criticism well and frequently argued with landing signal officers and other pilots. When they were talking about her landings, she would say things like "That's not what I saw," and she tried to blame every mistake on the people around her.

Kara and I planned to share a two-person stateroom on the USS *Abraham Lincoln,* and we moved our things into the room well in advance of our departure date. Kara was so anal about the way she packed her things that she was able to cram more stuff into her bags than a pack rat. She made efficient use of every inch of available space in our tiny room.

On the day of her accident she was in the first wave of planes to fly from Miramar out toward the ship, and I was in the second wave. Soon after my plane arrived overhead, we were told on the radio to expect a delay before landing. At the same time, all the nugget F-14 pilots were ordered to fly back to Miramar. I figured there had been some sort of mishap on the flight deck. And my concern deepened when the nugget pilots acknowledged their new instructions on the radio: everyone checked in except for Kara in aircraft number 103. It never even occurred to me that something catastrophic had happened to her.

After my plane landed on the ship, everything seemed normal. I got out of my flight gear, debriefed Maintenance, and picked up the key to my stateroom. Then I went to the ready room and started looking for Kara. I didn't see her, so I started asking questions. Was she down in Maintenance? Had she been sent to Medical? There were a bunch of gloomy faces staring back at me. Finally someone took me aside and said, "Look, I guess you haven't heard, but we lost a jet today. They recovered Shaggy [Lt. Matthew Klemish, the RIO], but they're still looking for Kara."

I was just devastated. I felt sick and lightheaded. My biggest fear was that Kara had been trapped in her ejection seat, and that the heavy seat had dragged her to the bottom of the ocean. As it turned out, of course, those disturbing thoughts and the horrible images that sprang into my mind were completely accurate.

Despite my grave concern for Kara, I had to fly again that night, and a strange sort of mental autopilot kicked in. I operated the Tomcat's radar and performed all my normal duties, and we made two uneventful traps. I don't know if naval aviators are insane or retarded or what; we just put our emotions on hold, and like robots we go out and do what needs to be done.

When I finally arrived in my stateroom that night, I was exhausted but couldn't sleep. I just lay there with the sink light on and looked around the room at Kara's family pictures and all the things she had packed so tightly into our limited space. Everything was in its place except for Kara herself. She was out there somewhere under the surface of the ocean, and she was never coming back.

The next morning Lt. Jana Raymond called and said, "I need your room key." They were switching our staterooms, and the news made me absolutely furious. The search for Kara was still in progress; she hadn't even been declared dead yet, but already they were telling me to pack up her things, and mine, and move. And I wasn't ready to give up on my friend that soon. I spent another night in our stateroom. The next day Jana and I took inventory of Kara's possessions, packed them up, and sent them to her parents in Texas.

Once our cruise actually began, my life improved immensely. I adapted to living on the ship almost immediately, and I was excited to be there. I looked forward to being at sea and dealing with the challenges of my job. I had good rapport with just about everyone in my squadron, and I enjoyed the work.

In many ways life at sea was easier than life at home: other people did the cooking and cleaning, I never had to worry about what to wear, and I could work out on the treadmill any time I liked.

I knew that some of the other women were having a tougher time adapting. Carey was still struggling and making excuses for her poor flying. But it never occurred to me that there was a conspiracy to ground the female pilots. When Carey was sent home, I didn't question the decision or see anything sinister in it.

My second cruise on the USS *Kitty Hawk* was even better. There was a brief time when I found myself in a melancholy funk, it's informally known in the navy as the "I hate this crap" syndrome. Being away from friends and family again so soon after the first cruise was hard, but my glum mood didn't last long.

Also, the female aviators on the *Kitty Hawk* had improved by leaps and bounds the second time around. Some, like Loree and Jana and me, had been to sea before. We were cruise-experienced, we had been to the Arabian Gulf, and we knew what to expect better than most of the guys. Also, the female nuggets on the *Kitty Hawk* had come straight from the training command—just like the guys. There were no senior women who had spent years in land-based assignments before being sent to the ship. The pipeline from training to sea duty was open, and the process was working as smoothly for the women as it ever did for the men.

There haven't been any more female pilots or RIOs assigned to my squadron, VF-213, since Kara was killed and Carey was grounded—but I'm certain that will change. There are women moving through the training pipeline right now, and I have no doubt that they will accomplish even more than we did.

Lt. Cdr. Linda Heid, Naval Flight Officer, VAQ-135

The start of our cruise aboard the USS *Abraham Lincoln* felt to me like a dream come true.

I was thirty-three years old at the time, and I had been in the navy eleven years. That made me one of the most senior women on the ship, and the fact that we were there was almost mind-boggling. One of my favorite memories came during workups. Pam Lyons and Brenda Scheufele and I were sitting in Kara Hultgreen's room, and all of us were so excited about the future. A year before all of us had gone to Washington to lobby Congress to change the combat exclusion law and allow women to fly in front-line squadrons. All of us had been complaining about the lack of opportunity for women in naval aviation. Then, suddenly, we were on the ship as members of combat squadrons, and we could hardly believe that circumstances had changed so fast. We were going to sea together, and we were full of high hopes and expectations.

Kara and I had flown together a lot when we were in Key West, and she was one of my very best friends. Back in 1990 I had become the first woman to eject from an E-6. We had a total hydraulic failure during an electronic warfare training exercise against the USS *Forrestal,* and the plane went out of control off the coast of Virginia. We declared an emergency, then ejected about three minutes later while the plane was at fifteen thousand feet and traveling about 270 knots. The pilot and I weren't injured, and we spent about an hour in the water before we got picked up.

Kara was our squadron's public affairs officer at the time, and I remember her taking pictures of me and writing a little story about the ejection as soon as I came back to Key West. To me the whole thing seemed like an occupational hazard. I was flying again within a couple of weeks, and I enjoyed being in the cockpit as much as ever.

I loved being in VAQ-135 at first. There were a bunch of great guys in that squadron, and they seemed to accept women right away. "Fast Eddie" Hasner was the commanding officer, and he was a superb leader and motivator who created good times. Things started to go downhill for the squadron on 6 May 1994. We were having a "Seis de Mayo" party at Whidbey Island when a couple of guys from our squadron got in a tiff with some P-3 guys. One of the P-3 guys sucker-punched our skipper—and the upshot was that our skipper got relieved of duty since he had been the most senior officer present.

Hasner's replacement wasn't nearly so supportive of women, and by the time Kara died, the squadron's whole personality had changed. People were openly hostile. The guys had been looking for an excuse to say women shouldn't be on the ship, and now they had one.

To this day it still pisses me off that they drag Kara's name through the mud. They stole her [flight training] records, they took things from them out of context. The fact that the navy stayed silent and allowed them to slam her was an affront. I flew with Kara, and she had the makings of a great fighter pilot. She had every right to be in an F-14. People more qualified and less qualified than Kara have been killed in naval aviation.

The day Kara died was the day our air wing's troubles really began. I'm a strong person, but I don't think I could have handled the pressure that Carey Lohrenz was under. Eventually she cracked.

In my squadron, I certainly wasn't my usual happy self. The guys would say, "C'mon, get over it. People die all the time." I found that I could compartmentalize my emotions in the airplane, but it was a strain. I flew a couple of days after Kara's accident, and it was a mistake. My mind wasn't there; I felt like crying. I just pushed myself through it and tried not to show my emotions in front of the guys. My way of dealing with the situation was to be outwardly bitchy.

Despite the poisonous atmosphere on the ship and my personal difficulties, I regard the Lincoln's cruise as the most thrilling, challenging, productive time of my life. I ran every day, I was in great physical shape, I was always busy, and I didn't let time go to waste. I loved flying on and off the boat. I loved everything about it.

An EA-6B has a four-person crew, and three of us flew together all the time. After a while we were so accustomed to working together that we could coordinate our actions in the airplane without even talking—we knew each other that well. We flew outside the [surface-to-air missile] sites in southern Iraq and protected the no-fly zone. We flew twice a day, and it was exhausting.

I spent most of my free time with Pam and Brenda, and I didn't see Loree very much. She was walking a very fine line. She was trying to become an LSO, and there was a certain distance between her and some of the other female pilots. She had a supportive squadron, and because she was in S-3s, she wasn't seen as such a threat to the male fighter and attack pilots. She didn't have to face the same degree of hostility as some of the other women —especially the women flying Hornets or Tomcats. The general feeling was that she had forgotten the adversity she had faced when she was in Hornet training.

Before the Lincoln cruise my career was on the fast track. People were saying that I would become the first female commanding officer of an EA-6B

Prowler squadron. By the time the cruise ended, however, I was burned out and bitter and I just wanted to get away from my squadron and Whidbey Island.

Instead of becoming an instructor in the field replacement squadron at Whidbey, I went to Washington, D.C., for three years in a nonflying assignment. I worked in Naval Intelligence, and it was one of the most satisfying times in my life. Being away from the constant hostility we had faced on the *Lincoln* repaired my soul and renewed my faith in the navy.

The whole time I was away from aviation, I agonized about whether to go back. I prayed about it and asked God what to do. I didn't feel that I could handle the pressure of being in the spotlight to that extent ever again. I had a reputation for being too outspoken in the aviation community, and I wasn't well liked. People kept telling me that the environment had changed for the better, but I wasn't sure what to think.

Also, my priorities had changed. I realized that if I went back to sea and devoted myself to my career, I would wake up one morning and realize that I was forty-five years old and had nothing. It took a lot of courage for me to resist going back. It would have been so easy to return to Whidbey Island. I still had friends there, and the church that I loved was there. But I left aviation and the fast track behind.

Sometimes I miss flying more than I can express. Right now "Tater," my pilot on the *Lincoln* cruise, is on the USS *Theodore Roosevelt* [in the Mediterranean Sea flying over Serbia]. I feel like I should be there, too. Instead, I'm working on a master's degree in computer science, and I have four and a half years left in the navy. My priorities are different than they were aboard the *Lincoln*. I'm thirty-seven years old, and I want to get married and have a family. Those are my new priorities—and they are more important to me than flying.

Appendix B: Investigation Documents

From: Commander Naval Air Force, U.S. Pacific Fleet

To: Office of the Judge Advocate General

Subj: INVESTIGATION INTO THE F-14 ACCIDENT THAT RESULTED
IN THE DEATH OF LT. KARA S. HULTGREEN

Shortly after 1500 on 25 October 1994, an F-14A aircraft belonging to VF-213 crashed into the ocean while attempting to land aboard USS *Abraham Lincoln*. The pilot, LT Kara Hultgreen, USN, died after ejecting from the aircraft. The radar intercept officer, LT Matthew Klemish, USN, also ejected and survived with minor injuries.

A complete understanding of all of the facets leading to this most unfortunate accident will never be known. After significant study of the video, detailed review of the investigation and discussions with numerous engineers and F-14 pilots, my analysis indicates the following:

LT Hultgreen started her landing approach to USS *Abraham Lincoln* from a slightly "close abeam" position. The approach was within established parameters through 90 degrees of turn. Sometime prior to turning onto the final approach course, the left engine malfunctioned, probably due to engine stall. The malfunction was most likely caused by a combination of a failed engine bleed air control valve coupled with more than normal side slip. Our best estimate is that neither of these conditions alone would have caused the engine to malfunction. There may have been other elements that contributed to this malfunction, but none could be positively identified. As the pilot rolled out on final and added power, only the right engine responded. This asymmetric thrust condition caused both the left side slip and the angle of attack to increase as the pilot attempted to slow the rate of descent with only one engine working correctly. The aircraft went from normal operating parameters to near stall in three seconds, and the rudders became ineffective. It is not clear if the crew realized that the left engine was malfunctioning, as there appears to have been no cockpit caution indications.

The correct response to recover from this flight condition would have been to use full throttle and forward stick to reduce the angle of attack and right rudder to level the wings, but this response had to be started within approximately three seconds after adding power. This action would most likely have appeared to the pilot to put the aircraft in danger of hitting the carrier. Within 10 seconds from the initial asymmetric engine condition, the aircraft departed controlled flight and crashed.

Analysis of LT Hultgreen's records indicates she was qualified, in a current flight status and had recently practiced single-engine approaches in a flight simulator. She had 217 flight hours in the F-14.

All too often we forget how narrow the margin of safety is in naval carrier aviation. This pilot did her best to keep this aircraft flying under conditions that were all but impossible.

R. J. Spane

From: Commander, Carrier Group Three

To: Office of the Judge Advocate General

Via: Commander, Naval Air Force, U.S. Pacific Fleet

Subj: INVESTIGATION INTO THE VFA-22 F/A-18 ACCIDENT ON 28 JANUARY 1995 THAT RESULTED IN THE DEATH OF LT. GLENNON J. KERSGIETER, USNR

On 28 January 1995, at 2035 local, aircraft 303 impacted the water immediately after a night catapult launch off Southern California. The pilot, LT Kersgieter, was killed during the mishap. LT Kersgieter was an outstanding pilot and fine officer who was killed as a result of no fault of his own. Aircraft 303 had flown three previous times that day. The pilot who flew the flight prior to the mishap . . . reported that a "basket slap" had occurred during an in-flight refueling. Aircraft 303 was inspected and no damage was discovered. As a result, aircraft 303 was certified safe for flight. The apparent cause of the mishap was a jammed Airstream Direction Sensing Unit (ADSU) which sent erroneous Angle of Attack input to aircraft 303's flight computer.

Disciplinary action is not warranted against any of the maintenance control personnel involved in this mishap. Personnel involved exercised that degree of care which had become the practice in the community over a period of years.

First priority needs to be to correct the F/A-18's flight control computer launch logic to prevent such catastrophic flight control inputs and provide better cockpit warning of critical failures.

R. M. Nutwell

From: Commander Naval Air Force, U.S. Pacific Fleet

To: Commander in Chief, U.S. Pacific Fleet

Subj: INVESTIGATION INTO THE CRASH OF AN F-14 AIRCRAFT WHICH OCCURRED NEAR NASHVILLE, TENNESSEE ON 29 JANUARY 1996

At 0948 on 29 January 1996, shortly after taking off from Nashville International Airport, a U.S. Navy F-14 Tomcat assigned to VF-213, crashed in Antioch, Tennessee. Several homes were damaged or destroyed by the resultant explosion, fire and debris. Mr. and Mrs. Elmer Newsom, along with a visiting friend, Mr. Ewing Wair, were killed instantly. The pilot in command, LCDR John Stacy Bates and his Radar Intercept Officer, LT Graham Alden Higgins, instantly perished upon impact. At the time of the mishap, the aircraft was departing Nashville for the return portion of a cross country flight. After becoming airborne, the mishap aircraft accelerated and climbed at an angle in excess of 50 degrees into Instrument Meteorological Conditions in violation of rules [prohibiting] such maneuvers. Shortly thereafter, the aircraft was observed descending below the cloud layer in a steep nose-down attitude, followed by a transition to slightly nose-up, left wing down attitude prior to impact with the ground.

While we may never know exactly what transpired between the takeoff and the crash, the investigation has determined that the loss of the aircraft was due to pilot error. Causal factors included faulty judgment leading to a prohibited takeoff maneuver into Instrument Meteorological Conditions;

weather; probable spatial disorientation; possible cockpit distraction; inadequate/improper recovery technique; and inadequate altitude for recovery. The investigation into this tragic loss of life has disclosed facts which include a squadron leadership mind set which was at times tolerant of mediocre performance, violation of established rules, and inattention to detail. . . .

Brent M. Bennitt

NAVAL INSPECTOR GENERAL INVESTIGATION

OF CARRIER AIR WING ELEVEN

10 February 1997

(Excerpts)

The initial deployment of women on the Lincoln in the Pacific fleet and the Eisenhower in the Atlantic fleet [had very different outcomes].

The Eisenhower Air Wing (CVW-3) deployed between October 1994 and April 1995. Nine of the ten female pilots assigned to CVW-3 tactical aviation squadrons successfully completed the deployment, although one was described as "one of the weaker pilots." The tenth pilot was found not suitable for carrier aviation, but permitted to transition to a non-carrier aviation community. No significant gender-related issues were reported, and no complaints relating to integration issues on that deployment were filed at any level.

The Lincoln Air Wing (CVW-11) deployed between April 1995 and October 1995. Of the eight female pilots assigned to CVW-11, one died in an aircraft mishap, one dropped on request, and two lost their flying status.

All but two of the women TACAIR pilots assigned to CVW-3 came straight through the training pipeline. By contrast, most of the women assigned to CVW-11 had prior experience that made them more senior (in rank, time-in-grade, and flight hours) than other "nuggets," but no more experienced in carrier landings or deployments.

Senior personnel in CVW-3, with the support of their superiors, targeted personnel to fill positions they considered important to a successful integration effort. For example, the most senior woman officer assigned to CVW-3 was the administrative assistant, a Lieutenant Commander, who was also an experienced NFO. She ran interference with other women for CAG, and provided him advice on issues of particular interest to women. By contrast, the CVW-11 CAG relied on the advice of his female [whited out], a first-tour Lieutenant. CVW-3 also obtained highly qualified and respected senior enlisted personnel, including a female command master chief. CVW-3 sought out LSOs for their "people skills" as well as their waving skills—not out of concern for women, but because its leaders preferred a more relaxed, less "in your face" debriefing style.

During its deployment, CVW-3 never called a "women only" meeting. The CVW-11 CAG called two; one at the start, the other at the end, of the CVW-11 deployment.

Although the policy of CVW-3 was "equal treatment," it never established or articulated a "gender neutral" policy by name. The unstated, but clearly understood leadership policy was that there would be an honest effort to help every member of the wing, male or female, do their best. By contrast, the CVW-11 policy required strict application of the "gender neutral" policy so that no action could be considered "preferential treatment" for women.

Two female nugget F/A-18 pilots in CVW-3 were top performers. The men felt challenged to do better, and the performance of both squadrons improved.

Although the Eisenhower was returning from its deployment as the Lincoln was preparing to depart, the CVW-3 CAG recalls no contacts with CVW-11 personnel attempting to discuss any issues relating to integration or obtain "lessons learned."

Military historians often have pointed out that at the most instinctive level, people do not fight for principle or for country, but only out of loyalty to leaders and shipmates. But if a commanding officer adopts the wrong interpretation of the gender neutral policy, blindly treating everyone alike without regard for their differences . . . then he or she will disengage from people, passively abdicate the role of leader, and consequently will not gain the trust and respect that results from the belief that the CO is looking out for every member of the command. That is what happened in some squadrons in CVW-11.

The weaker CVW-11 skippers thought the "gender neutral" policy prohibited them from providing individualized training for the women, or they used it as an excuse to avoid criticism they feared might come from subordinates and peers who were not favorably disposed to women in TACAIR. These skippers failed to recognize that all new pilots (male and female), especially in the high pressure environment of TACAIR, need individual attention. Naval aviation has been doing that since it was founded.

Gender neutral does not prevent giving a nugget, male or female, extra flights, an assigned mentor, additional debriefs or an encouraging word. Yet, unfortunately, that is how some applied it. In a real sense it paralyzed some commanding officers; they were afraid to be seen giving a woman any special attention, so they backed away from both the men and the women. They became managers of their squadrons; they gave up being their leaders.

In the extreme case, gender neutrality is nothing more than a code word for passive resistance to women in combat aviation.

The rift the [pregnancy testing] order created cannot be overemphasized. Virtually every woman interviewed identified it as a sore spot in the integration effort while most men could neither understand the women's dramatic opposition to it nor the command's significant retreat from it. It polarized men and women, and raised concerns about loyalty, both up and down. . . . It caused some women to doubt their superiors' commitment to integration.

Perhaps the most significant [communication problems] in the interaction between men and women concerned post-flight debriefs. Many of the female aviators saw the tone and mannerisms adopted by LSOs as hostile toward them, personally, and women, generally. The LSOs thought some of the women were "argumentative."

The LSOs encountered argumentative men, also. But they could deal with that problem easily. They would stick a finger in their chest, tell them to shut up, and continue with the debrief. They didn't think they could do that to a woman aviator. . . .

GENERAL RECOMMENDATIONS:

1) Pipeline Training: Introduce women into a new combat community in due course. No effort should be made to "accelerate" their introduction.

2) Leadership: Evaluate the Navy Leadership Continuum curriculum for diversity and gender differences training, and include/increase training as appropriate.

3) Media: Exercise an increased sensitivity for the potentially disruptive influence the media has when it is covering a story; and a recognition of the impact on individual members, particularly with respect to emotional and social issues.

4) Stress: Review the aviation training program . . . with respect to rec-

ognizing the signs and symptoms of maladaptive stress coping and impaired compartmentalization, and respective responsibilities of the individuals involved.

5) Field Naval Aviator Evaluation Board: Clarify the conditions under which [pilots may be allowed to switch from carrier-based to land-based aircraft].

6) Administrative Procedures: Emphasize the importance of record keeping . . . and other administrative documentation.

About the Authors

Loree Hirschman is the first female training-qualified landing signal officer in the U.S. Navy. As a pilot she has flown F/A-18 Hornets, S-3 Vikings, TA-4 Skyhawks, T-2 Buckeyes, and T-34 Mentor military aircraft. After graduating from the University of San Diego in 1989 with a degree in mathematics, she was commissioned a navy ensign and earned her navy wings in 1992. She successfully completed two six-month deployments to the Persian Gulf as a member of VS-29, a sea-control squadron based at NAS North Island in San Diego. She was a navy flight instructor in twin-engine S-3 Vikings and was promoted to lieutenant commander in June 1999. She left the navy in mid-1999 after completing her military service obligation and is pursuing a master's degree in business administration at the Wharton School of Business. She is married to Harry Hirschman.

Dave Hirschman is the author of *Hijacked: The True Story of the Heroes of Flight 705* and a business news reporter at the *Gazette* in Colorado Springs, Colorado. He received a bachelor's degree from the University of California San Diego in 1985 and a master's degree from the University of Michigan in 1987. He has won numerous journalism awards and was nominated for the Pulitzer Prize in beat reporting in 1994. He is a licensed commercial pilot and flight instructor with an FAA waiver to perform low-level aerobatics at air shows and flying competitions. He and his wife, Martha, have a three-year-old daughter, Kara, and an infant son, Nathan.

The Naval Institute Press is the book-publishing arm of the U.S. Naval Institute, a private, nonprofit, membership society for sea service professionals and others who share an interest in naval and maritime affairs. Established in 1873 at the U.S. Naval Academy in Annapolis, Maryland, where its offices remain today, the Naval Institute has members worldwide.

Members of the Naval Institute support the education programs of the society and receive the influential monthly magazine *Proceedings* and discounts on fine nautical prints and on ship and aircraft photos. They also have access to the transcripts of the Institute's Oral History Program and get discounted admission to any of the Institute-sponsored seminars offered around the country.

The Naval Institute also publishes *Naval History* magazine. This colorful bimonthly is filled with entertaining and thought-provoking articles, first-person reminiscences, and dramatic art and photography. Members receive a discount on *Naval History* subscriptions.

The Naval Institute's book-publishing program, begun in 1898 with basic guides to naval practices, has broadened its scope in recent years to include books of more general interest. Now the Naval Institute Press publishes about one hundred titles each year, ranging from how-to books on boating and navigation to battle histories, biographies, ship and aircraft guides, and novels. Institute members receive discounts of 20 to 50 percent on the Press's more than eight hundred books in print.

Full-time students are eligible for special half-price membership rates. Life memberships are also available.

For a free catalog describing Naval Institute Press books currently available, and for further information about subscribing to *Naval History* magazine or about joining the U.S. Naval Institute, please write to:

Membership Department
U.S. Naval Institute
291 Wood Road
Annapolis, MD 21402-5034
Telephone: (800) 233-8764
Fax: (410) 269-7940
Web address: www.usni.org